STUDENT'S BOOK

HUGH DELLAR AND ANDREW WALKLEY

INTERMEDIATE
OUTCOMES

HEINLE
CENGAGE Learning

Australia • Brazil • Japan • Korea • Mexico • Singapore • Spain • United Kingdom • United States

WELCOME TO *OUTCOMES*

Outcomes will help you learn the English you need and want. Each of the sixteen units has three double-pages linked by a common theme. Each double page is an individual lesson – and each teaches you some vocabulary or grammar and focuses on a different skill. The first lesson in each unit looks at conversation, the next two at reading or listening.

WRITING UNITS

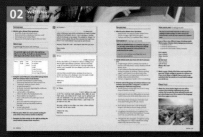

There are eight writing lessons in the *Outcomes* Student's Book, which teach different styles of writing. Each one has a model text as well as speaking tasks to do in pairs or groups. There are also extra vocabulary or grammar exercises to help you write each kind of text. In addition, there is a lot of writing practice in the *Outcomes* Workbook.

REVIEW UNITS

There are four Review Units in this book. Here you practise the core grammar and vocabulary of the previous four units. The first two pages of each unit feature learner training, a board game, a quiz and work on collocations and pronunciation (especially individual sounds). The next two pages feature a test of listening, grammar and vocabulary. This is marked out of 80 ... so you can see how you are progressing.

Clearly stated communicative goals in the unit menu, supported by grammar and vocabulary.

Grammar taught in context, with natural examples of usage and clear practice tasks.

Fuller explanations, more examples, and exercises are in the reference section at the back.

A translation exercise helps you think about how sentences work in your own language compared to English.

Speaking activities allow you to exchange information and ideas or comment on texts. A longer final speaking task ends every unit.

Tasks to practise a variety of skills.

Interesting texts and international contexts with tasks to practise a variety of skills.

02 FEELINGS

In this unit you learn how to:
- talk about how you feel – and why
- give responses to news
- use stress and intonation more effectively
- ask double questions

Grammar
- *be, look, seem* etc.
- *-ing / -ed* adjectives
- The present continuous
- Present continuous / simple questions

Vocabulary
- Feelings
- Adjective collocations

Reading
- It only takes Juan Mann to change the world!

Listening
- How's it going?
- How's it going at work?

VOCABULARY Feelings

A How are the people in the pictures feeling? Why? Can you use any of the words in the box to describe them?

exhausted	worried	fed up
confused	terrible	relaxed
stressed	in a good / bad mood	upset
furious	annoyed	disappointed
pleased	down	guilty

B Which of the words in A may show you are feeling: tired, ill, sad, happy, unsure, angry, or bad about something you did?

C Have you had any of these feelings recently? Why?

14 OUTCOMES

GRAMMAR *be, look, seem* etc

Be, feel, look, seem, and *sound* are all linking verbs that can be followed directly by an adjective.

A Match 1–8 with the reasons a–h for the feelings.
1 Are you OK? You look a bit stressed.
2 Are you all right? You look exhausted.
3 Is Julie OK? She sounded a bit disappointed.
4 Is Mike all right? He seems a bit down.
5 Are you OK? You look a bit ill.
6 Are you all right? You seem totally confused.
7 Have you seen Ann? She sounded so relaxed!
8 Hi. You look like you're in a good mood.

a Yeah, I've just found out I've got a new job. I'm really pleased.
b I am! My car broke down and I had to walk home.
c Yeah, I feel terrible. I think I'm going to throw up.
d I am. I'm really behind with work and I've got exams next week.
e Yeah, I don't get this. What am I supposed to do?
f Yeah. I think the week in the spa really helped her.
g He's just split up with Jo and he's quite upset.
h Yeah. I think she expected to get a better mark as she'd studied so much.

B Write your own responses to 1–8. Practise in pairs.

▶ Need help? Read the grammar reference on p. 138

LANGUAGE PATTERNS

Write the sentences in your language. Translate them back into English. Compare your English to the original.
She expected to get a better mark.
I expected London to be more modern.
I didn't expect to have so much homework.
We didn't expect it to take so long.
We didn't expect you to be so early.

SPEAKING

A Check you understand the words and expressions in bold. Then discuss the questions in groups.
1 How often do you do these things? In what situations?
- **hug** people
- **kiss** people **on the cheek** or lips
- walk **arm in arm** with people or hold hands
- **shake hands** or **bow**
- touch people on the arm or **put** your arm **round their shoulder**
2 Do you do any of these things more often or less often than most people in your country? Why?
I think I'm fairly typical. / I'm maybe a little bit unusual.
3 Have you been anywhere where they do these things differently to you? Where? What do they do?

READING

A Work in pairs. Look at the text *It only takes Juan Mann to change the world!* Discuss these questions.
- What is the man doing in the pictures? Why?
- What would you do if you saw someone like this?
- Are any people like him famous in your local area / country? What for? How do people feel about them?

B Read and see if you feel differently about the man afterwards.

C Work in pairs. Discuss these questions. Then read the article again to check your answers.
1 What made Juan Mann start his campaign?
2 How did he feel when he went out the first time?
3 Who first asked for a hug and why?
4 How did Mann become so famous?
5 Why does he feel surprised and lucky about what he does now?
6 What is Mann's theory about why people want hugs?

D Which adjectives went with these nouns?
connections ....
attempt ....
star ....
year ....
identity ....
skills ....
help ....
plan ....

16 OUTCOMES

Today's story

It Only Takes Juan Mann To Change The World!

In the modern world, it is not unusual for people to feel depressed or isolated. It can be hard to make **meaningful connections** with others. That was how 'Juan Mann' felt – until the day he decided to start giving free hugs. What started as a **desperate attempt** to change his own life has transformed him into an **international star**, thanks to the power of the Internet!

On returning to Sydney, Australia, in early 2004, after travelling in Europe, Mann had a **miserable year** in which his parents divorced and he found himself lonely and out of work. It was a depressing time. "I was alone. My family was elsewhere, my friends had all moved on. It was just me. It was just me, and I had to do something," said the famous hugger, who goes by the name of Juan Mann ('One man'), but who keeps his **true identity** secret.

"And I sat around for months doing nothing. Noticing, just watching the world. I didn't have a lot of contact with people. I was just on my own. And I thought I would try to step out of that and try and do something different."

DEVELOPING CONVERSATIONS
Response expressions

We use lots of short expressions to respond to news.

A Look at the following conversations and try to translate the expressions in **bold**. Are there any you cannot translate?

1 A: I can't drink at the moment. I'm pregnant.
   B: **Really? Congratulations!** When is the baby due?
2 A: I'm going to Canada to study English.
   B: **Wow, that's great!** How long are you going for?
3 A: I'm afraid I can't meet you tonight.
   B: **Oh, what a shame!** Are you sure?
4 A: My brother's not very well.
   B: **Oh no! I'm really sorry.** I hope it's not too serious.
5 A: I've lost my wallet.
   B: **On no, what a pain!** Did it have much in it?
6 A: I've found my wallet!
   B: **Phew, that's a relief!** Where was it?

Many expressions and grammatical patterns in spoken English are similar to other languages. These exercises help you practise those.

LISTENING

You are going to hear two conversations. The first is between two people talking about their friend Karim. The second is between two women, Belinda and Alisha.

A ♪ 2.1 Listen. How do these people feel?

Conversation 1	Conversation 2
Karim	Belinda
	Alisha

B Do you remember why they feel this way? Listen again and check.

NATIVE SPEAKER ENGLISH

How come?
People often use *How come?* instead of *Why?*
A: I can't come to your wedding, I'm afraid.
B: Oh what a shame. How come?
A: I've got an exam that day.

Listening exercises provide examples of the conversations you try in Conversation Practice.

Information on interesting bits of language common to native speakers of English.

SPEAKING

A Work in pairs. Discuss these questions.
- Do you find it easy to talk about your feelings? Who do you talk to if you have a problem?
- What would you do or say if a friend was upset? Would it be different if it was a man or a woman?
- What kind of things do you do to cheer yourself up?
- Are you good at sorting out problems?

PRONUNCIATION Responding

With positive responses our voice goes higher.

With negative responses our voice goes lower.

Pronunciation activities are integrated with the communicative goals.

A ♪ 2.2 Listen to the six responses from *Developing conversations* and copy the stress and intonation.

B Work in pairs. Practise 1–6 from *Developing conversations*. Try to continue them.

CONVERSATION PRACTICE

A Work in pairs. Think of a piece of good or bad news. Write a conversation like the ones you heard in *Listening*. Include response expressions.

B Try to remember your conversation. Act it out in front of another pair of students.

This section allows you to put together what you've learnt.

02 FEELINGS 15

And something different is exactly what he did!
Mann went to one of Sydney's main shopping districts holding a cardboard sign saying 'Free Hugs' and waited. He expected to last an hour at the most and asked a friend to come along to protect him, and left his wallet at home.

After 15 minutes, however, a woman approached and told him that her dog had died that morning and that it was also the first anniversary of the death of her daughter, and that she really needed a hug. Mann was happy to help!

His 'Free Hugs' campaign continued quietly for a couple of years until a friend made a film of him and posted it on YouTube, the online video sharing site. Since then, it has been seen by over 14 million people and fans have started copying him. Last year, the video clip was named the most inspiring on the site.

Mann finds this funny because at school he was told that he did not have the **social skills** to do humanitarian work. Yet he now seems to be a therapist for a whole city's problems.

"Every week a number of people will tell me their story, how they have suffered and how they got by, the mistakes they've made and the lessons they've learned," he said. "I'm very fortunate in what I do in that I learn from everyone else's mistakes as well as my own."

Mann claims many people need someone to listen to their problems – but are too embarrassed to call a help line or get **professional help**.

Mann's **original plan** was to personally take his campaign around the world, but he decided to stay in Sydney because "Now it all happens online." Mann is currently writing a book about his experiences and intends to carry on hugging people until nobody wants me." Until then, his message remains clear: have a hug. It will make you feel much better!

VOCABULARY Adjective collocations

A In the text, you read that 2004 was a depressing time for Juan Mann. Match these *–ing* adjectives with the nouns.

inspiring	disappointing	confusing
exciting	annoying	relaxing

1 ... holiday / bath / atmosphere / place / time
2 ... habit / person / noise / problem / spam
3 ...city / new development / discovery / opportunity
4 ...teacher / speech / story / book / film / video clip
5 ...instructions / message / grammar / explanation
6 ... response / news / loss / result / game / sales

B Write eight true sentences using the new collocations.

GRAMMAR –ing / –ed adjectives

Some adjectives, including those ending in –*ing*, only describe things which cause a feeling:
The film was so *boring* that I fell asleep.

The –*ed* and other adjectives in Vocabulary exercise A on p. 14 describe people's feelings:
I'm *exhausted*. I need to go to bed.

A Choose the correct word (in *italics*) in sentences 1–6 below.
1 I'm *confusing / confused*. What did he say?
2 This is really *interesting / interested*. I love Maths.
3 I got a *disappointing / disappointed* mark in my test.
4 I'm so *boring / bored*! I can't stand algebra!
5 I hate being in my Dad's class. He's so *embarrassing / embarrassed*!
6 Why do I have to sit next to him? He's so *scary / scared*!

B Now match 1–6 to the pictures

▶ Need help? Read the grammar reference on p. 138

Further grammar and vocabulary points presented and developed through the unit.

Visuals to help with new vocabulary.

SPEAKING

A Work in pairs. Discuss these questions.
- Does your town or area have any similar problems to Sydney?
- At one point the city council tried to stop Juan Mann's free hugs campaign. Why do you think they did that?
- Has your government tried to stop something popular? Why? Was it successful?
- Can you think of any other news stories which have been spread through the Internet?
- Have you ever posted anything on the Internet? What?

A longer final speaking task ends every unit.

02 FEELINGS 17

LEARNING

Research suggests words need lots of revision in context if you want to be able to use them with confidence. The authors of *Outcomes* have tried hard to make sure words reappear many different times in the course. Here are **twelve** ways to learn the word *mood*.

- see it and practise it in **Vocabulary** p. 14
- look it up in the *Outcomes* **Vocabulary Builder** p. 6
- use it again in **Grammar** p. 14
- hear it in a **Listening** exercise 2.1 p. 161
- say it in the final **Speaking** p. 19
- find an example in **Grammar reference** p. 138
- read it in a **Reading** text p. 30
- write, read and listen to it in the *Outcomes* **Workbook** Unit 2
- use it in **Writing** p. 134
- check the grammar in *Outcomes* **Vocabulary Builder** exercises p. 9
- revise it in square 5 of the game in **Review** p. 32
- test it with *Outcomes* **ExamView®**

Outcomes VOCABULARY BUILDER

The *Outcomes* **Vocabulary Builder** provides lists of key vocabulary with clear explanations, examples of common collocations and exercises focusing on the grammar of the words.

MyOutcomes
ONLINE

The pin code at the back of the Student's Book gives you access to a wide range of interactive, online exercises. We have created additional exercises to go with each unit from the book, so you can continue developing your English.
Visit Heinle **elt.heinle.com**

Grammar	Vocabulary	Reading	Listening	Developing conversations
• Question formation • Narrative tenses • Other uses of the past continuous	• Learning languages • Language words	• 'Language policy a disaster' says head teacher	• Getting to know people • Explaining why you were late	• Asking follow-up questions • *John was telling me …*
• *be, look, seem* etc • *-ing / -ed* adjectives • The present continuous • Present continuous / simple questions	• Feelings • Adjective collocations	• It only takes Juan Mann to save the world!	• How's it going? • How's it going at work?	• Response expressions • Making excuses
• Present perfect questions • The future	• Places of interest • Holiday problems • Weather	• Workers can't bank on holidays	• Deciding where to go sightseeing • Talking about your holiday plans	• Recommendations
• Frequency (present and past) • Duration (past simple and present perfect continuous)	• Evening and weekend activities • Problems and sports • Music	• The playlist of your life	• Did you have a good weekend? • A martial art	• *Are you any good?* • Music, films and books
• Rules: *have to, don't have to, can* • Rules: *allowed to, supposed to, should*	• Jobs • Workplaces and activities • *be used to, get used to*	• Terrible jobs not a thing of the past	• What does your job involve? • Rules at work	• *That must be …*
• *must*	• Describing souvenirs and presents • Clothes and accessories	• Shop till you drop!	• Negotiating prices • Comparing mobile phones • The best way to buy tickets for a gig	• Avoiding repetition • Responding to recommendations
• *after, once* and *when* • Zero and first conditionals	• Describing courses • Forming words • Schools, teachers and students	• Learning to be happy	• Describing how a course is going • Different aspects of education	• *How's the course going?*
• *tend to* • Second conditionals	• Describing food • Restaurants • *Over-*	• Food for thought	• Ordering dinner in a Peruvian restaurant • Conversations about restaurants and food	• Describing dishes

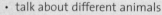

Grammar	Vocabulary	Reading	Listening	Developing conversations
• Comparing the past with now	• Describing where you live • Describing changes • Describing areas	• Priced out of the market	• Describing a flat • The area where you live	• Making comparisons • Asking about rules
• The future in the past	• Films, exhibitions and plays • Describing what's on • Describing an event	• What's on in Buenos Aires?	• Arranging a night out • How was it?	• Explaining where things are • Why you do not want to do things
• -ing clauses • Passives	• Animals • Keeping pets • Forming words	• Animals and the environment	• Unusual animal experiences • Pets	• Helping to tell stories
• used to and would • Expressing regrets (wish)	• Describing character • Synonyms	• Give me my space!	• Do you get on? • How do you know Nicolas?	• That's like …
• Third conditionals • should have	• Ways of travelling and travel problems • Phrasal verbs • Strong adjectives	• Journey to a new nation	• How was your journey? • Travel experiences	• Blaming people
• -ing forms and to-infinitives	• Computers • Talking about markets • Technology, programs and gadgets	• Here today, gone tomorrow!	• A computer problem • Gadgets and technology	• Responding to advice
• Reported speech • Reporting verbs	• Injuries and illness • Forming words • Explaining causes and results • Accidents and problems	• Fact or myth?	• At the doctor's • A big help	• Short questions with any
• Defining relative clauses	• Newspapers • Explaining who people are	• Seeking fame and fortune	• Stories in the news • Famous people	• Apparently

01 MY FIRST CLASS

In this unit you learn how to:
- ask and answer common questions
- maintain a conversation
- talk about language learning experiences
- tell stories

Grammar
- Question formation
- Narrative tenses
- Other uses of the past continuous

Vocabulary
- Learning languages
- Language words

Reading
- 'Language policy a disaster' says head teacher

Listening
- Getting to know people
- Explaining why you were late

NATIVE SPEAKER ENGLISH

I'm really into

In English, people often say *I'm really into* instead of *I really like*. It is generally used when talking about music, sport, films and free-time activities. This is particularly common among young people.
I'm really into cooking.
I'm really into jazz.

SPEAKING

A Did you have an interview before you began this course? What did they ask you?

B Work in pairs. Interview your partner for three minutes. Find out:
- information about your partner's life.
- about your partner's work / studies.
- where your partner learnt English.
- any other interesting information.

GRAMMAR Question formation

> We generally make questions by using the auxiliary verb (*be / have / do*) + the subject (*you / your parents / he / they*) and then a noun, adjective or verb.
>
> *Are you* a doctor?   *Have your parents left* already?
> What *did you do* yesterday?   What *are you doing* now?

A Complete the questions with the correct words.
1. A: Where .... from?
   B: Poland.
2. A: What .... do?
   B: I work in an office.
3. A: What .... studying?
   B: Law.
4. A: .... married?
   B: Not exactly. I live with my partner, but we're not married.
5. A: .... studied here before?
   B: Yeah, I was here last term, actually.
6. A: How long .... studying English?
   B: Ages. Probably ten years on and off.
7. A: What .... do when you're not working / studying?
   B: Oh, I'm really into surfing so I do that whenever I can. Apart from that, I like listening to music, shopping – that kind of thing.
8. A: .... any brothers or sisters?
   B: Yeah, I've got one sister.
9. A: How long .... study here?
   B: Probably till next June.
10. A: What .... do last weekend?
    B: Nothing special. I went out shopping on Saturday, but that's all really.

▶ Need help? Read the grammar reference on p. 136

LISTENING

You are going to hear Guy, a teacher at a language school, interviewing a new student, Olga.

A 🔊 **1.1 Listen. Answer the questions.**
1   Where is Olga from?
2   How long has she been studying English?
3   How long is she going to stay in Britain?

B   **Choose the words that you heard. Then listen again to check your answers.**
1   Hi. *Coming / Come in*. Sit down. Take a seat.
2   It's maybe 500 *kilometres / miles* from Moscow.
3   You haven't got a very *strange / strong* accent.
4   How long are you going to *study / stay* here?
5   How old are you, if you don't *mine / mind* me asking?
6   I'm going to put you in the *top / high* class.

LANGUAGE PATTERNS

Write the sentences in your language. Translate them back into English. Compare your English to the original.
I'd rather not say.
I'd rather not.
I'd rather not talk about it, if you don't mind.
I'd rather go somewhere else, if that's OK with you.
I'd rather do something else.

SPEAKING

A   **Work in pairs. Discuss these questions:**
•   Do you think many people from other countries know your home town? Why? / Why not?
•   Would you like to live and work abroad permanently? Why? / Why not?
•   Is it rude to ask someone their age?
•   Are there any other questions you should not ask when you do not know someone very well?

DEVELOPING CONVERSATIONS
Asking follow-up questions

We often follow up a question and answer by asking a related question to find out more details. Some of these questions are quite fixed.

A   **Can you remember the follow-up questions the teacher asked Olga after these questions?**
Where are you from?
How long have you been learning English?

B   **Match the questions 1–6 with the two possible follow-up questions a–f.**
1   What are you studying?
2   Have you studied here before?
3   What do you do when you're not studying?
4   Have you got any brothers or sisters?
5   What did you do at the weekend?
6   What do you do?

a   Whose class were you in? / Where did you learn your English?
b   What year are you in? / What does that involve?
c   Older or younger? / What do they do?
d   Where do you work? / Do you enjoy it?
e   Did you get anything nice? / Do you do that often?
f   How long have you been doing that? / What kind of music are you into?

C   🔊 **1.2 Listen and check your answers. You will only hear one of the follow-up questions in each case.**

D   **Can you think of one more follow-up question you might ask in 1–6 in exercise B?**

E   **Work in pairs. Have conversations using the six questions and the follow-up questions in exercise B.**

CONVERSATION PRACTICE

A   **Choose one of the people below. You are going to be this person. Do not tell anyone who you have chosen. Decide how to answer the questions we have looked at in this lesson.**

B   **Now have conversations with other students. Ask and answer the questions in the role of the person you chose.**

VOCABULARY Learning languages

A Work in pairs. Discuss what you think the words and phrases in **bold** mean.
1 Do you speak any other languages? How well?
 a I'm **fairly fluent** in Spanish. I **can maintain conversations on a range of topics**.
 b I **get by** if I'm travelling in Germany – I can do the basic things.
 c My Japanese is **very basic** – just a few words.
 d I'm more or less **bilingual** in English and Turkish.
 e I can have a conversation about some things in Italian if people **speak slowly**.
2 How did you learn your foreign language? Did you go to classes, **teach yourself**, or just **pick** it **up** off the street?
3 Do you find it easy to pick up a new language?
4 Why are you learning English?

B Look at question 1 and answers a–e in exercise A. Order the answers 1–5:
1 = the person who speaks the language best.
5 = the person who speaks the language worst.

C Work in groups. Answer the questions in exercise A. If you only speak English and your language, think of someone you know who speaks several languages and answer questions about them.

READING

You are going to read an article about British people and foreign languages.

A Look at these headings from the article. Discuss with a partner what you think is going to be said.
• 'Language policy a disaster' says head teacher
• Lack of motivation
• Lost trade
• Change to early teaching questioned

B Read the article and see if your ideas were correct.

C Decide if these sentences about the article are true or false.
1 UK students never have to study a foreign language.
2 Most British people only speak English.
3 Edward Jones' students never try to speak a foreign language.
4 Britain could do more business abroad.
5 The Government accepted there was a problem with their policy.
6 Learning languages earlier is definitely more effective.
7 The European Commission supports early teaching.
8 There aren't many opportunities for older people to learn.

EDUCATION

'Language policy a disaster' says head teacher

A **top head teacher** in the UK has called for a "review of languages policy" after the number of students taking exams in languages at sixteen fell by 14.4% because foreign languages are now optional after the age of fourteen.

Lack of motivation
Low levels of language learning are nothing new in Britain – over 60% of the population are unable to get by in a foreign language. As Edward Jones, a teacher from Manchester, says, "Many of my students lack **motivation** and, strangely, foreign travel doesn't really help. Often, they make an effort to speak French, or whatever, when they go abroad, but then find that local people reply in English and are more fluent than they are. They then feel embarrassed and just speak English after that. They come back to class asking 'What's **the point**?'"

> "Many primary school teachers don't have a good enough level to teach"

Lost trade
According to a recent report, the point is that Britain is losing millions of euros of trade because of the lack of language skills. **Relying on** everyone else to speak English is not enough.

Officials, however, defended their language policy. "We need to be realistic about what will improve language learning. Telling young people to learn a language at 16 won't help. It's better to give children the opportunity to learn a foreign language from the age of 7."

Change to early teaching questioned
While there have been similar changes

D Mark the text with a ✓ where you agree with what is said, a ✗ where you disagree, and a ! where something surprises you. Then work in pairs. Discuss your ideas.

E Work in pairs. Discuss what you think the words in **bold** in the text mean.

Speaking

A Read the short text about Brian Willis, the language expert from the article in *Reading*. Do you agree with the advice he gives? Why? / Why not?

B Have you ever had any embarrassing moments speaking a foreign language?

C What are your ideas about how best to learn a language? Use the following sentence starters to write five pieces of advice. Then work in groups. Compare your ideas.
It's important to …
It's best to …
Don't worry too much about …
Make sure you …
It's better to … than it is to …

in many countries, studies have questioned if it really is easier for younger children to learn languages. A European Commission report has noted that there is a lack of **evidence** about the usefulness of early teaching. Although the report is generally in favour, it suggests that the advantages of an early start depend on providing "a good **environment** for learning and **continuity** from one year to the next."

That can be difficult, according to Brian Willis, a language expert. "Many primary teachers have a basic level themselves and can't teach much. Also, students **progress at different speeds** – some pick things up quickly, some don't learn anything at all! When they go to secondary school, their teachers have to **deal with** a wide range of levels. It's very difficult." He suggests that making language learning **more available** to older learners is equally important. "They could provide cheap classes at work or in universities." Willis says it also helps if learners have more opportunities to hear foreign languages. "Places like Sweden and Holland show a lot of foreign films on TV and they don't dub foreign TV programmes and films into their own languages."

Brian Willis speaks eight different languages 'at various levels' and runs a company providing 'language solutions'.

People often say they have no talent for languages and so don't even try. It's nonsense. Everybody can learn to have basic conversations if they don't worry about feeling stupid sometimes. All fluent speakers have had experiences when they get things badly wrong, but it's important to keep practising.

I remember one mistake I made when I was teaching in Argentina. I had done a bit of Spanish before, but not much. In my first class, I was explaining to the students that I was a language learner too, so I knew how they felt. I told them – in Spanish – "Don't get embarrassed!" The students looked surprised and said "Embarazada?" "Yes," I said, "because if you're embarrassed, you can't talk" and acted being embarrassed. Several students laughed and we continued the class. I later found out I had used the wrong word and I'd actually said "Don't get pregnant!" I felt stupid, but it didn't stop me talking and learning. I just never made the same mistake again!

Vocabulary Language words

A It is a good idea to ask questions about the words you learn. Discuss the answers in teams.
1 What is the **adverb** of *fluent*? And what is the **noun**?
2 Is *lack* a **verb** or a noun or both?
3 Where is the **stress** when you say *available*?
4 How do you **pronounce** *foreign*?
5 What **preposition** follows the adjective *worried*?
6 What preposition follows the verb *rely*?
7 Can you say two **phrasal verbs** you have learnt in this unit?
8 What verb **collocates** (goes) with *mistake*?
9 What things can *improve*?
10 What's the **opposite** of a *slight accent*?

B Check with your teacher. Who had the most correct?

GRAMMAR Narrative tenses

A Without looking back at the article on p. 11, see if you can complete Brian Willis' story by putting the verbs in the correct tense. You will need to use:

> **The past simple:** I stayed in and watched TV. / I went to bed as soon as I got home. / I didn't hear you.
>
> **The past continuous:** I was chatting to him and he suddenly walked off. / I'm sorry. I wasn't listening.
>
> **The past perfect:** He told me he'd asked you. / In the morning, I realised I'd left my bag in the restaurant.

I remember one mistake I made when I ¹ .... (teach) in Argentina. I ² .... (do) a bit of Spanish before, but not much. In my first class, I ³ .... (explain) to the students that I was a language learner too, so I knew how they felt. I ⁴ .... (tell) them – in Spanish – "Don't get embarrassed!" The students ⁵ .... (look) surprised and ⁶ .... (say) "Embarazada?" "Yes," I said, "because if you're embarrassed, you can't talk" and ⁷ .... (act) being embarrassed. Several students laughed and we ⁸ .... (continue) the class. I later found out I ⁹ .... (use) the wrong word and I ¹⁰ .... (actually say) "Don't get pregnant!" I felt stupid, but it ¹¹ .... (not stop) me talking and learning. I just never made the same mistake again!

B Check your answers. Did you get any wrong? Why?

C Match the tense 1–3 with the usage a–c.
1 The past continuous
2 The past perfect
3 The past simple

a .... emphasises an action that happened before another past action, time or event
b .... shows an action was unfinished when another past action happened.
c .... shows completed actions that follow one after the other.

▶ Need help? Read the grammar reference on p. 137

D Work in pairs. Tell your partner about one of the following occasions:
- a time when you made a mistake.
- a time when someone didn't understand what you said.
- a time when something funny happened at school.

LISTENING

You are going to hear a conversation between two English-speaking students, Martin and Anna. They are studying Spanish in Spain.

A Work in pairs. Discuss these questions.
- Have you been late for a class or appointment recently?
- How late were you? Why were you late? What happened when you finally arrived?
- How many reasons for being late can you think of?

B 🔊 1.3 Listen to the conversation and find out why they both got to class late.

C In pairs, explain in detail why each person was late to class using the three narrative tenses.

D Look at the audioscript on p. 160. Did you use the tenses in the same way?

E Work in pairs. Would you rent the room. Why? / Why not?

GRAMMAR
Other uses of the past continuous

> Sometimes we use the past continuous to emphasise an activity and the fact that it went on for a period of time.
>
> I was banging on the door and shouting, but nothing. I'm looking for a flat to rent and I was phoning round a few places this morning before class.

A Complete the sentences with the past continuous form of the verbs in the box.

build	chat	cry	look for
drive	do	have	sort out

1 I didn't sleep very well last night. The baby .... all night.
2 A: My brother lived in Copenhagen for four years.
   B: What .... he .... there?
   A: He's a civil engineer and they .... a metro line there.
3 Sorry. I'm late. I .... to a friend and I forgot the time.
4 Sorry. I .... a coffee over the road.
5 Sorry I'm late. I .... a problem at work.
6 Sorry I'm late. I .... a parking space.
   I .... round in circles for about half an hour.

▶ Need help? Read the grammar reference on p. 137

B Work in pairs. Take turns saying sorry for being late. Give a different excuse each time. Reply with some of the expressions below.

Oh well. Never mind. At least you're here now.
It's OK. I've only just got here myself.
Don't worry about it. I haven't been waiting long.

SPEAKING

A Work in pairs. Use the pictures to help you tell the story of why Steve failed his exam.

B Have you ever missed or been late for an exam / important meeting / date? What happened?

DEVELOPING CONVERSATIONS

John was telling me ...

> We often use *X was telling me (that)* to report what someone said, and then continue the conversation by adding a comment or a question.

A Can you remember the example of this in the conversation between Anna and Martin in *Listening*? What did they say?

B Work in pairs. Have conversations using the words below. Try to continue each conversation for as long as possible. For example:

like tennis / play much

A: John was telling me you like tennis.
B: Yeah, that's right.
A: Do you play much?

1 lived in Germany / doing there?
2 play golf / any good?
3 just been on holiday / you go?
4 getting married / Congratulations / big day?
5 looking for a flat at the moment / any luck?

C Work in pairs. Report some of the things other students told you in the first part of this unit. Have conversations like this:
A: *X was telling me he / she listens to a lot of music.*
B: *Oh yeah? What kind?*

02 FEELINGS

VOCABULARY Feelings

A How are the people in the pictures feeling? Why? Can you use any of the words in the box to describe them?

exhausted	worried	fed up
confused	terrible	relaxed
stressed	in a good / bad mood	upset
furious	annoyed	disappointed
pleased	down	guilty

B Which of the words in A may show you are feeling: *tired, ill, sad, happy, unsure, angry,* or *bad* about something you did?

C Have you had any of these feelings recently? Why?

GRAMMAR *be, look, seem* etc

> *Be, feel, look, seem,* and *sound* are all linking verbs that can be followed directly by an adjective.

A Match 1–8 with the reasons a–h for the feelings.
1 Are you OK? You look a bit stressed.
2 Are you all right? You look exhausted.
3 Is Julie OK? She sounded a bit disappointed.
4 Is Mike all right? He seems a bit down.
5 Are you OK? You look a bit ill.
6 Are you all right? You seem totally confused.
7 Have you seen Ann? She sounded so relaxed!
8 Hi. You look like you're in a good mood.

a Yeah, I've just found out I've got a new job. I'm really pleased.
b I am! My car broke down and I had to walk home.
c Yeah, I feel terrible. I think I'm going to throw up.
d I am. I'm really behind with work and I've got exams next week.
e Yeah, I don't get this. What am I supposed to do?
f Yeah. I think the week in the spa really helped her.
g He's just split up with Jo and he's quite upset.
h Yeah. I think she expected to get a better mark as she'd studied so much.

B Write your own responses to 1–8. Practise in pairs.

▶ Need help? Read the grammar reference on p. 138

LANGUAGE PATTERNS

Write the sentences in your language. Translate them back into English. Compare your English to the original.
She expected to get a better mark.
I expected London to be more modern.
I didn't expect to have so much homework.
We didn't expect it to take so long.
We didn't expect you to be so early.

LISTENING

You are going to hear two conversations. The first is between two people talking about their friend Karim. The second is between two women, Belinda and Alisha.

A 🎵 2.1 **Listen. How do these people feel?**

Conversation 1		Conversation 2	
Karim	....	Belinda	....
		Alisha	....

B **Do you remember why they feel this way? Listen again and check.**

NATIVE SPEAKER ENGLISH

How come?

People often use *How come?* instead of *Why?*
A: *I can't come to your wedding, I'm afraid.*
B: *Oh what a shame. How come?*
A: *I've got an exam that day.*

SPEAKING

A **Work in pairs. Discuss these questions.**

- Do you find it easy to talk about your feelings? Who do you talk to if you have a problem?
- What would you do or say if a friend was upset? Would it be different if it was a man or a woman?
- What kind of things do you do to cheer yourself up?
- Are you good at sorting out problems?

DEVELOPING CONVERSATIONS
Response expressions

We use lots of short expressions to respond to news.

A **Look at the following conversations and try to translate the expressions in bold. Are there any you cannot translate?**

1. A: I can't drink at the moment. I'm pregnant.
   B: **Really? Congratulations!** When is the baby due?
2. A: I'm going to Canada to study English.
   B: **Wow, that's great!** How long are you going for?
3. A: I'm afraid I can't meet you tonight.
   B: **Oh, what a shame!** Are you sure?
4. A: My brother's not very well.
   B: **Oh no! I'm really sorry.** I hope it's not too serious.
5. A: I've lost my wallet.
   B: **On no, what a pain!** Did it have much in it?
6. A: I've found my wallet!
   B: **Phew, that's a relief!** Where was it?

PRONUNCIATION Responding

With positive responses our voice goes higher.

With negative responses our voice goes lower.

A 🎵 2.2 **Listen to the six responses from *Developing conversations* and copy the stress and intonation.**

B **Work in pairs. Practise 1–6 from *Developing conversations*. Try to continue them.**

CONVERSATION PRACTICE

A **Work in pairs. Think of a piece of good or bad news. Write a conversation like the ones you heard in *Listening*. Include response expressions.**

B **Try to remember your conversation. Act it out in front of another pair of students.**

SPEAKING

A Check you understand the words and expressions in **bold**. Then discuss the questions in groups.

1   How often do you do these things? In what situations?
  · **hug** people
  · **kiss** people **on the cheek** or **lips**
  · walk **arm in arm** with people or **hold hands**
  · **shake hands** or **bow**
  · touch people on the arm or **put** your arm **round their shoulder**

2   Do you do any of these things more often or less often than most people in your country? Why?
  I think I'm fairly typical. / I'm maybe a little bit unusual.

3   Have you been anywhere where they do these things differently to you? Where? What do they do?

READING

A Work in pairs. Look at the text *It only takes Juan Mann to change the world!* Discuss these questions.
  · What is the man doing in the pictures? Why?
  · What would you do if you saw someone like this?
  · Are any people like him famous in your local area / country? What for? How do people feel about them?

B Read and see if you feel differently about the man afterwards.

C Work in pairs. Discuss these questions. Then read the article again to check your answers.

1   What made Juan Mann start his campaign?
2   How did he feel when he went out the first time?
3   Who first asked for a hug and why?
4   How did Mann become so famous?
5   Why does he feel surprised and lucky about what he does now?
6   What is Mann's theory about why people want hugs?

D Which adjectives went with these nouns?

connections	....
attempt	....
star	....
year	....
identity	....
skills	....
help	....
plan	....

It Only Takes Juan Mann To Change The World!

In the modern world, it is not unusual for people to feel depressed or isolated. It can be hard to make **meaningful connections** with others. That was how 'Juan Mann' felt – until the day he decided to start giving free hugs. What started as a **desperate attempt** to change his own life has transformed him into an **international star**, thanks to the power of the Internet!

On returning to Sydney, Australia, in early 2004, after travelling in Europe, Mann had a **miserable year** in which his parents divorced and he found himself lonely and out of work. It was a depressing time. "I was alone. My family was elsewhere; my friends had all moved on. It was just me. It was just me, and I had to do something," said the famous hugger, who goes by the name of Juan Mann ('One man'), but who keeps his **true identity** secret.

"And I sat around for months doing nothing. Noticing, just watching the world. I didn't have a lot of contact with people. I was just on my own. And I thought I would try to step out of that and try and do something different."

And something different is exactly what he did! Mann went to one of Sydney's main shopping districts holding a cardboard sign saying 'Free Hugs' – and waited. He expected to last an hour at the most and asked a friend to come along to protect him, and left his wallet at home.

After 15 minutes, however, a woman approached and told him that her dog had died that morning and that it was also the first anniversary of the death of her daughter, and that she really needed a hug. Mann was happy to help!

His 'Free Hugs' campaign continued quietly for a couple of years until a friend made a film of him and posted it on YouTube, the online video sharing site. Since then, it has been seen by over 14 million people and fans have started copying him. Last year, the video clip was named the most inspiring on the site.

Mann finds this funny because at school he was told that he did not have the **social skills** to do humanitarian work. Yet he now seems to be a therapist for a whole city's problems.

"Every week a number of people will tell me their story, how they have suffered and how they get by, the mistakes they've made and the lessons they've learned," he said. "I'm very fortunate in what I do in that I learn from everyone else's mistakes as well as my own."

Mann claims many people need someone to listen to their problems – but are too embarrassed to call a help line or get **professional help**.

Mann's **original plan** was to personally take his campaign around the world, but he decided to stay in Sydney because "Now it all happens online."

Mann is currently writing a book about his experiences and intends to carry on hugging people "until nobody wants me." Until then, his message remains clear: have a hug. It will make you feel much better!

VOCABULARY Adjective collocations

A In the text, you read that 2004 was a depress*ing* time for Juan Mann. Match these *–ing* adjectives with the nouns.

inspiring	disappointing	confusing
exciting	annoying	relaxing

1 … holiday / bath / atmosphere / place / time
2 … habit / person / noise / problem / spam
3 … city / new development / discovery / opportunity
4 … teacher / speech / story / book / film / video clip
5 … instructions / message / grammar / explanation
6 … response / news / loss / result / game / sales

B Write eight true sentences using the new collocations.

GRAMMAR *–ing* / *–ed* adjectives

> Some adjectives, including those ending in *–ing*, only describe things which cause a feeling:
> The film was so *boring* that I fell asleep.
>
> The *–ed* and other adjectives in Vocabulary exercise A on p. 14 describe people's feelings:
> I'm *exhausted*. I need to go to bed.

A Choose the correct word (in *italics*) in sentences 1–6 below.
1 I'm *confusing / confused*. What did he say?
2 This is really *interesting / interested*. I love Maths.
3 I got a *disappointing / disappointed* mark in my test.
4 I'm so *boring / bored*! I can't stand algebra!
5 I hate being in my Dad's class. He's so *embarrassing / embarrassed*!
6 Why do I have to sit next to him? He's so *scary / scared*!

B Now match 1–6 to the pictures

▶ Need help? Read the grammar reference on p. 138

SPEAKING

A Work in pairs. Discuss these questions.
- Does your town or area have any similar problems to Sydney?
- At one point the city council tried to stop Juan Mann's free hugs campaign. Why do you think they did that?
- Has your government tried to stop something popular? Why? Was it successful?
- Can you think of any other news stories which have been spread through the Internet?
- Have you ever posted anything on the Internet? What?

LISTENING

You are going to hear two friends talking. Sarah has just met Louise in front of a shop.

A **What things do you think they will say? Have the conversation.**

B **♦ 2.3 Listen. Do the adjectives in the box describe Sarah or Louise?**

| annoyed | exhausted | happy |
| mysterious | shocked | stressed |

C **Why are they *annoyed, happy, being mysterious*, etc.? Listen again if you need to.**

GRAMMAR Present continuous

A **Write the missing words from *Listening* in the present continuous.**
1 I .... quite hard at the moment. We .... at nine most days!
2 So what .... here? ....?
3 Not really. I .... a friend here. I'm a bit early.
4 I .... someone from work.
5 Why .... so mysterious about it? It's unlike you. You normally tell me everything.
6 I .... any more money or anything. I .... something different.
7 What .... on Friday? Do you fancy meeting?
8 I'm afraid I can't. I play badminton on Fridays and this Friday .... for a meal afterwards.

B **Work in pairs. Discuss the questions.**
1 Which examples of the present continuous in 1–8 in exercise A:
   a show an action is temporary and / or unfinished?
   b show something in the future that involves an arrangement with other people?
2 Which sentence in exercise A uses the verb *be* in the present continuous form? Why?

▶ **Need help? Read the grammar reference on p. 139**

GRAMMAR Present continuous / present simple questions

> Double questions are very common in English. Notice these examples from *Listening*.
>
> So what *are you doing here? Are you window shopping?*
> What *are you doing* on Friday? *Do you fancy* meeting?

A **Make double questions in the present continuous or present simple with the ideas in 1–8.**
1 How / your course / go? you / still / enjoy / it?
2 What / you / do / now? you / fancy / going for a coffee?
3 What / your sister / do / these days? she / still / study?
4 you / work / this weekend? you / want / go for a picnic?
5 I / need / a coat? it / still / raining outside?
6 What / you / do here? you / work / near here?
7 What / you / do? you / wait / to be served?
8 What / be / the matter with her? Why / she / shout / me?

B **Match the answers a–h with the questions 1–8 in exercise A.**
a I'm afraid so. I could meet you later today though, if you like.
b Yeah, it's pouring down. I've got an umbrella, if you need one.
c I don't know. She's been in a bad mood all day. Just ignore her.
d Yeah, the assistant is just sorting out this lady's problem.
e Sorry, I'm in a rush. My friend's waiting for me.
f Yeah, she graduated last year, but now she's doing a Masters.
g Yeah, although I'm finding it a lot harder than before.
h No, I'm just visiting a client. I'm just getting a sandwich before I go there.

C **Work in pairs. Have conversations asking and answering 1–4 below. Add second questions to make double questions. Try to continue each conversation for as long as you can. For example:**
A: *What are you doing these days? Are you still studying?*
B: *No, I'm working in a bank now. And what are you doing these days? Are you still teaching?*
A: *Yes, but I'm not enjoying it!*

1 What are you doing these days?
2 What are you doing here?
3 What are you doing after the class?
4 What's the matter with him?

DEVELOPING CONVERSATIONS
Making excuses

Look at the example from *Listening*. We often use the present simple or continuous to explain why we can't or don't want to do something.

A: *What are you doing on Friday? Do you fancy meeting? It'd be nice to hear more of your news.*
B: *I'm afraid I can't. I play badminton on Fridays.*
OR *I'm going away for the weekend.*

A Give reasons for refusing the following requests:
1 A: Do you think you could help me with this?
  B: No, sorry, but I can't. ...
2 A: We're going out for dinner later. Would you like to join us?
  B: Oh, I'd love to, but I can't. ...
3 A: Can I just check my email on your computer?
  B: No, sorry. ...
4 A: Do you really like this kind of music? Can I just turn it off?
  B: No, don't! ...
5 A: This is rubbish! Is it OK if I change the channel?
  B: No, it's not! ...
6 A: I was wondering if you wanted to go out somewhere with me on Friday?
  B: Oh, it's nice of you to ask me, but I can't. ...

B Work in pairs. Take turns reading out the questions. Read your response and continue the conversation.

SPEAKING

A Look at the pictures below. Are they your idea of holiday heaven or of holiday hell? Why?

B Read the short text about other people's ideas of heaven and hell. Work in pairs. Discuss which of the ideas you agree with. What is your favourite comment? Why?

C Write your own idea of heaven and hell. Explain why. Use language from this unit or the text such as:
verbs: *love, annoy, hate, can't stand, depress, bore, etc.*
adjectives: *relaxing, annoying, boring, fantastic, amazing, etc.*

D Tell different students your ideas. Do they agree with you?

MY IDEA OF HEAVEN IS:

MY IDEA OF HELL IS:

...having a long hot bath at the end of the day with candles and a glass of wine – it's just so relaxing.
Carla, 35, Scotland

...playing with my five-year-old son. It always puts me in a good mood. Hamid, 28, Morocco

...driving round in my sports car in the summer with the roof down and the Rolling Stones playing on the CD. I love it. Brad, 49, Australia

...being stuck in a lift with Brad Pitt. Patricia, 23, Mexico

...having a barbecue with my family. Zeynep, 14, Turkey

...being in a quiet room with a good book. Shirley, 67, England

...scoring the winning goal at football. It's the best feeling ever. Pavel, 13, Czech Republic

...going skiing. It's exciting. You're in amazing scenery, and it's fantastic! In-ha, 20, South Korea

...having to drive anywhere. I hate it! And other drivers just annoy me. Joan Carles, 43, Spain

...sunbathing on a beach. I can't stand the heat and I find it incredibly boring. Frank, 19, Germany

...looking after my baby brother. He's so annoying. Celine, 15, France

...watching the news. It depresses me too much! Concha, 21, Peru

...walking anywhere with my parents. I can't stand it. We never go anywhere interesting. Daffyd, 10, Wales

...being stuck in a lift with any politician. Imagine, a boring situation with someone who bores you! Sofia, 19, Italy

...taking an exam. I get so nervous. It's awful. Cissy, 17, Hong Kong

03 TIME OFF

In this unit you learn how to:
- describe interesting places
- ask for and make recommendations
- talk about problems
- talk about the weather

Grammar
- Present perfect questions
- The future

Vocabulary
- Places of interest
- Holiday problems
- Weather

Reading
- Workers can't bank on holidays

Listening
- Deciding where to go sightseeing
- Talking about your holiday plans

SPEAKING

A Work in pairs. Discuss the question.
What are the main tourist attractions locally /
regionally / nationally?

VOCABULARY Places of interest

A Complete the sentences with the words in the boxes.

galleries	lake	market	palace	square

1 There's a huge .... about ten miles outside
   of town, which is a great place to go fishing.
2 There's a great street .... out in the east of
   the city.
3 There are lots of nice cafés and restaurants in the
   main ....
4 There's an old royal .... down by the river.
   They were restoring it for years and they've just
   reopened it.
5 It's a very cultural city. There are lots of great
   museums and .... there.

old town	castle	mosque	ruins	theme park

6 There's an incredible .... there, where the
   Royal Family spend their holidays.
7 There's a really fun .... down by the beach.
   They've got some great rides there.
8 There are some historic buildings in the ....
9 There are lots of ancient .... to go and see all
   along the coast.
10 There's a beautiful .... near here. You'll hear
    the call to prayer in the morning.

B Complete the expressions with prepositions from exercise A.
a **about** ten miles / sixty kilometres / an hour
   .... **of town**
b .... **in the** west of the city / desert / country
c .... **by the** river / beach / lake
d **all** .... **the** coast / river / canal

**C Think of five towns / cities / areas in your country
that contain places of interest. Choose language from
exercises A and B to describe the places of interest.
Then work in pairs. Have conversations like this:**
A: Have you ever been to ...?
B: No, never. What's it like?
A: Oh, it's great. There are some / lots of amazing ... there.
   There's a / an incredible / great ... there.
B: Oh really? It sounds great.

LISTENING

You are going to hear a conversation between a tourist and a hotel receptionist in Kraków, Poland.

A Look at the places to visit in and around the city. Work in pairs. Decide which you would go and see and why.

B 🔊 3.1 Listen. Which of the things in Kraków are discussed? What does the tourist, Claire, decide to do? Work in pairs and compare your ideas.

C Complete the sentences. Then listen again to check your answers.
1 I .... if you can help me.
2 I'm .... of going sightseeing today.
3 Can you .... anywhere good to go?
4 It depends .... you like.
5 I'm not really a big .... of churches, to be honest.
6 Well, in that case, you .... try Kazimierz.
7 .... about a guided tour of Nowa Huta?
8 I can call and .... a .... for you, if you want.

DEVELOPING CONVERSATIONS
Recommendations

A **Put the two conversations into the correct order.**
...... Well, **you could try** Oxford Street. There are lots of big department stores there.
...... Oh, OK. Well, **in that case, how about** Portobello Road? It's a big street market. You can find lots of bargains there.
...... **To be honest, I'm not really a big fan of** department stores.
...... Oh, that sounds great. I love that kind of thing. Is it easy to get to?
_1_ **I'm thinking of** doing some shopping today. Can you recommend anywhere?
...... Yes, very. Here. I'll show you on the map.

...... Right. I'm not really into museums, to be honest.
...... Well, you could try the local museum. That's quite close to here. They've got lots of interesting things in there.
...... No, it's quite cheap. It should only be about $10.
...... I'm thinking of doing some sightseeing today. Can you recommend anywhere?
...... Oh, that sounds better. Is it expensive to get into?
...... That's OK. In that case, how about going to the Roman ruins down by the lake? There are also some nice cafés and you can swim there.

B Work in pairs. Practise reading the conversations.

CONVERSATION PRACTICE

A Work in pairs. Role-play a conversation between a tourist and a hotel receptionist in the place where you live. When you have finished, change roles and start again.
Student A: you are the tourist. You are thinking of going sightseeing. Ask for recommendations. Reject some before deciding on one.
Student B: you are the hotel receptionist. Suggest some different places to the tourist. Explain why they are good.

Kraków

Rynek Glowny
The main market square in Kraków – a huge medieval square in the centre of the old town.

Full-day tour to Auschwitz-Birkenau Museum
Auschwitz-Birkenau was a Nazi concentration camp, where over a million Jews were killed during World War II.

Half-day tour to Wieliczka Salt Mine
These ancient mines are now a World Heritage Site.

Full-day tour to the Tatras mountains
Enjoy a day's walking in this beautiful location.

Tour of Nowa Huta
Visit the old Communist housing district built during Stalin's time.

Alchemia
Great local bar/club with live music six nights a week.

Kazimierz
The old Jewish district, now a lively area with excellent nightlife.

St. Mary's Church
The city's most important church, built in the sixteenth century.

VOCABULARY Holiday problems

A **What problems are the people having in each of the pictures?**

B **Complete the sentences with the pairs of words from the box.**

arguing + angry	stole + spoilt
stuck + hours	crowded + space
upset + threw up	poured + windy
ripped off + charged	missed + lost

1 Our flight was delayed so we .... our connecting flight. Then they .... our luggage.
2 Two days before we left, we got robbed. Someone .... my bag with my camera, purse and passport. We'd actually had a lovely time up till then, but that rather .... the holiday.
3 The beach was always really .... You could hardly find a .... to put your towel.
4 The weather was awful. It .... with rain most of the time and it was really .... as well.
5 I don't know if it was the food or the water, but I had a really bad .... stomach. I was in and out of the toilet for three days and I .... twice.
6 We got .... a couple of times. In one restaurant, they .... €20 for a salad.
7 My sisters didn't stop .... with each other the whole time we were away, and then my parents got .... with them. It was a nightmare!
8 There was an accident on the motorway. We were .... in a traffic jam for ....

C **Have any of these things happened to you? When?**

READING

You are going to read an article about public holidays and workers' holiday entitlement in different countries. Note that public holidays are known as *bank holidays* in the UK.

A **Work in pairs. Discuss these questions.**
- How many public holidays are there where you live? Do you take all of them?
- What is your favourite public holiday? Are there any you do not like? Why?
- What did you do on the last public holiday?

B **Read these Holiday facts. Is there anything you find surprising? Why?**

> **HOLIDAY FACTS**
> - The legal minimum holiday entitlement in the EU is 20 days per year, excluding weekends.
> - The UK only gets eight public holidays a year, compared to a European average of 10.8.
> - Slovenia has the most public holidays in the EU with 16.
> - UK workers have no legal right to have public holidays.
> - Germany takes the most time off on average at 43 days a year, with Finland next on 39.
> - Japan actually allows 17.5 days per year, but on average workers only take 9.

C **Now read the article opposite. Answer these questions.**
1 Why does the writer refer to the August bank holiday as an 'annual horror show'?
2 What are the unions complaining about?
3 What changes do the unions want?
4 What is *karoshi* and why is it mentioned?
5 What problems are caused by the high number of public holidays in Puerto Rico?

D **Work in pairs. What do these numbers in the article refer to?**

millions	20	16	hundreds
eight	one	three	twenty-one

E **Work in small groups. Discuss these questions.**
- Do you think the union is right? Why? / Why not?
- Do you think your country needs more public holidays? Why? / Why not?

Workers Can't Bank on Holidays

The August bank holiday is here again. The busiest weekend of the year will see millions of people get stuck in traffic on the motorway; bored children ask, "Are we there yet?"; delays at airports and accidents on the roads. Hundreds of people will get sunburnt on crowded beaches; children will throw up after eating too much ice cream; adults will drink too much beer; families will argue and kids will scream "It's not fair!" Then it's home: more traffic jams, more delays, more arguments.

You might think that anyone who is going to miss this annual horror show is lucky. However, British trade unions are using this weekend to highlight the low number of public holidays in Britain compared to the rest of Europe. They also want to draw attention to the fact that a large number of workers are not getting their legal entitlement of twenty days' holiday per year.

A trade union spokesman said yesterday, "British workers get fewer public holidays than workers in any other European country, and the government also allows companies to include those eight days within the compulsory 20. British workers are being ripped off and it needs to change." The unions want the government to start by declaring three new public holidays. Britain has just eight public holidays compared to 16 in Slovenia.

The unions also say there is a worrying trend for some workers not to take their full entitlement to holiday because they have too much work. In Japan, lack of holidays has been linked to the problem of *karoshi*: dying from overworking.

While Britain and Japan may want more, other countries are debating whether to reduce the number of holidays. France cancelled one holiday in May to help pay for the care of old people. In Puerto Rico, businesses have complained that the high number of holidays – government workers take twenty-one – is damaging the economy. They argue they increase costs, raise unemployment, and mean higher prices for everyone.

SPEAKING

You are going to read different people's experiences of the issues in the article.

A Work in groups of three.
Student A, read about **Maggie** on p. 156.
Student B, read about **Luca** on p. 157.
Student C, read about **Ethan** on p. 158.

Don't look back at the texts. Role-play a conversation asking and answering these questions.
- What do you do?
- How much holiday do you get per year?
- Is that the same for everyone in the UK / Italy / the US? Are you happy with what you get now?
- Have you been away on holiday recently? Where did you go?

B When you finish, discuss these questions.
- Is it OK to miss school to go on holiday?
- Whose last holiday was the best: Maggie's, Luca's or Ethan's? Why?
- Which of the three people is most like you?

GRAMMAR Present perfect questions

> Look at this possible exchange from the role-play in *Speaking*.
>
> A: *Have you been* away on holiday recently?
> B: Yes, I went camping in Tuscany. *Have you* ever *been* there?
> A: No, never. What's it like?
>
> To ask about general experiences before now, we often use the present perfect simple. Don't just give a *Yes* or *No* answer – add a comment.

A Add *Yes* or *No, never* to the front of the following answers to the question *Have you (ever) been to X?*
...... What's it like?
...... It's supposed to be amazing.
...... Several times.
...... I've never really fancied it.
...... I'd love to, though.
...... It's great. You should go.
...... I wouldn't go there, if I were you. It's not worth it.
...... but I'm actually going to go there this summer.
...... Have you? I've heard it's quite nice.

▶ Need help? Read the grammar reference on p. 140

B Think of six places you have been to for which you would give the answers in exercise A. Write only the names of the places on a clean piece of paper.

C Work in pairs. Swap your piece of paper with a partner. Ask 'Have you been to ...' questions about the places on your partner's list.

VOCABULARY Weather

A Match the sentence halves.

1 It said it'll be hot and humid during the day, and so
2 They said it's going to be really windy, so
3 Apparently, it's going to be really sunny, so
4 They said it's going to be freezing and
5 They said it's going to be boiling hot all week and
6 Apparently, it's going to pour down tomorrow, so
7 They said it's going to be generally quite warm, but
8 The same as today: grey, cloudy, cold, but

a it might drop to minus 10°.
b on Tuesday it might reach 36°. I hate the heat!
c there might possibly be a storm this evening.
d we should take down the parasol or it'll blow away.
e I'll probably stay at home and keep out of the rain!
f hopefully I might get a bit of a suntan!
g they said it might clear up next week!
h it might be a bit chilly, especially at night.

B Spend two minutes memorising the sentence endings in exercise A. Then work in pairs.
Student A: say 1–8.
Student B: close your book and say the endings.

C Work in pairs. Discuss these questions:
* Do you know what the forecast is for tomorrow / the weekend / next week?
* Are there any bad times to visit where you live because of the weather? Why? And when is the best time to visit?
* How many of the different kinds of weather in exercise A have you had in the last year?

LISTENING

You are going to hear two English people discussing their plans for the coming Easter holiday. They also talk about the weather in Italy and the UK.

A Before you listen, work in pairs. Discuss why the people might describe the weather as annoying or worrying.

B ◈ 3.2 Now listen and complete the table.

	Cristina	Andrew
Plans		
Weather		

LANGUAGE PATTERNS

Write the sentences in your language. Translate them back into English. Compare your English to the original.
It depends on the weather.
It depends (on) whether it's raining (or not).
It depends (on) how much it costs.
It depends (on) how far it is to walk.
It depends (on) how long it'll take.
It depends (on) what time I get up.

SPEAKING

A Work in pairs. Discuss the question.
What is the most important thing for you when choosing a holiday? Why?
* the countryside
* being near a beach or a pool
* the nightlife
* guaranteed good weather
* the local sights
* peace and quiet
* the history
* the food

GRAMMAR The future

A We use lots of different forms to talk about the future. How many do you know?

B Match the structures 1–7 from *Listening* with a–d below. Some structures match more than once.

1 I'**m** not **going to** be here. `a`
2 I'**ve got** a week off work. ☐
3 It'**ll probably** clear up later. ☐
4 We'**re thinking of** go**ing** to Palermo. ☐
5 I'**ve got to** work. ☐ ☐
6 I'**m** hav**ing** lunch with my parents. ☐
7 I **might** go for a picnic in the park. ☐ ☐

a Something which is definite / planned / organised.
b Something which is uncertain / unplanned.
c An obligation.
d Only a 50% certainty.

▶ **Need help? Read the grammar reference on p. 141**

C Complete the conversations with the words in the box.

| going to | 'll | thinking | might |
| meeting | 's got | 've got to | might |

A: Are you going away in the summer?
B: Probably, but we're ¹ .... of leaving it to the last minute to book, and trying to get some cheap package deal to Greece or somewhere like that. What about you?
A: Not abroad. We ² .... probably just go to my parents' in Scotland at some point. I suppose we ³ .... go camping if the weather's OK, but it really depends on my wife. She's not a big fan of camping.

A: Have you got any plans for the weekend?
B: Yeah, I'm probably ⁴ .... a friend on Sunday, but I'm waiting for him to confirm. He ⁵ .... an exam next week, so he ⁶ .... have to study on Sunday – it depends how much he gets done on Saturday. Anyway, he is ⁷ .... ring me at some point on Saturday evening to confirm. Why? What about you?
A: Well, unfortunately, I ⁸ .... do some shopping at some point, as I've got nothing in the fridge. Apart from that, no plans at all.
B: Well, we could meet up on Saturday, if you like.

D Work in pairs. Discuss these questions.
· Are you going away in the summer?
· Have you got any plans for the weekend?
· What are you doing after the class?
· Are you going to do anything for your birthday?
· Are you going to continue studying English after this course?
· What are you going to do after you leave school / graduate?
· Have you got any plans to change jobs?

SPEAKING

A Look at the calendar at the bottom of the page.

There is a public holiday on the Tuesday. You also have three days annual holiday till the end of the year, so you could take more time off if you want. It might rain on Saturday or Sunday and be a bit chilly, but it is going to clear up and get hotter during the week. Write in the calendar:

· two nice things you are going to do.
· one other appointment.
· one thing you have got to do.

Think about other things you might possibly do and when.

B Work in pairs. Role-play a conversation. Try to arrange to do something together during the week. In the conversation, try to use some of the language you have learnt in this unit. Start by asking: *So what are you doing ...?*

OCTOBER

Sunday 1st	Monday 2nd	Tuesday 3rd
		public holiday
Wednesday 4th	**Thursday 5th**	**Friday 6th**
	dentist 11 a.m.	

04 INTERESTS

In this unit you learn how to:
- talk about free-time activities
- talk about sports
- talk about music
- pronounce, and understand, groups of words

Grammar
- Frequency (present and past)
- Duration (past simple and present perfect continuous)

Vocabulary
- Evening and weekend activities
- Problems and sports
- Music

Reading
- The playlist of your life

Listening
- Did you have a good weekend?
- A martial art

SPEAKING

A Work in groups. Discuss these questions:
- Look at the picture. Do you have any hobbies like these?
- What did you do at the weekend?
- What did you do last night?

VOCABULARY
Evening and weekend activities

A Which of the four endings are not correct?
1 I stayed in and ...
   studied / played football / took it easy / tidied up.
2 I played ...
   roller-blading / on the computer / golf / tennis.
3 I went ...
   clubbing / a run / cycling / walking in the country.
4 I went for ...
   a meal / a ride on my bike / the gym / a swim.
5 I went to ...
   the cinema / shopping / Karen's house for dinner / a bar to watch the football.

B Think of two more ways you could finish each sentence starter in exercise A.

LISTENING

A 🔊 4.1 Listen to four short conversations and find out what the speakers did and when.

B Listen again. Note down the questions asked.

C Do you remember what the answers to the questions were? Role-play the conversations.

PRONUNCIATION Connected speech

Hearing words in groups can be confusing. Fluent speakers join words together – especially when final consonants are followed by vowels.
Not as much as I used to

They also don't pronounce certain letters – such as when final consonants are followed by a word beginning with another consonant.
Not as much as I used to

A 🔊 4.1 Listen to the fourth conversation (between Jason and Mohammed) again – and read the audioscript on p. 162. Notice the linking and missing sounds. Practise reading the conversation.

LANGUAGE PATTERNS

Write the sentences in your language. Translate them back into English. Compare your English to the original.
Nearly every day, unless I'm really busy.
Most weekends, unless it's raining.
I usually play on Saturdays, unless I'm away on business.
I never missed a lesson, unless I was really ill.
He used to see us every day, unless we were away.

C Work in groups of three or four. Ask about habits using the questions and patterns in Exercise A.

▶ **Need help? Read the grammar reference on** **p. 142**

GRAMMAR
Frequency (present and past)

We can ask about frequency in the present with these patterns:

Do you + verb + *much / a lot*?
How often do you + verb?
Do you ever + verb?

A Complete the sentences with the words in the box.

every	used	quite	all	hardly	'd	that

1 A: So do you read much?
   B: Yeah, ... the time. I read at least a book a week.
2 A: Do you go swimming a lot?
   B: Yeah, nearly .... day, unless I'm really busy.
3 A: Do you go to the cinema much?
   B: Yeah, ... a lot. I probably go once every two weeks.
4 A: How often do you play games on the computer?
   B: Not .... often, actually. It's not really my kind of thing.
5 A: So how often do you go to the gym?
   B: .... ever now, to be honest. Today was the first time in ages. I used to go more often.
6 A: Do you ever watch your favourite team play?
   B: Yeah, but not as much as I .... like to. I only went four times last season.
7 A: Do you eat out a lot?
   B: Not as much as we .... to. Before we were married, we went out all the time.

B Underline all the frequency expressions. Translate them. Then discuss these questions.
- What tense do we use in English when talking about frequency in the present?
- Which two structures do we use in English when talking about frequency in the past?

DEVELOPING CONVERSATIONS
Are you any good?

Look at this extract from the fourth conversation in *Listening*. Notice how the short answer is explained.
A: *So are you any good?*
B: *I'm OK. I'm quite good in defence, but I'm useless at shooting. I think the last time I scored a goal was about three years ago.*

A Decide which of these activities the people are talking about in sentences 1–8.

basketball	rollerblading	judo	football
swimming	table tennis	tennis	skiing

1 **No, I'm useless**. I usually hit the ball out of the court or into the net.
2 No, I'm useless. I can't even kick the ball in a straight line.
3 **No, not really**. I can do a hundred metres breaststroke, but that's all. I can't do the front crawl.
4 No, not really. I can stand up and go in a straight line, but that's all. I can't do turns or go backwards.
5 **I'm OK**. We had a table at home, so I used to play quite a lot.
6 I'm OK. I can do the basic moves, but nothing complicated.
7 **Yeah, quite good**. I can do black runs, but I go down them slowly!
8 Yeah, quite good. I used to be in a team. I used to be good at free throws.

B Ask each other about your abilities in sports, music etc., using *Are you any good ...?* Explain your answers fully.

CONVERSATION PRACTICE

A Have a similar conversation to the one in File 6 on p. 157, but choose a different sport or activity. Spend two minutes thinking about how to answer the questions. Start by saying 'So did you have a nice weekend'?

LISTENING

You are going to hear a conversation about a martial art between Ian and Rika. They are both sales reps for a large publishing company. Ian is visiting Rika in Japan.

A Before you listen, work in pairs. Discuss these questions:
- Which martial arts do you know?
- Have you ever done any martial arts?
- Have you ever entered any sports tournaments or competitions? How did you get on?

B 🔊 4.2 Listen and answer these questions.
1 Why is Rika famous?
2 How often does she practise her martial art?
3 Why didn't Ian know about this?

C Work in pairs. Decide if these sentences about the conversation are true or false. Can you remember what Ian and Rika actually said? Listen again and check if you need to.
1 Someone asked Rika to sign a piece of paper.
2 Rika won the judo tournament she entered.
3 You need to be tall to do judo.
4 Rika started doing judo when she was a child.
5 Her teachers at school persuaded her to start doing it.
6 Rika boasts about how good she is.
7 She hurt herself last year because she had not prepared for her fight properly.
8 Rika found it easy to start fighting again after her injury.

D Work in groups of three. Discuss these questions:
- Do you know anyone who does something in their free time that other people might find surprising?
- Do you know anyone who was bullied at school? Why?
- Do you know anyone who is big-headed? In what way?

NATIVE SPEAKER ENGLISH

kind of
People often use *kind of* to modify an adjective or a verb. It means *more or less, but not exactly*.
He's been on TV a few times, so he's kind of famous now!
I didn't really plan to do it. It just kind of happened!

VOCABULARY
Problems and sports

Rika hurt her back fighting in a competition. Here are some other problems you can have during or after sports activities.

A Complete the sentences with the words in the box.

banged	fell	stiff	unfit
bloody	broke	beat	pulled

1 I went running with a friend, but I had to stop after ten minutes. I'm so ....!
2 We did a twenty-mile walk yesterday, so my legs are really .... this morning.
3 I didn't really warm up before we started playing and so I .... a muscle in my leg.
4 I hadn't played for ages, which is why he .... me so easily.
5 I was playing football and .... my leg. It was in plaster for six weeks.
6 I fell off my bike and .... my head. Luckily, I was wearing a helmet.
7 My son kicked a ball in my face and gave me a .... nose.
8 I injured my back skating. I tried to stand up and I slipped and .... backwards.

B Have you ever had any of the problems in exercise A? What happened?

GRAMMAR Duration

A **Find the grammatical mistakes in these sentences from the conversation in *Listening*. Correct the mistakes.**

1 Rika usually practises all the techniques during at least an hour a day.
2 After her injury, Rika didn't fight since a couple of months.
3 She's doing quite a lot of yoga for the last few months.
4 She used to get into fights since she was at school.
5 She's been doing judo ever from she was a kid.

B **Compare the sentences with the audioscript on pp. 162–163 and complete the rules.**

> **Rules**
> Use .... (not *during*) with periods of time in the past and present.
> Use .... to show the *start* of a period of time from the past to now.
> Use the .... tense to talk about periods including now.
> Use the .... tense to talk about periods of time which are finished.

C **Choose the correct word or words in italics.**

1 A: I've been doing yoga off and on *for / since* January, but I didn't warm up before the class one day and pulled a muscle, so I didn't go *for / during* a while.
  B: Really? You need to be careful.
2 A: I played him every week *from / for* about five years, but only managed to beat him once!
  B: I'm not surprised you gave up.
3 A: My brother's been able to ski *from / ever since* I can remember. He does a lot of off-piste skiing.
  B: Wow. That's amazing. *I'm / I've been* learning for a week now and I can only go about 100 metres before I fall down!
4 A: I think I spent too long in the gym yesterday. I'm really stiff this morning.
  B: How long *were you / have you been* there for?
  A: About two hours!
5 A: I've got my judo class tonight.
  B: How long *are you / have you been* doing that?
  A: *Since / For* last year. I feel so much fitter – and I've also managed to lose five kilos.
6 A: I used to play for a local team.
  B: How long *did you do / have you been doing* that?
  A: *Until / Since* quite recently, actually. I injured my knee really badly last season and had to give up.

D **Work in pairs. Tell your partner about a sport or hobby you do now, and one you used to do in the past. Your partner should reply:**
Really? How long have you been ...?
Really? How long did you ...?

Ask further questions to develop the conversation.

▶ **Need help? Read the grammar reference on p. 143**

PRONUNCIATION Auxiliaries

How long is used with other tenses as well as the past simple and the present perfect continuous. It is easy to mishear these questions because the auxiliary verb is pronounced very softly.

A 🔊 **4.3 Listen to these words from some questions. Repeat them.**

was your	do you	were you	did it
are you	will it	have you	does it

B 🔊 **4.4 Listen and write down the eight *How long ...?* questions.**

SPEAKING

A **Work in groups of three or four. Look at the list below. Find out who 'wins' each category in the list. Try to win as many categories as you can by talking about yourself or about people you know. Take turns to start. Ask *How long ...?* questions to find out extra details. For example:**
A: I think my grandparents have had the longest marriage.
B: Why? How long have they been married?
A: 51 years!

- the longest marriage
- the shortest journey to this class today
- the longest journey to work
- studying English the shortest length of time
- the longest flight
- the most time spent on their homework
- the longest wait for a plane or train
- the shortest time in their current house
- the longest film you have seen

DEVELOPING CONVERSATIONS
Music, films and books

We often move from more general questions to more specific.

A Put the conversation into the correct order.

...... Erm, I don't know ... Girls Rock!, Soul Train, **stuff like that**.

...... **All sorts** really, **but mainly** pop music and R&B.

...... Oh right. **Anyone in particular?**

...... Yeah, all the time.

...... So **have** you bought **anything good recently?**

...... **What kind of** music **are you into?**

..1.. **Do you** listen to music **much?**

...... Well, I downloaded this great song by K Boy. It's fantastic.

B 🔊 **4.5 Listen and check your answers.**

C Have similar conversations about music, books, films, and TV programmes. Try and re-use the expressions in bold in exercise A.

VOCABULARY Music

pop	jazz
blues	heavy metal
folk	techno
hip-hop	R&B / Soul
classical	salsa

A Look at the adjectives in bold in 1–10 below. Discuss which adjectives you would personally use to describe the kinds of music in the box.

1 If a song is **catchy**, you quickly want to sing it and can't stop.
2 If music is **repetitive**, it has the same boom, boom beat all the way through.
3 If it's **heavy** or loud, it's very noisy.
4 If it's **soft**, it's quiet.
5 If we say the music or lyrics – the words to the song – are **sentimental,** they are romantic or sad in a bad way.
6 If we say a song is very **commercial**, it is a negative way of saying it is written to sell lots of records.
7 If music or songs are **moving**, they make you cry.
8 If music is **bland**, it's boring.
9 If music is **uplifting**, it makes you happy or hopeful.
10 If music is **depressing**, it makes you sad.

THE PLAYLIST OF YOUR LIFE

Now that even your grandmother can download music, it seems albums are a thing of the past. You just create your own playlist to suit every mood and occasion. We set our readers 'a playlist challenge'. Here is their response.

All time classics playlist
The top of any all-time classic list has to be *Hey Jude* by the Beatles. It's a song you immediately want to sing along with. The Beatles are why I learnt English. *Love Phantom* is by B'z, a Japanese band. I saw them live and they were loud and energetic – incredible. *[Toshi, Japan]*

All time classics playlist

Hey Jude The Beatles
Love Phantom B'z
Stairway to Heaven Led Zeppelin
Yellow Coldplay
Hotel California The Eagles

That was a great year playlist
JXL's remix of *A Little Less Conversation* by Elvis Presley reminds me of 2003, which I spent studying in Amsterdam. There were loads of other foreigners studying there and we became very close. We all worked hard, but we partied hard as well. Whenever this song came on at a party or club, we all jumped up and danced – it didn't matter how tired we were. There's a great video that goes with it too. I sometimes watch it online. *[Corina, Germany]*

That was a great year playlist

A Little Less Conversation Elvis Vs JXL
I'm Not A Girl, Not Yet A Woman Britney Spears
Hey Ya! Outkast
Fell In Love With A Boy Joss Stone
I Can Nas

Music when I'm down playlist

I've put Vivaldi's *The Four Seasons,* but I actually only play two seasons! The winter section is sad and moving, but then I play the spring section because it's so uplifting. I'd actually like it played at my funeral! There was life before me, there will be life after me, like spring that comes again after winter.

Julieta Venegas' *Limón Y Sal* also cheers me up. My boyfriend bought it for me. The lyrics basically say 'I love you however you are; you don't have to change anything.' *[Kari, Chile]*

Music when I'm down playlist

The Four Seasons Vivaldi
Limón Y Sal Julieta Venegas
Bridge over Troubled Water Simon & Garfunkel
Happy The Rolling Stones
I'm Like A Bird Nelly Furtado

My family playlist

My dad's a big jazz fan and always has music on in the background. Personally, jazz doesn't do anything for me – I just find it strange. However, he used to play one song for me – *I Wanna Be Like You* from the film *The Jungle Book*. Now we play it to my baby brother and it always makes him laugh.

Underneath is for my sister. We both love indie music and it's by a new Hungarian band called Lincoln that we've been listening to a lot recently. They're going to be big. *[Natalia, Hungary]*

My family playlist

I Wanna Be Like You Louis Prima
Underneath Lincoln
A Love Supreme John Coltrane
Country House Blur
Not Quite Right Wohllebe

Music for my worst enemy playlist

This was difficult to choose. I hate Céline Dion's *My Heart Will Go On*. I can't stand commercial pop music – it's so sentimental. However, the worst is *The Birdie Song*. It reminds me of weddings and people doing the stupid dance. The problem is it's so catchy! The other day I heard it as the ring-tone on a mobile phone and I couldn't get it out of my head all morning! It was really annoying. *[Kevin, Scotland]*

Music for my worst enemy playlist

My Heart Will Go On Céline Dion
The Birdie Song The Tweets
Agadoo Black Lace
The Final Countdown Europe
I Will Always Love You Whitney Houston

READING

You are going to read about some pieces of music.

A Before you read, work in pairs. Look at the song titles and artists. Do you know any of them? Do you like them?

> *Hey Jude* (The Beatles)
> *Love Phantom* (B'z)
> *A Little Less Conversation* (Elvis Vs JXL)
> *The Four Seasons* (Vivaldi)
> *Limón Y Sal* (Julieta Venegas)
> *I Wanna Be Like You* (from The Jungle Book)
> *Underneath* (Lincoln)
> *My Heart Will Go On* (Céline Dion)
> *The Birdie Song* (The Tweets)

B Read the magazine article and find out if the readers like the songs in exercise A or not – and if they do, why.

C Work in pairs. Discuss these questions. Which of the people you read about:
1 likes different kinds of music to her father?
2 finds some songs drive him mad?
3 uses the Internet to access music?
4 went to a concert by one of his favourite bands?
5 predicts that one band will become famous?
6 talks about special ceremonies?

D Correct the words in *italics* with words in the article. Then work in pairs. Discuss if any of the sentences are true for you.
1 I love singing *together* with songs. I like karaoke.
2 I've seen lots of bands *lively*.
3 There's a song which really *remembers* me of my father.
4 There's a song I dance to whenever it *puts* on in a club.
5 If I'm sad, I like to play something sad to *same* my mood.
6 I like to study with music on in the *behind*.
7 Classical music doesn't *feel* anything for me. It's bland.
8 I don't like *sensitive* songs about love and romance.
9 I've sometimes *made* a stupid dance to some music.

SPEAKING

A Work in pairs. Choose three of the following playlist titles and make a list of three songs you would have. Compare lists with your partner.
- My current favourites
- That reminds me of …
- Party music
- Music I can't stand
- Music for my funeral
- Music to sleep to
- Music for a romantic evening
- I can't get it out of my head

01 REVIEW

LEARNER TRAINING

Work in groups of three. Discuss these questions:
- Do you write notes in your coursebook or do you use a separate exercise book? Why?
- Compare the notes you have taken in the last few lessons. Are all of your notes similar? Discuss the reasons for any differences.
- What do you do with your notes after class? Tell each other any ideas you have about how to write and use your notes better. Use these sentence starters:

It's important to...   It's best to...   Don't worry too much about...   Make sure you...   It's better to... than it is to...

GAME

Work in pairs. Student A use *only* the green squares; student B use *only* the yellow squares. Spend 5 minutes looking at your questions and revising the answers. Then take turns tossing a coin: Heads = move one of your squares; Tails = move two of your squares. When you land on a square, your partner looks at the relevant page in the book to check your answers, but *you don't*! If you are right, move forward one space (but don't answer the question until your next turn). If you aren't right, your partner tells you the right answer, and you miss a go. When you've finished the game, change colours and play again.

Start	**1** *Native English note*, p. 8: if you can say what the *Native English note* was, throw again.	**2** *Language Patterns* p. 9: say three endings to *I'd rather ... .*	**3** *Developing Conversations* p. 9: your partner will say 1-6. Can you remember one follow-up question in each case?	**4** *Grammar* p. 12: give four different reaso for being late, using the past continuous.
5 *Vocabulary* p. 14: can you remember eight feelings mentioned in the exercise?	**6** *Native English note*, p. 15: if you can say what the *Native English note* was, throw again.	**7** **Miss a go!**	**8** *Developing Conversations* p. 15: your partner will say student A's lines. Can you remember the correct response expression?	**9** *Vocabulary* p. 17: your partner will say the adjectives and you should give two collocations each time.
10 *Vocabulary* p. 22: tell your partner about a terrible holiday. Use at least five of the expressions in the exercise.	**11** *Grammar* p. 23: say four replies to the question *Have you ever been to X?* using different tenses.	**12** *Vocabulary* p. 24: can you remember eight words and expressions about the weather?	**13** *Native English note*, p. 25: if you can say what the *Native English note* was, throw again.	**14** **Miss a go!**
15 *Vocabulary* p. 26: say two endings to each of these verbs: *I stayed in and ... / I played ... / I went ... / I went for ... / I went to ......*	**16** *Native English note*, p. 28: if you can say what the *Native English note* was, throw again.	**17** *Grammar Reference* p. 143: say five *how long* questions using three different tenses.	**18** *Vocabulary* p. 30: your partner will read out the meanings. Can you remember eight of the ten words?	**Finish**

For each of the activities below, work in groups of three. Use the Vocabulary Builder if you want to.

CONVERSATION PRACTICE

Choose one of these *Conversation Practice* activities:
My first class p. 9
Feelings p. 15
Time off p. 21
Interests p. 27

Two of you should do the task. The third person should listen and give a mark of between 1 and 10. Explain your decision. Then change roles.

ACT OR DRAW

One person should act or draw as many of these words as you can in three minutes. Your partners should try to guess the words. Do not speak while you are acting or drawing!

seat	bang your head	split up	hug
grab	can't stand	score	kick
a ride	be stuck in a lift	suntan	ruins
restore	approach someone	a mine	net
hum	bully someone	luggage	bow
court	swim breaststroke	warm up	shoot
unfit	pull a muscle	whistle	hurt
prayer	sign something	decorate	lake

QUIZ

Answer as many of the questions as possible.
1 What does **a head teacher** do?
2 What's the difference between **holding hands** and **shaking hands**?
3 Say two things you can **sort out**.
4 How do you feel if you **get ripped off**? Why?
5 Why would you be **in a rush**? Why would you **rush** somebody to hospital?
6 Is it good to get **sunburnt**?
7 Why would you **ignore** somebody?
8 Say three things people **boast** about.
9 Say three things that can **break down**.
10 When do you need to **warm up**?
11 What do you usually **get promoted** to?
12 Can you **hurt** a car?
13 What's the difference between **practise** and **play**?
14 Why might you **need cheering up**?
15 Say two things that are often **due**.

COLLOCATIONS

Take turns to read out collocation lists from unit 1 of the Vocabulary Builder. Where there is a '~', say 'blah' instead. Your partner should guess as many words as they can. Each time you change roles, move to the next unit.

PRONUNCIATION Vowel sounds

A ⏺ R 1.1 Listen and repeat the sounds and the words.

/ iː /	/ ɪ /	/ ʊ /	/ uː /
cheek	rip	pull	boots
....	....	....	....
/ e /	/ ə /	/ ɜː /	/ ɔː /
upset	gallery	hurt	sort
....	....	....	....
/ æ /	/ ʌ /	/ ɑː /	/ ɒ /
bang	hum	spa	loss
....	....	....	....

B Add the words below to the appropriate box, according to how the underlined sounds are pronounced.

exhausted	therapist	accent	mosque
confirm	marks	wonder	skills
relief	due	attempt	bully

C Which sounds do you find hardest to pronounce?

CONNECTED SPEECH

A ⏺ R 1.2 Listen and say the sentences. The stressed sounds are marked for you.
1 At least you're here now.
2 Fair enough.
3 I'm sure it'll sort itself out.
4 I think I'll join you.
5 It's not worth it.
6 Apart from that
7 Not as much as I should.
8 Whenever I get the chance
9 Ten years on and off.
10 On in the background
11 I can't get it out of my head.
12 It doesn't do anything for me.

B Work in pairs. Mark the expressions in exercise A in the following ways:
• Mark where sounds disappear.
• Mark where the consonant at the end of a word joins with the following vowel sound.

C Listen again and check your ideas with the audioscript on p. 163.

LISTENING

A 🎧 **R 1.3 Listen to four people describing how they feel about different things. Decide what each speaker is talking about. There is one extra topic below that you do not need.**

a ...... People's habits in different countries

b ...... A free-time activity

c ...... A language they speak

d ...... Future plans

e ...... A holiday

B Listen again and decide how they feel – or felt. There is one extra feeling below that you do not need.

a ...... a bit confused and sometimes embarrassed

b ...... fed up and disappointed

c ...... relaxed

d ...... shocked at something

e ...... pleased with themselves

[... / 8]

GRAMMAR

Complete the conversation with one word in each gap.

A: I need to lose some weight.

B: Really? You don't ¹........................... very fat.

A: I've put on 6 kilos ²........................... March.

B: Really? ³........................... you do much exercise?

A: Not as much as I ⁴........................... to. I ⁵........................... running every day when I was at university, but since I started work, I've ⁶........................... going less and less and then in March I ⁷........................... an accident, so I more or less stopped completely.

B: Oh dear. What ⁸...........................?

A: Well, I went running near my house and it was already dark as I'd ⁹........................... back from work late. Anyway, I was ¹⁰........................... along a narrow street and suddenly I slipped and ¹¹........................... backwards. I looked back and someone ¹²........................... dropped a banana skin on the floor.

B: You're joking!

A: No, honestly. Anyway. It was really painful and I can't run at the moment.

B: Why don't you go swimming? I ¹³........................... once or twice a week.

A: Maybe. I'm not very good ¹⁴........................... swimming.

B: Well, I don't go very fast. What ¹⁵........................... you doing tomorrow? I'm ¹⁶........................... to my local pool in the evening. You could come with me.

A: I've got ¹⁷........................... work late tomorrow, but maybe some other time.

B: Well, I ¹⁸........................... probably go on Saturday as well.

A: I need to check my diary, but that ¹⁹........................... be better. I'll ²⁰........................... you later to confirm. It'd be nice to go with someone.

[... / 20]

PRESENT PERFECT QUESTIONS AND ANSWERS

Complete the answers to the present perfect questions with the correct form of the verbs in brackets.

1 A: Have you been to the old town yet?
   B: Yeah, we .... there last night. It's lovely. (walk round)

2 A: Have you seen Ricardo today?
   B: No, but I .... him for lunch later. (meet)

3 A: Have you decided what you're doing this weekend?
   B: Not really. I .... at home. I'm exhausted. (probably stay)

4 A: Have you been to Mexico before?
   B: Yeah, I .... a few times on business. (be)

5 A: Have you heard that new song by *The Love Machine*?
   B: No, but it .... quite catchy. (be)

[... / 5]

▶ **Find this difficult? Look back at grammar reference p. 140.**

-ing / ed ADJECTIVES

Choose the correct form.

1 I was a bit *disappointed / disappointing* when I saw the castle in real life. I expected it to be bigger.

2 We went on this really *scary / scared* ride at a theme park. My dad was *terrifying / terrified*.

3 There's a really *fascinating / fascinated* museum there about the history of farming.

4 I saw this new Russian film at the weekend. It was great – really *moved / moving*.

5 My friend said the play was really *depressing / depressed*, but I thought the ending was quite *uplifting / uplifted*.

[... / 7]

▶ **Find this difficult? Look back at grammar reference p. 138.**

DEVELOPING CONVERSATIONS

Match 1-8 to the responses a-h.
1 I've locked myself out of the house.
2 To be honest, I'm not a big sports fan.
3 He's really into windsurfing.
4 I'm thinking of eating out. Can you recommend anywhere?
5 Are you any good at tennis?
6 What kind of music are you into?
7 My husband used to teach English.
8 I've just heard I got a place at university.

a Oh well, in that case, how about going to a museum instead?
b All sorts.
c Really? How long did he do that for?
d No, I'm useless, but I still enjoy playing.
e Congratulations! Are you doing anything to celebrate?
f On no, what a pain! How are you going to get in?
g How long has he been doing that?
h Well, you could try that place round the corner.

[... / 8]

COLLOCATIONS

Match the verbs with the words they go with.
1 restore   a my connecting flight
2 reach   b some trainers to play tennis
3 go   c the holiday
4 borrow   d if you want to go out
5 pour   e an old church
6 spoil   f in a straight line
7 hit   g 45 degrees in the shade
8 miss   h the museum free
9 wonder   i the ball into the net
10 get into   j with rain

[... / 10]

FORMING WORDS

Complete the sentences with the noun forms of the words in CAPITALS.
1 There's plenty of cheap .... available in the town, if you want to stay. ACCOMMODATE
2 We got a very good .... from the advert. RESPOND
3 It looks like the company is going to make a big .... this year. LOSE
4 I just can't deal with the .... at all. HOT
5 I didn't use my full holiday .... ENTITLE

[... / 5]

▶ **Find this difficult? Look for other words in the same word family when you learn a new word.**

LANGUAGE PATTERNS

Correct the mistake in each of the sentences.
1 How much did that cost, if you don't mind me to ask?
2 I'd rather not to sit in the front row, if you don't mind.
3 We didn't expect to have so difficulty finding a place.
4 I only brought a T-shirt as I expected that it be warmer.
5 It depends of my dad whether I can go or not.
6 It depends how much does it cost.
7 She goes swimming every day – if she's busy.
8 I never managed that I won – not even once!

[... / 8]

VOCABULARY

Complete the short news stories by choosing the correct word.

Joey Chestnut has [1]...... Japanese speed eating legend Takeru Kobayashi to win Nathan's Hot dog Eating Contest in Coney Island. Kobayashi had never [2]...... in America and was [3]...... to win the competition for the seventh year running. Chestnut also [4]...... a new world record by eating 66 hot dogs in just 12 minutes.

1	A won	B lost	C beaten
2	A lost	B defended	C missed
3	A attempting	B pretending	C wishing
4	A won	B set	C gave

A conference is being held this weekend to [5]...... the health problems caused by global warming. There's [6]...... that climate change has led to [7]...... in skin cancer and it is also being [8]...... to greater risks of food poisoning and infectious diseases as the planet gets hotter. A spokesman for the conference said, 'We are [9]...... progress in understanding these problems, but we need to do more'.

5	A draw attention	B tell	C highlight
6	A evidence	B fact	C show
7	A improvements	B increases	C more
8	A proved	B caused	C linked
9	A finding out	B doing	C making

[... / 9]

  [Total ... /80]

05 WORKING LIFE

1

2

3

4

VOCABULARY Jobs

A Which of the jobs in the box can you see in the photos? Label the photos.

civil servant	estate agent	security guard
plumber	labourer	electrician
engineer	lawyer	graphic designer
surgeon	accountant	programmer

B Use the extra information in sentences 1–10 to guess the meanings of the words in bold. Translate the sentences into your language.

1 It's very **competitive**. It's difficult to find a good job.
2 It's very **well-paid**. He gets £60,000 a year as well as a bonus at the end of the year.
3 It's quite **rewarding**. You really help people and that makes you feel good.
4 It's quite **insecure**. You are often self-employed or have a temporary contract and it's quite badly-paid.
5 You don't have any **responsibility**. Once your day's finished, you don't have to worry about anything.
6 You need to be quite **creative**. You have to think of a lot of new ideas and new ways of doing things.
7 It's very **stressful**. You're under a lot of time pressure.
8 It's **physically demanding**. You have to be strong and fit.
9 It's very **varied**. You get to do lots of different things.
10 There's a lot of **paperwork** – writing reports, filling in forms, things like that.

C Work in groups. Discuss these questions.

· Are the jobs in Exercise A good jobs to have in your country at the moment? Would you do any of them?
· Do you know anyone who does any of these jobs? Who do they work for? Do they enjoy it?

LISTENING

You are going to hear two people, Ivan and Amanda, talking about work.

A ◎ 5.1 Listen and answer the questions.

1 What do they do now?
2 What jobs have they done in the past?
3 What are Ivan's plans for the future? Why?
4 How old are they both now?

B Decide which words in *italics* you heard. Then listen again and check.

1 I'm involved *in / on* designing what you see on the screen.
2 How did you *getting / get into* that?
3 Vodafone were recruiting people so I *applied / replied* and I got a job.
4 It's like any job. It has its boring *moments / minutes*.
5 It depends if we have a deadline to *complete / meet*.
6 I do *something / anything* like fifty or sixty hours a week.
7 That must be *stressed / stressful*.
8 I sometimes work better *under / in* pressure.

5

6

C Work in pairs. Discuss the questions:
- Would you ever work for no money? Why? / Why not?
- Are there any jobs for life in your country? Do you think it is good? Why? / Why not?

LANGUAGE PATTERNS

Write the sentences in your language. Translate them back into English. Compare your English to the original.
It's quite a creative job, which is nice.
It's quite well-paid, which is good.
I have to work 14 hours a day, which is really tiring.
I didn't get the promotion, which was a bit disappointing.
My old office overlooked a park, which was nice.

VOCABULARY Workplaces and activities

A **Match 1–5 with the specific job descriptions a–e.**
1 I work in the warehouse.
2 I'm in the accounts department.
3 I work in human resources.
4 I'm in sales.
5 I'm part of the marketing team.

a I am mainly involved in planning the campaigns.
b I'm the rep for the whole of the south of Italy.
c I am responsible for packing all the orders and doing all the admin for the delivery.
d I am responsible for recruitment contracts and working conditions.
e I deal with all the pay and finances.

B **Work in pairs. Use the words and phrases in exercise A to have conversations like this:**
A: What do you do?
B: I work for a .... company.
A: Oh yeah? Doing what?
B: I'm in sales. I'm the rep for the whole of the south.

NATIVE SPEAKER ENGLISH

Rep

Rep is short for *representative*. You can be *a sales rep, a holiday rep, a class rep,* etc. We also use *admin* instead of *administration* and *HR* instead of *human resources*.

DEVELOPING CONVERSATIONS
That must be …

In conversations we often give our opinion of what we think of the other speaker's job or situation using *That must be* + adjective.

A: Sometimes I do something like fifty or sixty hours a week.
B: Really? *That must be* stressful.

A **Respond to these sentences with *That must be …***
1 I'm the sales manager for Europe. I'm in charge of thirty reps.
2 I travel a lot round Europe and the Middle East.
3 I care for people who are dying.
4 Basically, I just sit in front of a TV screen all day.
5 I often can't explain myself clearly in English.
6 I really see the kids develop and improve.

B 🔊 **5.2 Listen to six conversations. Which three short answers do the speakers use to respond to *That must be …*?**

C **Practise reading the conversations in exercise B.**

CONVERSATION PRACTICE

A **Choose a job from these pages or a different job. Work in pairs. Describe the job in as much detail as you can, using language from these pages. Your partner must guess the job.**

GRAMMAR *Have to, don't have to, can*

A Complete the sentences with the correct form of *have to, don't have to* or *can.*

1. I .... wear a stupid uniform. I really hate it!
2. It's just round the corner, so I .... travel very far to work.
3. I work flexi-time, so I .... start and finish more or less whenever I want.
4. I .... speak English over the phone, which can be difficult for me.
5. We .... wear whatever we want in the office.
6. I work hard, but at least I .... work weekends!
7. I sometimes .... deal with some really awful people and my boss isn't very supportive.
8. I .... usually take time off if I need to.
9. We always .... show our ID cards to get into the building.

> We use *have to* to talk about rules. We also use *have to* for things that we feel are essential to do.
>
> We use *don't have to* for something which is not necessary. We also use *don't have to* when there is no rule (the person can choose to do something or not).
>
> We use *can* to show something is possible.
>
> *I have to work* really long hours sometimes.
> I'm glad *I don't have to work* tonight!
> *I can walk* to work. The office is really close to my flat.

B Tick the sentences in exercise A that are true for the place you study / work in. Then make three more true sentences. Work in pairs to discuss your ideas.

C Work in pairs. Discuss which jobs you can see in the pictures. Do you think they are good jobs or bad jobs? Why? Make sentences about the jobs using *have to, don't have to* and *can.*

▶ Need help? Read the grammar reference on p. 144

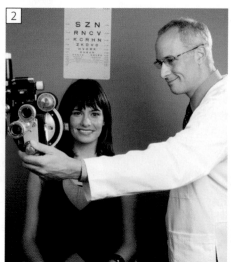

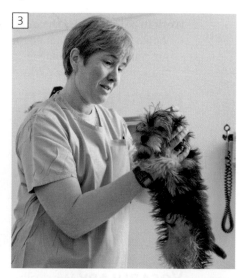

LISTENING

You are going to hear three conversations about rules at work.

A Before you listen, work in pairs. Discuss these questions:
- Why do you think companies have the rules below?
- Do you think they are sensible and fair?

1 Women have to wear skirts or dresses at work.
2 We have to go outside to smoke.
3 We have to agree holidays with our boss. We can't take time off when we want.
4 We have to ask the admin assistant to make photocopies for us. We can't just do them ourselves.
5 We have to take our breaks at set times.
6 We have to wear a hard hat at all times.
7 We can't surf the web on company computers.
8 We can't call mobile phones from the office.
9 We can't talk to each other while we're working.

B 🔊 5.3 Listen and decide which of the rules in exercise A they talk about in each conversation.

Conversation 1 ......
Conversation 2 ......
Conversation 3 ......

C Work in pairs. Match the words used in the conversations. Then listen to check your answers.

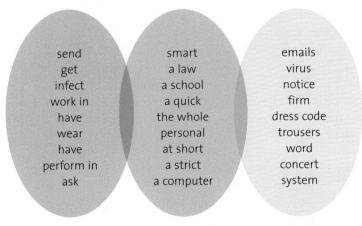

send	smart	emails
get	a law	virus
infect	a school	notice
work in	a quick	firm
have	the whole	dress code
wear	personal	trousers
have	at short	word
perform in	a strict	concert
ask	a computer	system

D Do you think the rules are fair in exercise B? Why? / Why not?

GRAMMAR Talking about rules

We sometimes use *be allowed to* instead of *can* to talk about permission. We use *be supposed to* and *should really* instead of *have to*, especially when the rules are often broken.

....

They have a strict dress code – woman *aren't* even *allowed to wear* smart trousers.
You're not supposed to use the company computers.
You should really arrange time off with me a month in advance.

A Choose the correct form in *italics*.
1 Sorry, *you're not allowed to / you don't have to* smoke in here. Can you go outside please?
2 *I'm supposed to / I don't have to* have my ID at all times, but nobody ever asks me for it!
3 I *can't / have to* start really early some days, but at least I *have to / I'm allowed to* go home early.
4 You're *supposed / allowed to* dress smartly, but no one's said anything when I've worn jeans.
5 *We are supposed to / We are allowed to* belong to a trade union, but our manager doesn't really like it when we do.
6 We *shouldn't really / don't have to* come out here on the roof of the building, but it's a really nice place to have a break!
7 I know *I'm allowed to / I should really* turn off my phone before I come in, but I'm expecting a really important call!
8 *You can't / You're not really supposed to* eat or drink in the classroom, so please tidy everything up after you finish your coffee.

B What rules are being broken in the pictures?

C Work in pairs. Discuss these questions. Use *should / shouldn't really* and *(not) supposed to* where appropriate.
- Are there any rules where you work / study which you do not like? Do you follow them?
- Are there any laws in your country that people often break? How do you feel about that?
- Are there any other rules or laws you would like to see introduced at work / school / in your country?

▶ Need help? Read the grammar reference on p. 144

READING

A Read the opening of a magazine article and decide:
1 why the author wrote the article.
2 what the rest of the article will be about.

TERRIBLE JOBS NOT A THING OF THE PAST.

The Channel Four series *The Worst Jobs in History* returns this week with the nineteenth century. Among the jobs that will be looked at are rat catcher, (which involved killing rats by hand) and boot boy (endlessly cleaning and polishing the shoes of the rich). It would be easy to think that such terrible jobs were a thing of the past, but the reality is that they have largely been replaced by other jobs where you might be exposed to dangerous chemicals or have to put up with high levels of noise; where you might die of boredom – or simply die!

B Think of different jobs where the workers:
1 are exposed to chemicals, dust or dirt.
2 risk their lives.
3 risk catching a disease.
4 work very long hours.
5 do not have much space to work in.
6 have to bend over a lot or lift heavy objects.
7 get a lot of abuse.
8 are standing all day.

C Read the rest of the article and decide which job in the article involves the problems in exercise B. Some jobs may match with more than one problem.

D Work in pairs. Discuss these questions about the jobs in the article:
- Did anybody like any aspects of their job? Why?
- What other reasons did the people give for doing the jobs?
- Do you think they are good reasons?

HUMAN GUINEA PIGS

Hundreds of people take part in tests of new medicines (called **drug trials**) every year. For between €45 and €4,500 they take a new drug to test for any **side effects** such as vomiting or headaches. Some students join drug trials as a relatively **quick and easy way** of earning money. John Spiral, a history student from Dublin, regularly does them. "You might go to the hospital three or four times, maybe eight hours 'work'. I had a really upset stomach once, and another time I got strange red marks on my skin, but that's all. Usually it's fine, and you're helping science!"

EMBALMERS

Embalmers preserve dead bodies in preparation for funerals. They work anything up to 50 hours a week for a salary of around £15,000 a year, far less than the **national average**. They spend most of the day standing and generally work bent over a table. They also have to work with very strong-smelling chemicals. "I do suffer from backache, but the job's not as bad as you might think", says Frank McCreary. "I'm even used to the smell now – I don't even notice it. And the job is quite rewarding too. The families of the dead are usually **very grateful** for the job I've done."

CALL CENTRE WORKER

Many banks and other companies have call centres abroad where customers can ring for information or to complain. Levels of stress among workers are very high. They often work in **cramped conditions**, have to stare at a computer all day, and have little opportunity to laugh or joke with their co-workers.

One worker, from an Indian call centre, said, "People can be very abusive. They shout and swear, but often there is nothing you can do about their complaint. They then **slam down the phone**, and another person calls you straightaway. It's awful. I'd like to leave, but the money's quite good and there's a lot of competition for jobs here in Mumbai."

RECYCLING PLANT WORKER

You are supposed to sort your own rubbish and put glass in one bag, paper in another, but unfortunately many people still do not do this. So workers in a recycling plant have to find the recyclable items from a big pile of rubbish, and all for a **minimum wage**. Apart from the smell, they have to handle dirty nappies, rotting meat, used needles. "I've heard of people catching hepatitis from working in those places," says Solomon Iwenofu. "I did it for a while when I first arrived in America. I actually **got on with** the people working there. We used to laugh about some of the things we found. After a while, I even got used to being dirty all the time, but, you know, I wanted to do better for myself and my family."

E **Without looking at the text, complete the sentences.**

1 I'm lucky, because I .... on really well with my colleagues.

2 There are six people living in a two-bedroom flat, so they have to put up with very .... conditions.

3 It's a quick and easy .... of sending large video files.

4 Honestly, I was getting so angry I couldn't continue talking to him, so I just .... down the phone.

5 Thank you so much. I'm very .... for all your help.

6 The boss is so mean! He basically just pays the minimum .... That's it!

7 The drug was taken off the market after serious side .... were reported.

8 Unemployment in the city is 25% – well above the national ....

F **Put the jobs in the article in order from the best to the worst (best = 1, worst = 4). Work in pairs. Compare your answers and explain your decisions. Are there any other jobs you would hate to do?**

VOCABULARY *Be used to, get used to*

We use *be used to* when a habit or situation is normal for us because of our experience. This habit might be difficult for other people.
Some people find working with kids difficult, but *I'm used to it*. I have five brothers and sisters who are younger than me.

. . . .

We use *get used to* when a habit or situation is changing from being difficult to being normal / easy. We use it with lots of tenses.
I never had to wear a suit and tie before I had this job. I'd still prefer something less formal, but *I'm slowly getting used to it*.

A **Look back at the article, *Terrible jobs not a thing of the past* on p. 40, and find one example of *be used to* and one example of *get used to*.**

B **Complete the dialogues by putting the words in brackets in the correct order.**

1 A: It must be difficult getting up so early.
   B: Oh, ... (to / I'm / it / used). I had to get up at five in my last job.

2 A: How are you finding the new job? It must be hard having to do everything in English.
   B: It is difficult, but .... (getting / slowly / to / it / I'm / used). The people I work with are being very supportive.

3 A: How are you finding your new job?
   B: Not that good, to be honest. I hate sitting at a desk all day, but I need the money, so I guess .... (to / I'll / get / used / to / just / have / it).

4 A: How do you find working shifts?
   B: OK, although it .... (get / to / me / a / while / used / took / to) working nights. I couldn't sleep during the day to begin with, but it's fine now.

5 A: How do you find working nights? It must be quite difficult.
   B: It was to begin with, yeah, but .... (it / totally / now / I'm / to / used).

6 A: How are you finding your new job?
   B: The job's OK, but I hate the journey to work. .... (I'll / think / don't / ever / I / used / to / get) the crowded trains! I'm actually thinking of leaving.

C **Underline the six expressions using *be used to / get used* to in exercise B. Translate them into your language. Does your language use a similar structure to *be used to / get used to*?**

D **Now practise reading the conversations.**

SPEAKING

Work in pairs. You both have new jobs in Britain or America and are discussing how you are finding your work and life.

A **Decide what your jobs are and where you live. Decide the questions you will ask. For example:**

- How are you finding your job?
- Do you get on with the other people at work?
- How are you finding living here?
- What's your flat / the area you live in like?
- What do you think of the weather / food?

B **Role-play a conversation. Use at least two *be / get used to* comments.**

06 GOING SHOPPING

In this unit you learn how to
- describe things you buy
- describe clothes
- compare products
- make, and respond to, recommendations

Grammar
- *must*

Vocabulary
- Describing souvenirs and presents
- Clothes and accessories

Reading
- Shop till you drop!

Listening
- Negotiating prices
- Comparing mobile phones
- The best way to buy tickets for a gig

VOCABULARY
Describing souvenirs and presents

A Put the words in the box into three groups:
1 opinion
2 how things are produced
3 material

hand-made	silk	gorgeous	cute
beautiful	clay	horrible	carved
hand-painted	lovely	plastic	leather
hand-printed	wooden	machine-woven	tacky

B Use the words to describe the things in the pictures.

C Complete the sentences with the descriptions in the box.

traditional hand-carved	lovely silver
little hand-woven	really cute
lovely hand-painted	tacky plastic
beautiful hand-printed silk	nice clay

1 My dad bought me what he thought was a .... scarf, but it was horrible! I'm never going to wear it!
2 He bought me this .... model of the Eiffel Tower. I don't know what to do with it. It's horrible.
3 I bought this really .... pot for cooking. It's really heavy.
4 She bought me this .... teddy bear. I keep it on my bed.
5 They bought me this .... plate. It looks like it was quite expensive.
6 He bought me this .... ring when we were in Paris. I've been wearing it ever since.
7 I bought this .... African mask. I'm going to hang it on my wall. It's great.
8 I bought this .... rug. I've put it on the floor by my bed.

D Work in pairs. Tell your partner about souvenirs that you have bought or that people have bought for you.

LISTENING

You are going to hear a tourist buying a small rug. The tourist is negotiating with the seller.

A Before you listen, work in pairs. Discuss these questions:
- What reasons might the tourist give for paying less?
- What reasons might the seller give for paying more?

B ♦ 6.1 Listen to the conversation and find out what reasons they give.

PRONUNCIATION Intonation

> When negotiating prices, we express surprise about a price using high intonation. To make an alternative offer or to agree, we use lower intonation.

A 🔊 6.1 Listen to the conversation again and read the audioscript on p. 164. Notice the numbers where the intonation rises and those where it drops.

B Work in pairs. Practice reading the conversation, using high and low intonation.

C Work in pairs. Student A is the owner of one of the shops in the picture. Student B is a tourist who wants to buy a souvenir. Negotiate the price.

DEVELOPING CONVERSATIONS
Avoiding repetition

We often use *one / ones* to avoid repeating words when we compare the difference between two things.

A Match the sentence halves about two mobile phones.
1 This phone has an MP3 player,
2 This one only has 75 megabytes of memory,
3 This one is only £43.99,
4 These phones are on special offer,
5 These ones all use a lithium battery,
6 You can store up to 100 messages on this one,

a whereas this one is 87.
b whereas this one has a hundred.
c whereas this one doesn't.
d whereas that one only has room for 50.
e whereas those use a nickel cadmium one, which isn't as good.
f whereas those ones aren't.

B Work in groups. Compare the features of any mobile phones you have.

LISTENING

You are going to hear a man in a mobile phone shop. His phone company, Blue, has offered him the S620 and he is thinking of getting a better upgrade by changing company. The assistant offers him an N5703.

A 🔊 6.2 Listen and complete the table. Then work in pairs to compare your answers.

Features	N5703	S620
Kind of battery?		
Camera (mega-pixels)?		
Comes with memory card?		
Comes with MP3?		
Minutes: free calls?		
Number of free text messages?		

B The assistant starts by offering one number of free calls and messages, and ends by offering another. Would you accept her final offer?

C Correct the information in *italics*.
1 The N5703 is *slightly* better quality.
2 The lithium battery lasts *a bit* longer than the other one.
3 The camera on the N5703 is *more than* twice as powerful.
4 With the memory card, the N5703 stores *slightly fewer* photos than the S620.
5 The sound quality of the MP3 is *much worse* than on a normal player.

D Listen and read through the audioscript on pp. 164–165 to check your answers.

CONVERSATION PRACTICE

Work in pairs. You are going to role-play a conversation in a phone shop between a customer and a salesperson, similar to the one in *Listening*.

A Look through the audioscript on pp. 164–165 and underline any expressions you could use.

B Student A, read File 2 on p. 156. Student B, read File 8 on p. 158. Role-play the conversation.

VOCABULARY
Clothes and accessories

A Decide which is the odd one out in each group and explain your decision.

1 necklace / bracelet / chain / belt / ring
2 top / shirt / jacket / skirt / jumper
3 jeans / trousers / earrings / tracksuit bottoms / leggings
4 socks / trainers / sandals / boots / high heels
5 scarf / gloves / T-Shirt / woolly hat / thick jumper
6 scruffy / trendy / smart/ cool / nice
7 colourful / stripy / tight / bright / plain / checked

B Work in pairs. Say what you think of the way the people in the picture below are dressed. Use some of the language from exercise A. You might also want to use some of these expressions:

- That top / shirt *doesn't fit* him / her *properly.*
- Those trainers / earrings *don't suit* him / her.
- Those trainers *don't match / don't go with* that / those …

READING

You are going to read a questionnaire from a magazine to find out your attitudes to shopping, fashion and money.

A Work in two groups: Group A and Group B. See how many of the words in the box you know. Look up any words you do not know in the *Vocabulary Builder*.

GROUP A	GROUP B
avoid something	out-of-town shopping mall
last a long time	force a company out of business
can't really afford it	a label
do without something	in the sales
come back empty-handed	designer brands
shop around	an overdraft
go window-shopping	owe money
get ripped off	retail therapy
an outfit	an exception
price tag	second-hand

B Now work in pairs: one person from Group A, the other from Group B. Go through the questionnaire together and discuss your answers. Explain the new words from exercise A to each other if you need to.

C When you have finished, look at File 4 on p. 157. Calculate your marks and read the appropriate description. Tell your partner if the description of you is accurate. Why? / Why not?

LANGUAGE PATTERNS

Write the sentences in your language. Translate them back into English. Compare your English to the original.
It's not worth getting upset about.
It's not worth arguing about. He won't change his mind.
It's not worth doing. Nobody is interested.
It's not worth the trouble. It's a long way to travel.
It's not worth a hundred pounds. It's really bad quality.

SHOP TILL YOU DROP!

1 What do you think of shopping?
a Boring and often stressful. I avoid it if I can.
b OK if you go with friends, or have nothing else to do.
c Fantastic. I love it.

2 What's the most important thing when you buy clothes?
a They're cheap.
b They will last a long time.
c They look good on me.

3 If you see something you really like, but can't really afford, what do you do?
a I just do without it. I don't really need it anyway.
b I save up and buy it when I have enough money or when it's in the sales.
c I buy it with a credit card.

4 If you go shopping and come back empty-handed, how do you feel?
a A bit frustrated, but I like to shop around for the best bargains and sometimes it takes time.
b I don't mind. Sometimes it's nice to go window-shopping.
c I never come back empty-handed! What's the point of going shopping if you don't buy anything?

5 Have you ever lied about the price of something?
a Yes. I didn't want them to realise how little I'd spent.
b No, never. Why should I?
c Yes. I didn't want them to realise how much I'd spent.

6 If you get ripped off, how do you feel?
a Angry. I complain and try to get my money back.
b A bit annoyed, but these things happen from time to time. It's not worth getting upset about. You can't do anything about it.
c I never get ripped off.

7 When you include trainers, boots and sandals, how many pairs of shoes do you have?
a 5 pairs or fewer.
b 6–19 pairs.
c I've lost count. It must be at least 20.

8 Do you have any clothes you only wear at home?
a Yes, they have holes in, but they're OK to wear around the house.
b Yes. They're not fashionable, but they're comfortable.
c No. You never know who will call at your house. I always look my best.

9 Do you have any clothing you haven't worn much?
a Not really, but I have one outfit I only wear on special occasions.
b Yes. It doesn't fit me at the moment, but it will once I lose some weight!
c Yes. One piece still has the price tag.

10 Do you ever shop in big out-of-town shopping centres / malls?
a No. They're a nightmare. They're forcing small independent shops out of business.
b Sometimes. They're quite convenient. It's nice to have such a wide choice in one place.
c Yes, I love them. I go all the time.

11 If people comment on your clothes, what do they normally say?
a I look a bit scruffy.
b I look smart or my clothes suit me.
c I look very trendy.

12 Are there any shops you normally avoid going to?
a Yes, because I don't like the politics connected with the shop.
b No, not really. I sometimes worry about how things were made, but I also love a bargain!
c Not really. I don't really like shops full of cheap, nasty clothes, but they're still worth looking in.

13 Do you ever buy designer brands?
a Never. They're a rip-off. You're just paying for the label.
b Sometimes – especially if they are in the sales.
c All the time. Designer brands are better.

14 Do you have money left at the end of the month?
a Usually. I often put money away in a savings account.
b Sometimes, but sometimes I go into overdraft.
c Hardly ever. I often have an overdraft or owe money on my credit card.

15 Do you believe in retail therapy?
a Not at all. Buying things doesn't make you happy.
b Shopping isn't the first thing I think of to cheer myself up, but it does work sometimes.
c Absolutely. If I'm feeling down, going shopping or buying something always cheers me up.

16 Have you ever had to buy an extra bag to bring home all the purchases you made on holiday?
a Never. Holidays are supposed to be relaxing and the last thing I want to do is go shopping.
b Once I did, but it was an exception.
c I usually make sure I have plenty of space in my luggage before I go because I know I'll do loads of shopping.

17 Do you ever buy second-hand clothes?
a Only if they fit me OK and they're really cheap!
b No. I can't stand the idea of wearing something that someone else wore before me!
c Of course! You can find some incredible vintage clothes in second-hand shops.

18 How often do you look at fashion magazines?
a Never. They are stupid. A complete waste of time.
b Sometimes. If they are in a waiting room or someone else has bought them, I like to have a look.
c I regularly buy them.

LISTENING

You are going to hear two friends, Leo and Noel, talking about buying tickets for a gig. *A gig* is a rock concert, usually in a small venue.

A **Work in pairs. Discuss these questions:**
- Do you ever go to gigs? What was the last band you saw?
- What is the most you have ever paid for a ticket for something?
- Where is the best place to buy tickets for concerts / sports events?

B 🎧 **6.3 Listen and answer these questions.**
1 Who does Leo want to see?
2 Is Noel going to the gig?
3 Why is Leo surprised that tickets have sold out?
4 Why does Leo want to go to the gig?
5 What two things does Noel suggest he should do?
6 How does Leo respond to each of Noel's suggestions?

C **Work in pairs. Discuss these questions:**
- Do you think Noel's suggestions to Leo were good?
- Do you ever use online auction sites like eBay? What for?
- What is the best birthday present you have ever received?

GRAMMAR *must*

In *Listening*, you heard the speakers say:
a *I must try and book some tickets for a gig next week*
b *You must be able to get tickets somewhere*
c *If you like The Brain Police, you must go and see Spook Train.*

A **Look at the three examples of using *must* above. Match the examples with rules 1–3.**
1 We often use *must* to make guesses about things, based on what we know. *Must* shows we believe something is very probably true. ☐
2 We can use *You must* to strongly recommend things like films, books, shops or tourist attractions. ☐
3 We use *I must* when we feel something is very important for us to do. We use *I mustn't* when it is important for us not to do something. ☐

B **Match a–i to the uses of *must* 1–3 in exercise A.**
a You must try the local food while you're there. It's great.
b You must be able to find it cheaper somewhere else.
c I must make sure I send them the money today.
d That's your third helping! You must be really hungry.
e I mustn't forget to thank her for all her help.
f It must get really cold there in the winter.
g You must go to Virgo. They've got a sale on.
h It's amazing. You must go and see it if you have time.
i I really must try and buy a few souvenirs today.

C **Work in pairs. Compare your answers.**

▶ **Need help? Read the grammar reference on p. 145**

D Complete these sentences with *must* or *mustn't*.

1 Can you remind me later? I .... remember to buy a present for my sister before I leave.
2 I .... just go and say 'hello' to someone. I'll be right back.
3 I have an appointment at half past two. I .... be late.
4 Remind me – I .... forget to phone my mum when we get to the hotel.
5 You really .... try the grilled squid they do here.
6 Whatever else you do, you simply .... take the ferry across to the islands. It's amazing!
7 I'd love some cake, but I really .... I'm on a diet!
8 I .... forget to pay my rent – or I'll be in big trouble.
9 I .... just let my boss know that the time of her flight has been changed.
10 I'm sure you're very busy. I .... keep you any longer.

E Make a list of the following. Then work in pairs to discuss your ideas.

- two things you must remember to do this week
- two things you mustn't forget to do this week
- five things visitors to your town simply must do / see / try

F Work in pairs. Look at the photos below. Have conversations like this …

A: *How old do you think .... is?*
B: *I'm not sure. He / She must be something like …*

Explain your guesses.

> If you use *must* and *mustn't* to tell other people what to do, it often sounds rude and aggressive.
> It is better to use other structures in these situations. For example:
> ....
> *Don't buy* it here. It's too expensive. *Wait* till you get back home.
> *(If I were you,) I'd take* it *back* to the shop and ask for a refund.
> I'm sorry, but smoking's *not allowed* in the store.

DEVELOPING CONVERSATIONS
Responding to recommendations

When you ask two or more people to recommend things, you often get different opinions. Look at this example:

A: *I'm thinking of going shopping for clothes while I'm here. Can you recommend anywhere?*
B: *Well, you could try Oxford Street. There are lots of big department stores there.*
C: *No, you don't want to go there! It's a rip-off! I'd go to a street market instead. There's more choice – and they're cheaper.*

A Put the two conversations in the correct order. In each conversation, there are three speakers.

Conversation 1

...... No, it's too late for that. They won't be able to deliver the tickets in time.
..*1*.. I'm thinking of trying to get a ticket for the match tonight.
...... You don't want to do that. It's illegal. You might get arrested. I'd try the Internet instead.
...... It's totally sold out. You've got no chance. I guess you could go and hang around outside the stadium and buy one from a ticket tout.

Conversation 2

...... There isn't time! He doesn't want to miss the plane!
...... No, I wouldn't do that! It's more expensive. You'd be better getting something in town.
...... I want to get a present for my girlfriend before I go back.
...... Just get something at the airport in Duty Free.
...... It's OK. My flight's not till three. I think I've got time. Where's the best place to go?

> **NATIVE SPEAKER ENGLISH**
>
> ***You don't want to***
> When we want to tell friends what we think they should or should not do, we often use sentences beginning with *You want to* or *You don't want to.*
> *You want to be careful if you go to the market.*
> *You don't want to get ripped off.*
> *You don't want to buy that! It doesn't suit you.*

SPEAKING

A Work in groups of three. You are going to role-play a conversation between a tourist and two local people where you live.

Student A: you are the tourist. You want to go shopping for some different things. Ask for recommendations.
Students B and C: you are locals. Suggest some different places. Explain why your ideas are good – and why the other ideas are bad!

07 SCHOOL AND STUDYING

SPEAKING

A Work in pairs. Discuss these questions:
- What kind of courses do you think the people in the pictures are doing?
- Have you ever done any courses like this?
- Would you like to?

B Have you ever done any of the courses in the box or any similar courses? Work in pairs. Tell your partner about:
- where you did the course.
- why you did it.
- how long it lasted.
- what the tutors / other students were like.
- whether or not it was worth doing.

a postgraduate course	a first-aid course
an evening course	an online course
a training course	an IT course

VOCABULARY Describing courses

A Add the nouns in the box to the groups of words they go with a–h.

deadline	essay	exams	lecture
modules	seminar	tutor(s)	workload

a write an ~ / hand in an ~ / a fifteen-hundred word ~
b dedicated and supportive ~ / my personal ~ / very helpful ~
c my end-of-year ~ / my final ~ / pass all my ~ / fail my ~
d have a weekly ~ / a group ~ / go to a ~ / ~ discussions
e give a ~ / fall asleep in a ~ / a fascinating ~ / ~ theatre
f a heavy ~ / a lighter ~ / increase the ~ / cope with the ~
g a very tight ~ / miss the ~ / extend a ~ / the ~ is Friday
h choose which ~ to do / core ~ / optional ~ / the ~ are hard

B Work in pairs. Use five of the collocations in exercise A to talk about the course you discussed in *Speaking* exercise B, or another course you have done.

DEVELOPING CONVERSATIONS
How's the course going?

A Look at the answers 1–6 to the question *How's the course going?* Two words in each answer are in the wrong position. Underline them. For example:

Really well. I'm really <u>progress</u> it. I can't believe how much <u>enjoying</u> I've already made!

1 I've had a few ups and supportive of course, but the tutors have been really helpful and downs.
2 Quite well, actually. The seminar can be a bit boring, but the lectures work in groups is great.
3 OK, but I've got my final revision next week, so I'm having to do lots of exams at the moment.
4 OK, but I'm really busy. I have to hand in an deadline next week – and if I miss the essay, I'll fail!
5 Actually, I'm struggling at the moment. I just can't demanding with the workload. It's really cope.
6 To be honest, I'm finding it really term. The modules I'm doing this difficult are really hard!

B Work in pairs. Take turns asking *How's the course going?* Give different answers each time.

LISTENING

You are going to hear two friends, Daniel and Paulina, talking about a course Paulina is doing.

A 🔊 7.1 Listen and complete the questions.
1 How's the course going? Are you ....?
2 So what does that involve, then? I mean, what .... do you have to study?
3 And what are the other students like? Do you .... them OK?
4 And what about the tutors? What are they ....?
5 How long does the course last? When ....?
6 And what are you going to do once the course has finished? Have .... yet?

B Listen again. Take notes on the answers to the questions.

LANGUAGE PATTERNS

Write the sentences in your language. Translate them back into English. Compare your English to the original.

I'm glad (that) it's going well.
I'm glad (that) you're feeling better.
I'm glad (that) you like the present.
I'm glad (that) everything is OK.
I'm glad to hear the accident wasn't that serious.
I'm glad to see they've finally fixed the lift!

GRAMMAR *After, once and when*

When a clause starts with *after, once* or *when*, we can then use the present simple or present perfect although we're referring to the future. Using the present perfect emphasises a finished action.

What are you going to do once *the course has finished?*
When I'm there, I might look for a job.
After I get back from Australia, I'll just start looking for a proper job.

A Rewrite each of the pairs of sentences as one sentence.
1 I'm going to leave school next month. Then I might go away for a few weeks.
After ...., I ....
2 The course finishes soon. Then I'll have to start paying back all my debts.
Once ...., I'll ....
3 You are going to move to Germany soon. Are you going to look for a job there?
Are .... when ....?
4 I'll call you this weekend. I need to finish my essay first.
I'll .... when ....
5 My workload should lighten in the future. Then I'm going to start going swimming regularly again.
Once ...., I'm ....
6 I'm in a lecture at the moment. It finishes at three. Then I'll call you back.
I'll .... after ....

B Work in pairs. Think of possible endings for these questions about your English course / other studies / your holiday / work plans, etc. Take turns asking and answering your questions.
1 What are you going to do once ....?
2 Where are you going to stay when ....?
3 Where are you going to go after ....?

▶ Need help? Read the grammar reference on p. 146

CONVERSATION PRACTICE

A Work in pairs. Role-play a similar conversation to the one in *Listening*, but choose a different course. Think about how to answer the six pairs of questions from exercise A in *Listening*. Start the conversation like this: *How's the course going? Are you still enjoying it?*

SPEAKING

A Read the short text about a Korean school student. Then work in pairs. Discuss these questions:
- Do you have any subjects like *Tongjon* at your school?
- Would you like to do a course where you choose what you study?
- What do you think are the advantages and disadvantages of this kind of study?

It's 9 a.m. on Monday morning and seventh-year student Nan-Joo Yoon is reading the story *The Goat and the Goatherd* in English. Nan-Joo studies at a private boarding school in the mountains of central Korea. The story is part of a subject called *Tongjon*, where students decide what they study. Nan-Joo chose to study goats – which has involved reading assignments, biology, looking at the star constellation Capricorn, and making a field trip to observe some real goats.

READING

A Read the article about alternative ideas about education. Answer the questions.
1 What caused the writer to write the article?
2 Why does the writer talk about her daughter?
3 Why does she mention the main industry in Patagonia?
4 Why does she mention PSHE?
5 Why does she talk about *Tongjon*?
6 Why does she quote the Russian poet Pushkin?

B Work in pairs. Discuss what you think the words in bold in the article mean.

C Work in pairs. Look at the article again and try to find:
- something which is the same for you.
- something which is similar in your country.
- something which you found surprising.
- something which does not happen in your country.
- something that made you smile.
- an opinion you agree with and one you disagree with.

Compare your ideas and explain your choices.

NATIVE SPEAKER ENGLISH

in mind

If you have something *in mind*, you are thinking of this thing.
Such ideas are not really what Oliver James has in mind.
Have you got anywhere in mind for your holiday?
I've got three people in mind for the new job.
What have you got in mind?
I'll keep you in mind if I hear of any opportunities for work.

VOCABULARY Forming words

One way to build your vocabulary is to learn word families: words which all have the same root, like *innovate*, *innovative* and *innovation*. These words are often next to each other in a dictionary, so they are easy to look up. Make sure you try to learn the collocations that go with these words as well.

A Add the missing words to these word families. One of each of the forms is in the article.

noun	verb
state	**educate** children privately
feel like a	**fail** your exam
a big	**achieve** all your ambitions
do a **calculation**	.... the answer in my head
wine **appreciation**	.... the good things in life
give a lot of **encouragement**	.... me to work hard
have no	**inspire** me to success

B Work in groups. Discuss these questions:
- Do you think state education is better than private education?
- Have you ever done something that you saw as a failure?
- What has been your biggest achievement so far?
- Has anyone been an inspiration to you? How?

Sioban Flanagan finds food for thought in Oliver James' new book *Affluenza*.

LEARNING TO BE HAPPY

Reading Oliver James' new book *Affluenza*, I was reminded of a regular scene in our house. My 12-year-old daughter is in tears. "I've got a test tomorrow. I don't understand any of it," she screams. After shouting and slamming her door, she calms down enough to **go through** her notes. The following day I ask her how the test went and she just says "OK. I got a nine".

"Wow, that's brilliant! Well done!" I say, before she finishes with "But I never get a ten!"

According to James, this obsession with getting top marks has been a bad development, which encourages people to think of education in terms of work and consumption. To test this idea, I asked my daughter why she was so concerned about her tests. She looked at me as if I was **thick**. "Well, if I don't get good grades, I won't get into university. Then I probably won't get a good job and if I don't have a good job, I won't be able to afford nice things like a car and stuff."

I was quite shocked, because I do not consider myself a **pushy** parent. But James suggests showing any interest in grades sends the message

that what is important is results and it leaves students feeling failures even if they are very **bright**. He **points to** the Danish system of education as a better model. Creating happy citizens who have good social skills is seen as more important than high academic achievement or the needs of business.

The strange thing is that so little of what we learn at school is actually **relevant** to most jobs. I cannot remember the last time I had to calculate the area of a circle, **recite** a Shakespeare poem or grammar rules. I have lived a happy life, despite the fact I have forgotten Boyle's Law and the main industry in Patagonia. What I really needed to learn at school was how to make polite conversation, or how to avoid getting into debt, or how to control my own children!

To be fair, both the responsibilities of **parenthood** and personal finances are now sometimes taught as part of Personal, Social and Health Education (PSHE), which also covers areas such as citizenship and the abuse of illegal drugs. Many EU countries also teach citizenship as a **core** subject, although not everyone agrees what it should aim to teach. Norway includes lessons on respecting nature. France aims to teach 'republican values' – and some politicians have also talked of teaching students to appreciate the importance of wine in French culture.

Such ideas are not really what Oliver James has in mind, though. He seems to

be looking for schools where students are encouraged to find and follow their own interests, something more like *Tongjon*. *Tongjon* has been developed in some Korean private schools as an alternative to the more **rigid** system of learning things by heart that is used in Korea, and indeed in many other school systems around the world. The irony of this is that *Tongjon* is now seen by some as answering economic needs. It is thought that schooling which gives students more freedom will provide more of the creative and innovative thinkers the future Korean economy needs.

As the Russian poet Pushkin said, "Inspiration is needed in geometry just as much as in poetry", and inspiration does not come from endlessly revising for tests or getting upset about them.

SPEAKING

A Work in pairs. Discuss what might be good / bad about going to each of the schools in the pictures. Explain your decisions.

VOCABULARY
Schools, teachers and students

A Work in pairs. Read sentences 1–16 and decide:
- whether each describes a school, a teacher or a student.
- if they are positive or negative descriptions.

1 She's very patient.
2 It's quite rough.
3 She's very studious.
4 He's good at controlling the class.
5 It's got a very good reputation for sport.
6 She's quite traditional.
7 He really pushes us.
8 She never pays attention in class.
9 Discipline is very good there.
10 She thinks she knows it all.
11 It has a very good headmaster.
12 She's very encouraging.
13 He's very bright.
14 She's in serious trouble because she keeps skipping classes.
15 He's lively and makes things fun.
16 There are hardly any facilities.

B Work in pairs. Use some of the language from exercise A to talk about:
- what kind of student you are.
- the good and bad teachers you have had.
- the school you go / went to.

LISTENING

You are going to hear four conversations about different aspects of education.

A 🔊 7.2 Listen and decide who the main speaker is in each case. Note that there is one person you do not need to use.
a a parent
b a school teacher
c a university lecturer
d an overseas student
e a postgraduate student

conversation 1 ....
conversation 2 ....
conversation 3 ....
conversation 4 ....

B Work in pairs. Answer these questions. Then listen again to check your answers.
1 Why is the teacher annoyed? What advice is she given?
2 Why is the overseas student unhappy? What is she going to do?
3 What rule does the lecturer explain? Are there any exceptions to the rule?
4 Why is the parent happy?

C Try to remember which verbs went with these nouns in the four conversations. Work in pairs to discuss your ideas. Then compare your ideas with the audioscript on p. 146.
1 attention   each other   their respect
2 one of the questions   my score   the test
3 a deadline   an exception   any excuses
4 the kids   classes   a good reputation

D Work in pairs. Discuss these questions:
- Do you agree that teachers should be strict?
- Have you ever made a stupid mistake in an exam / test? How?
- Do you know anyone who has changed schools? Why?

GRAMMAR Zero conditionals and first conditionals

A Work in pairs. Look at these sentences from *Listening*. Try to remember how each sentence finished.

1 If I try to explain something, ...
2 If they talk, ...
3 If they don't accept me on the course, ...
4 If you miss a deadline that your tutor has set, ...
5 If you have any problems which are affecting your coursework, ...

B 🔊 7.3 Listen and write down the second half of each sentence in exercise A. Which verb forms are used in each part of the sentences?

We use present tenses in the *if* clause to talk either a) about real present situations or b) possible future situations. The other half of the sentence uses different verb forms, according to their normal meanings.

In zero conditionals, we use the present simple to talk about real repeated actions in the present.

In first conditionals, we use *will* to talk about definite decisions and consequences in the future. *Might* is used to talk about possible ones.

In some conditional sentences, we use imperatives and *should* to give advice.

▶ Need help? Read the grammar reference on p. 146

C Complete the first conditional sentences with the verbs in the correct form.

A: What are you going to do when you graduate?
B: It depends on my grades. If I .... good grades, I .... a master's in Business Administration. (get / probably do)
A: And what if you don't?
B: Well it depends on how much I'm in debt. If I .... enough money, I .... travelling for a while and maybe get a job abroad. (have / go)
A: And what if you haven't got enough money?
B: I suppose I .... get a job – and quickly! (have to)

D Write your own ideas to answer these questions.

1 A: What are you going to study at university?
  B: It depends .... If ...., ...

2 A: How long are you going to stay in your job?
  B: It depends .... If ...., ...

3 A: Do you want to go out later?
  B: It depends .... If ...., ...

E Work in pairs. Role-play the three conversations in exercise D using your ideas. Your partner should continue the conversations by saying *And what if ...*

SPEAKING

A Look at the school rules and their consequences. Work in pairs. Discuss these questions:
- Which rules do you think are fair?
- Are any the same as you have / had at school?

B Invent five new rules for your own class.

- If you say something while the teacher is talking, you get a warning. If you do it again, you have to stand in the corner for five minutes. If you do it a third time, you have to go and see the headmaster.
- If you are caught running in the corridors, you have to write on a piece of paper 'I must not run in the corridors' 200 times.
- If you are caught bullying, you have to meet the victim and his / her parents and listen to how your bullying has affected them.
- If you fail your end-of-term exams, you have to repeat the whole school year.
- If you are caught skipping class, you are suspended from school for three days.
- If you are caught dropping litter, you have to stay behind after school and sweep the whole school.
- If you are late to school more than three times in a term, you get a letter sent home to your parents.
- If you are caught smoking in the school, you get expelled.
- If you get caught cheating in an exam, you fail all your exams.

08 EATING

SPEAKING

A Work in pairs. Discuss these questions:
- Can you cook? What is your best dish?
- Who does the cooking in your house?
- What kind of thing do you usually eat?
- Are you a fussy eater, an unadventurous eater or an adventurous eater?
- Do you prefer to eat out at a restaurant or at home? When you eat at home, what do you like to cook?

VOCABULARY Describing food

A Which of the ways of cooking in the box can you see in the picture?

grill	slice	mash	steam	deep-fry
roast	boil	grate	stir-fry	marinate

B Which food in the picture do you think might be:
1 spicy?   3 tasty?   5 bland?
2 fattening?   4 greasy?   6 filling?

C Work in pairs. Look at the pictures in File 9 on p. 158. Do you know anyone who cannot – or does not – eat any of these things? Explain why not.

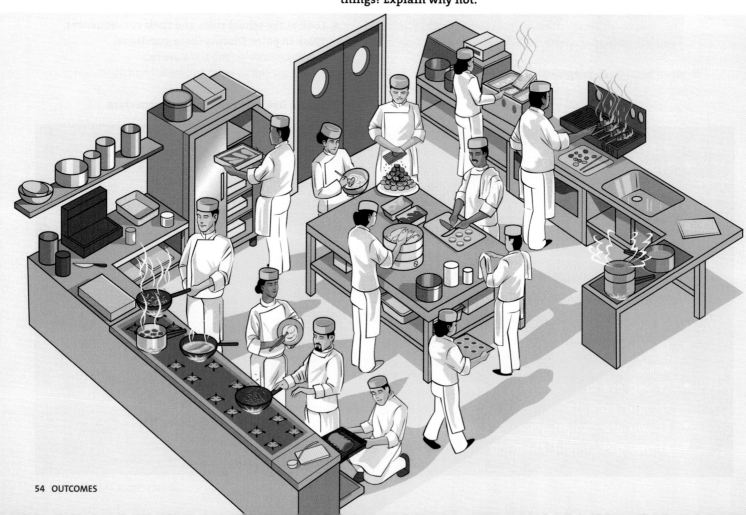

LISTENING

You are going to hear a conversation between Aurora, a Peruvian businesswoman, and Claes who is visiting Peru. Aurora explains the things on the menu below.

A Before you listen, discuss these questions:
- Do you eat much foreign food? What is your favourite?
- Have you ever tried Peruvian food? Do you know anything about it?
- Do you have any idea what any of the dishes on the menu below might be?

MENU

PAPA RELLENA
ANTICUCHOS
CEVICHE
SOPA DE CARNE
TALLARÍN CON MARISCOS

BISTEC APANADO
ARROZ CON MARISCOS
ARROZ CON PATO
LOMO SALTADO
SECO DE CABRITO

ARROZ CON LECHE
CREMA VOTEADA
HELADO DE LÚCUMA
MAZAMORRA MORADA

B ♨ 8.1 Listen to the conversation. Cross out the dishes Claes rejects, and tick ✓ the dishes he decides to order.

C How much can you remember about each of the dishes that were mentioned?

D Work in pairs. Try to complete the sentences. Then listen again to check your answers.
1 They don't have an English menu, I'm ....
2 You'll just have to talk me .... it.
3 That's balls of mashed potato, ... with beef, raisins and olives.
4 It's sliced cow's heart, very .... and ....
5 I'll go .... that.
6 That's steak, sliced very .... and then fried and .... with rice.
7 It's a bit .... a Spanish paella, but ....
8 It's a .... of stew with goat's meat in.
9 That sounds very ....

DEVELOPING CONVERSATIONS
Describing dishes

> When we have to explain different foods or dishes, we often use the patterns below.
>
> *It's a kind of* vegetable / side dish / spice.
> *It's a bit like* an oyster, *but* smaller.
> *It's a bit like* vodka, *but not as* strong.
> *It's made from* pig's blood / a special kind of bean.

A Think of four different kinds of fruit, vegetables, drinks, dishes, etc. from your country. Decide how to explain them using the structures above.

B Work in pairs. Describe your choices and see if your partner can guess what you are describing.

CONVERSATION PRACTICE

A Write a typical menu for a restaurant in your country. Write it in your own language.

B Work in pairs. You're trying to decide what to eat.
Student A: you're visiting the country on holiday or on business. You don't speak the local language.
Student B: talk Student A through the menu.
Student A: reject at least two things. Explain why. Then decide what you'd like to eat for starter, main course and dessert.

SPEAKING

A Read the introduction to an article about people living abroad and getting used to foreign food. Then work in pairs. Discuss these questions:
- Are there many specialist shops selling foreign food in your town / city? Are there any near where you live?
- Do you ever shop in any of them? Why? / Why not?
- What food from your country would you miss if you went to live abroad?

Food for thought

They say that the last thing you get used to when living abroad is the food. Look around any big city and you're bound to find a wide range of specialist shops selling imported goods for foreigners living there. Supermarkets have also started to realise there's money to be made by stocking Polish bread and beer, Chinese vegetables and Indian spices. We decided to interview four people about their experiences of living overseas to find out how they were coping with the food and with meal times. Here's what they told us.

READING

A Work in two groups. Group A, read the texts on the right. Group B, read the texts in File 3 on p. 156. As you read, answer these questions.
1 Where are the two people in your texts from?
2 Where are they living now? Why?
3 What do they like about the food and the way people eat there?
4 Is there anything they miss about their home?
5 What do they still find strange or annoying?
6 What do you think they'll never get used to? Why?

B Work in pairs with a student from the other group. Ask each other the questions in exercise A.

C Continue working with a partner from the other group. Complete the sentences with words from the texts. The definitions in brackets will help you.
1 Ian said 'stinky tofu' smells like sweaty socks and rotting fish and it's really .... (*making you not want to eat it*)
2 Ian said Americans usually just .... the bill. (*divide equally*)
3 Isabella didn't like having dinner at 6 in the evening. She was always .... by bedtime. (*really hungry*)
4 She said she was .... about eating new food before going to Scotland. (*not brave*)
5 Ya-Wen described blue cheese as .... cow fat. (*rotten*)
6 She said she sometimes ordered things that didn't .... very nice. (*end up being*)
7 Alan is now happy either pouring olive oil or .... butter on his bread. (*putting*)
8 He says people in Britain eat a lot of .... meals instead of cooking fresh food. (*pre-cooked*)

D Work in groups. Discuss these questions:
- Do you do or eat any of the things the four people found strange / annoying?
- What was the strangest thing the four people mentioned?
- What food and eating habits in your country do you think foreigners might find strange?

Ian (American)

I moved to Taiwan five years ago because my wife is from Taipei, and I love it here. We eat out a lot, and there are lots of good, cheap restaurants and street snacks. I'm vegetarian and there's a long tradition of veggie food here so it's great for me. Having said that, I'll never get used to 'stinky tofu'. The name is very accurate – it smells like sweaty socks mixed with rotting fish! I tried it once. The sauce was actually OK, but that smell is just so off-putting!

When you go to restaurants here, generally speaking, you all just order lots of different dishes and then everyone shares, which is nice. The first time I went out with my wife's family, my father in-law insisted on paying, which is pretty normal I suppose. What is still a bit strange for me, though, is when you go out with people of your own age and *all* the men always offer to pay for everything. There's sometimes almost a fight to get hold of the bill first! Generally speaking, back home we just split the bill between everyone.

One final thing I find a bit annoying here is how surprised everyone is that I can use chopsticks. I mean, just because you're foreign, it doesn't mean you can't learn how to use chopsticks!

Isabella (Spanish)

I've been studying in Glasgow for two years now, and it's a great city. When I first moved here, I spent six months living with a host family and they provided me with my first experience of the food. British food has got a bad reputation, but they served great stuff. They introduced me to some really interesting things like the Scottish national dish, haggis. It's a bit like a Spanish blood sausage called *morcilla*, but bigger.

There were a couple of things I just couldn't get used to, though. The first thing was that they always ate everything with bread and butter. It really made me miss olive oil! The other thing was that they used to have dinner at 6 o'clock every evening. I was starving by bedtime and it didn't give me time to do anything beforehand!

Another cultural difference is that lots of people here go for a drink after work. They tend not to eat while they're drinking, and only get something to eat when the pub finally closes: usually fish and chips, pizzas, that kind of thing. I've even seen deep-fried bars of chocolate! With food like that, it's no wonder there are so many foreign restaurants here!

Having said that, I think I was actually quite unadventurous before coming here, but the Scottish have introduced me to food from other countries – Indian, Thai, Mexican, all of which I love now.

LANGUAGE PATTERNS

Write the sentences in your language. Translate them back into English. Compare your English to the original.

Just because you're foreign, it doesn't mean (that) you can't learn how to use chopsticks!
Just because I'm a man, it doesn't mean (that) I can't cook.
Just because I'm young, it doesn't mean (that) I'm stupid, OK!
Just because you can it doesn't mean (that) you should.

GRAMMAR *tend to*

In *Reading*, the different people said:
The portions here *tend to be* enormous.
People *tend to buy* fresh food every day and cook
They *tend not to eat* while they're drinking.

We use *tend to* before a verb to mean *usually, but not always*. The negative form is *tend not to* or *don't tend to*.

A **Rewrite these sentences replacing the adverbs and adverbial phrases with *tend to / tend not to*.**
1 My family generally eats a lot of ready meals, as both my parents work full-time.
2 We don't normally keep food which is left over after dinner.
3 Generally speaking, people here eat food with their hands.
4 I usually skip breakfast during the week unless I have a late start at work.
5 Generally speaking, our family doesn't eat out unless it's a special occasion.
6 People don't usually leave tips here unless it was an exceptionally good meal.
7 I hardly ever have a dessert when I go out for dinner.
8 Most of the time people here avoid making any noises while they're eating. It's seen as bad manners.
9 I don't usually have time to have a big lunch, so I normally just have a sandwich.

B **Work in pairs. Discuss which of the sentences in exercise A are true for you and your country. For example:**
My wife and I *tend not to eat* ready meals, unless we're both really busy. We *tend to buy* fresh food and we cook most evenings.

C **Work in pairs. Write five more sentences about your country using *tend (not) to*. The sentences could be about food, eating, shopping, work, education or character. Then tell your partner your sentences and see if they agree with you or are surprised by anything.**

▶ Need help? Read the grammar reference on p. 147

VOCABULARY Restaurants

A **In pairs, discuss whether each of these sentences about restaurants is a good thing or a bad thing. Why?**

It's always packed.	It's home-style cooking.
It's always deserted.	It only does seafood.
It looks out over the sea.	It's got trendy décor.
The portions are huge.	The food's quite greasy.
The food's very rich.	It's all organic.

SPEAKING

A **Work in pairs. Discuss these questions:**
- Do you and your family eat out much? Where?
- Do you know any restaurants:
  - with strange or unusual décor?
  - where you get huge portions?
  - that are always packed?
  - which serve the local speciality?
  - where you can eat really cheaply?
  - which have a great view?
  - which aren't very good?

LISTENING

You are going to hear four conversations about restaurants and food.

A 🔊 **8.2 Listen and answer the questions.**
1 In conversation 1, what reasons do they give for going to a restaurant further away?
2 In conversation 2, why do they think they need to do up the restaurant?
3 In conversation 3, why does the woman want to swap dishes?
4 In conversation 4, why is the man threatening to leave without paying?

B **Work in pairs. Choose the words that were used in each conversation. Listen again and check.**
1 a The terrace *gives onto / looks out over* the river.
  b They *do / make* some really nice snacks.
  c The walk will give you *hunger / an appetite*.
2 a The menu's a bit *limited / short*.
  b The restaurant doesn't look very *interesting / inviting*.
3 a The sauce is quite spicy so it really *overcooks / overpowers* the taste of everything else.
  b That steak is so *tender / tough*!
4 a The restaurant doesn't *deserve / merit* the money.
  b The portions weren't very *great / generous*.

C **Work in pairs. Role-play two conversations.**
1 Decide where to go for something to eat or drink. One of you should reject at least one suggestion.
2 You are having dinner together in a restaurant. Ask each other about the dishes you have ordered. Use the menu on p. 55 for ideas, if you need to.

VOCABULARY *over-*

> In *Listening*, you heard that the vegetables were *overcooked*. We add *over-* to some verbs to mean *too much*.
>
> ....
>
> The vegetables were *overcooked* because they had been cooked too long, so they tasted watery.

A **Complete the sentences with the words in the box.**

overcharged	overdid	overcooked
overheated	overestimated	overate
overreacted	overslept	

1 It was a great meal. In fact, my only complaint would be that the food was so good that I completely ....!
2 When I checked the bill, I realised we'd been ....
3 He .... it at the gym. He should be more careful.
4 It was so hot, the car .... on our way there.
5 It was a mistake. I .... how much food we needed.
6 It was a bit of a disaster, because I .... the pasta.
7 I know the waiter was a bit rude, but I still think you ....
8 No wonder he .... this morning! He didn't get to bed till three last night.

B **Work in pairs. Discuss these questions:**
- What do you think happened in each of the situations described in exercise A?
- Have any of these things ever happened to you?

NATIVE SPEAKER ENGLISH

No wonder
If you say *(It's) no wonder* something happened, it means you are not surprised about it.
No wonder he overslept this morning! He didn't get to bed till three last night.
A: *I'm starving. I haven't eaten all day.*
B: *No wonder you're hungry!*

GRAMMAR Second conditionals

A Look at these examples from the conversations in *Listening* and then complete the explanation.

They might attract a few more people if they redecorated.
It would be better if it didn't have so much sauce on it!
What would happen if they called the police?

> These sentences are all examples of the second conditional. The *if* part of the sentence is in the .... simple (or continuous). This shows the speaker thinks a situation in the .... or in the future is impossible to change or is not actually going to take place. The other part of the sentence uses either .... + base form – to show a definite result or .... + base form – to show a possible result.

▶ **Need help? Read the grammar reference on p. 147**

B Complete these sentences so they are true for you.
1 If I had to wait half an hour to pay the bill, I'd...
2 If I spilt Coca-Cola all over someone's clothes, I'd...
3 If a waiter was being very rude to me, I'd...
4 If I forgot my wallet and couldn't pay for my meal, I'd...
5 If I was undercharged, I'd...

C Complete these sentences by putting the verbs in the correct form to make second conditionals.
1 A: How's your steak?
  B: It's OK, but it .... (taste) better if it .... (be) a bit more rare.
2 A: How's the soup?
  B: It's a bit bland. It .... (be) better if it .... (have) some spices in it.
3 A: Would you like any more?
  B: No thanks. No. I .... (explode) if I .... (eat) any more.
4 A: I keep putting on weight.
  B: No wonder! You're stuck in front of that computer all day. It .... (help) if you .... (do) more exercise.
5 A: They told us we'd have a table in five minutes, but we had to wait for an hour.
  B: That's awful! I hate it when that kind of thing happens. It .... (be) better if they just .... (tell) the truth at times like that.
6 A: They should do something about the décor. It looks so cold and bare in there.
  B: I know. It .... (look) a lot more inviting if they .... (paint) it a warmer colour and .... (change) the lighting.

D Write some sentences explaining how the following could be improved – and why they need to be.
- The canteen / food where you work or study.
- The way people eat and drink in your country.
- Your job, university or school.
- Public transport.

E Work in pairs. Tell a partner your ideas.

SPEAKING

A Have you seen anything in the news about the following things connected to food and drinking? What was the story?

the amount people drink   farming
famine   obesity
diets   anorexia
school meals

B 🔊 8.3 Listen. Answer the questions. Then work in pairs to check your answers.
1 What problem does the person talk about?
2 What example from the media does she give?
3 What does she think the solution is?

C Discuss these questions as a class:
- Do you think the situation in exercise B is a problem in your country?
- Do you agree with the solution the speaker suggested?

D Work in groups. Look at these suggestions about how to deal with some of the issues in exercise A. Say if you agree or disagree with them, and why. Use these sentence starters, or other second conditionals.
If they did that, ...
It'd be better if ...

- Fashion magazines shouldn't be sold to anyone under 16.
- They should ban the sale of chocolate and ice cream.
- Students should be given two pieces of fruit a day at school.
- The legal age for drinking should be raised to 21.
- Farmers shouldn't get any money from the government.
- All the extra food which is produced in Europe should be given to developing countries free.
- Children should discuss issues connected to nutrition more in school.

02 REVIEW

LEARNER TRAINING

Work in groups of three. Look at the different ways of revising vocabulary and then discuss the questions.

- Do you do any of these things? Why / Why not?
- What do you think is good or bad about these ways?
- Have you got any other ways of learning vocabulary?

> I try to put new words into a story.

> I write an alphabetical list of single words and translations.

> I put an expression on a card with the translation on the back.

> I write new vocabulary on a paper and stick it on my fridge.

GAME

Work in pairs. Student A use *only* the green squares; student B use *only* the yellow squares. Spend 5 minutes looking at your questions and revising the answers. Then take turns tossing a coin: Heads = move one of your squares; Tails = move two of your squares. When you land on a square, your partner looks at the relevant page in the book to check your answers, but *you don't*! If you are right, move forward one space (but don't answer the question until your next turn). If you aren't right, your partner tells you the right answer, and you miss a go. When you've finished the game, change colours and play again.

Start

1
Vocabulary p. 36: say eight of the jobs in the box.

2
Native English note, p. 37: if you can say what the *Native English* note was, throw again.

3
Grammar p. 39: can you say five rules using a different structure each time?

4
Vocabulary p. 41: can you remember 5 of the 6 *be/get used* to expressions?

5
Vocabulary p. 42: tell your partner four souvenirs you could buy on holiday. Use two different adjectives to describe each present.

6
Vocabulary p. 44: cover the words and describe the pictures using at least ten of the words.

7
Grammar p. 46: give an example for each of the three different uses of *must*.

8
Miss a go!

9
Native English note, p. 47: if you can say what the *Native English* note was, throw again.

10
Vocabulary p. 48: your partner will say the nouns. You should give two collocations each time.

11
Miss a go!

12
Native English note, p. 50: if you can say what the *Native English* note was, throw again.

13
Forming Words p. 50: your partner will say the verbs and you should say the noun form.

14
Vocabulary p. 52: talk about a teacher, a school and a student you know, using five of the expressions.

15
Vocabulary p. 54: say eight adjectives to describe food.

16
Native English note, p. 58: if you can say what the *Native English* note was, throw again.

17
Vocabulary p. 58: describe a restaurant you know, using four of the expressions.

18
Vocabulary p. 58: say six of the eight verbs starting with *over-* that mean 'too much'.

Finish

For each of the activities below, work in groups of three. Use the Vocabulary Builder if you want to.

CONVERSATION PRACTICE

Choose one of these *Conversation Practice* activities:
Working life p. 37
Going shopping p. 43
School and studying p. 49
Eating p. 55

Two of you should do the task. The third person should listen and give a mark of between 1 and 10. Explain your decision. Then change roles.

ACT OR DRAW

One person should act or draw as many of these words as you can in three minutes. Your partners should try to guess the words. Do not speak while you are acting or drawing!

dirt	dust	bend over	slam
stare	roast	a warehouse	rotting
pot	bracelet	starving	trainers
carved	scruffy	stripy	stew
price tag	hang	an outfit	a gig
queue	a ferry	whisper	an essay

QUIZ

Answer as many of the questions as possible.
1 Why might you not be **accepted** on a course?
2 If something is **tacky**, is it nice?
3 What might you **upgrade**, and why?
4 Why might a school be described as **rough**?
5 What is the opposite of someone who is **very bright**?
6 What are **postgraduate** courses?
7 If you work in **HR**, what do you do?
8 What should you do if you **owe someone money**?
9 What is the difference between **it doesn't suit you** and **it doesn't fit**?
10 Say two things which might make food **off-putting**.
11 Why might a company or shop **go out of business**?
12 What is the problem if you work in **cramped conditions**?
13 Why might a drug be **taken off the market**?
14 What do **pushy parents** do?
15 Name three things that are **fattening**.

COLLOCATIONS

Take turns to read out collocation lists from Unit 5 of the Vocabulary Builder. Where there is a '~', say '*blah*' instead. Your partner should guess as many words as they can. Each time you change roles, move to the next unit.

PRONUNCIATION Consonant sounds

A ◆ R 2.1 Listen and repeat the sounds and the words.

/p/ apply permanent	/t/ training tutor	/tʃ/ cheat overcharge	/k/ accounts contract
/b/ bland diabetic	/d/ discipline avoid	/dʒ/ gorgeous rigid	/g/ rug gig
/f/ afford fake	/s/ civil service juicy	/l/ label lecture	/ʃ/ sugary portion
/v/ venue woven	/z/ overseas raise	/r/ rep research	/w/ warehouse swear

B Which sounds do you find hardest to pronounce?

Notice that when you say /p/, /t/, /f/, /tʃ/, /k/ and /s/ it is important to push more air out of your mouth as you make the sound.

C A group of consonants at the start of a word is called a consonant cluster, such as *str* in *straight*. Always try to say these sounds very clearly when they are at the beginning of a word. If you make a pronunciation mistake here, it can be especially difficult for people to understand you.

Try saying these words.
trainers	swap
skip	pretty
stripy	spread
squid	greasy
grade	brand
bright	playground

▶ Find this difficult? Try adding a short /ə/ sound between the consonants and then speed up. People will still understand you.

LISTENING

You are going to hear five people talk about things connected with food and restaurants.

A 🔊 R 2.2 **Listen. Which of the things in the box does each person do?**

businessman	chef	teacher	model
factory worker	student	waiter	

Speaker 1 ....   Speaker 4 ....

Speaker 2 ....   Speaker 5 ....

Speaker 3 ....

B **Listen again and decide which speaker:**
a has changed jobs and is worried about getting fat.
b has an injury from work and stopped eating something.
c never goes on a diet and wants to change jobs.
d compares his job to the past and keeps strong discipline.
e enjoys the job, but complains about co-workers.

[... / 10]

GRAMMAR Talking about rules

Complete the second sentence using the word in brackets, so it has a similar meaning to the first one.

1 You must hand in your essay on Tuesday.
You .... your essay later than Tuesday. (can)
2 You must tell me in advance if you want a day off.
You .... sooner if you want a day off. (supposed)
3 It's not a problem if you use the Internet at any time.
You .... the Internet whenever you like. (allowed)
4 You mustn't go there. It's a rip-off.
.... there, if I were you. It's a waste of money. (would)
5 You can skip the queue if you have a ticket.
You .... if you don't have a ticket. (have)
6 You should go if you're busy.
You .... stay behind if you're busy. (have)
7 I need to ask for a doctor's certificate.
.... forget to get a doctor's certificate. (must)
8 Is taking photos inside the gallery prohibited?
.... photos inside the gallery? (allowed)

[... / 8]

▶ **Find this difficult? Look back at grammar reference p. 144.**

CONDITIONALS

Choose the correct words a–d to complete the sentences.

1 ...... I get another job soon, I'm going to get into debt.
  a When   b Since
  c Unless   d If
2 Honestly, I think I'd explode ...... I ate another thing.
  a unless   b when
  c after   d if
3 He ...... his homework unless you stand over him and force him to do it.
  a didn't do   b doesn't do
  c hasn't done   d wouldn't do
4 If he ...... hard, he'd probably pass, but he's just very lazy.
  a will work   b would work
  c worked   d works
5 If she ...... it, she can take it back to the shop.
  a will like   b won't like
  c wouldn't like   d doesn't like
6 We can get a sandwich before the film, if you ....
  a ate   b won't eat
  c don't eat   d haven't eaten
7 If you have any problems, ... me a ring.
  a just give   b you'll just give
  c just you give   d you gave
8 If I could work anywhere, I .... a job with Google.
  a would get   b got
  c can get   d will get

[... / 8]

▶ **Find this difficult? Look back at grammar reference pp. 146 and 147.**

ADVERBS AND PREPOSITIONS

Choose the correct preposition or adverb.

1 I work *as / like* a rep for a small company.
2 I'm *in / of* charge of the whole department.
3 He's *away / off* sick. Hopefully, he'll back at work soon.
4 I'm sorry to ask you *to / at* such short notice, but I need you to work this weekend.
5 People near the factory are exposed *with / to* dangerous chemicals.
6 He's stressed. He's *under / below* a lot of pressure at work.
7 There's so much competition now, I don't know if we can stay *in / on* business for much longer.
8 He insisted *of / on* paying for everything. He wouldn't let me pay a penny!
9 We're having some friends *at / round* for dinner. Would you like to come as well?
10 They've got some books *of / on* special offer – three for two.

[... / 10]

COLLOCATION

Decide which word does not collocate with the word in bold.

1 a well-paid / temporary / scruffy / stressful / demanding **job**
2 filling / deserted / sugary / vegan / chewy / disgusting **food**
3 a hard / post-graduate / evening / struggling / online **course**
4 thick / rewarding / trendy / smart / plain / colourful **clothes**
5 a hand-painted / mass-produced / china / plastic / silk **plate**
6 grated / mashed / boiled / steamed / sliced / limited **carrot**

[... / 6]

DEVELOPING CONVERSATIONS

Complete the dialogues with one word in each gap.

1 A: What's the difference between these phones?
   B: Well, firstly, this one is pay-as-you-go, ... that .... requires a contract.
2 A: What are *kakis*?
   B: Oh they're a .... of fruit. They're a bit .... big tomatoes, but they are creamier and they're sweeter.
3 A: I spend a lot of time travelling round Asia.
   B: Really. That .... be really interesting.
   A: Yeah, it .... be, but unfortunately I often only see the hotel!
4 A: How's the course ....?
   B: Great – but I'm very busy. I have to .... in an essay at the end of the week.

[... / 8]

VERB – NOUN COLLOCATIONS

Match the pairs of verbs with a noun.

1 ask for / split   breakfast
2 cheat in / fail   a tip
3 owe / save   litter
4 ask for / fill in   the rules
5 drop / pick up   the deadline
6 skip / have   the bill
7 leave / deserve   an exam
8 get into / pay back   an application form
9 set / break   debt
10 extend / miss   money

[... / 10]

▶ **Find this difficult? Remember the Vocabulary Builder has information on new collocations.**

FORMING WORDS

Complete 1–8 with the adjectives of the words in bold.

1 The mobile phone business is incredibly .... **compete**
2 It's a very .... environment at work. **support**
3 When it comes to food, she's not very .... **adventure**
4 The course was really useful – just very .... **practice**
5 She's very .... She always does her homework. **study**
6 He's very .... about history. **know**
7 Some parents are .... and pay for private tutors. **push**
8 My tutor's .... and tells us we're doing well. **encourage**
9 The menu for the school dinners isn't very .... **variety**
10 It's a .... investment: you can lose a lot of money. **risk**

[... / 10]

VOCABULARY

Complete the words in the two short articles. The first letters are given.

An organisation which deals with people who are in debt has said the situation is getting worse. It says people often [1]o........................ £20,000 on credit cards and regularly go into overdraft on their bank [2]ac........................ . It blames a mixture of consumerism and low salaries. It wants the government to raise the minimum [3]w........................, and suggests banks should [4]av........................ giving loans to people who can't afford to pay them back. It says that those in debt should be sensible. They should do [5]w........................ the latest trendy clothes and should wait to buy things in the [6]s........................ when things are cheaper.

A school headmaster has called for schools to reduce the amount of [7]ho........................ children are given. He says it does not affect students' level of achievement and, as evidence of this, he [8]po........................ to the success of Finland where students [9]t........................ to have a lighter [10]wo........................ outside school.

[... / 10]

■   [Total ... /80]

In this unit you learn how to:
· describe flats, houses and areas
· add emphasis
· make comparisons
· ask about rules

Grammar
· Comparing the past with now

Vocabulary
· Describing where you live
· Describing changes
· Describing areas

Reading
· Priced out of the market

Listening
· Describing a flat
· The area where you live

VOCABULARY
Describing where you live

A Which of the words in the box can you see in the pictures?

a courtyard	a garage
a swimming pool	a patio
gas central heating	an open fire
a back garden	a balcony
a loft	a tiled floor
a roof terrace	a basement

B Work in pairs. Which of the things in exercise A have you got where you live? Are there any things you are happy not having?

C Use the extra information in sentences 1–10 to guess the meanings of the words in **bold**. Translate the sentences into your language.

1 It's only a one-bedroom flat, so now we have the baby and all the extra baby stuff, it's quite **cramped**.
2 We've got huge windows, so we get a lot of sunlight, which means it's nice and **bright** in the summer.
3 It's very **conveniently located**. There's a shop just round the corner and it's five minutes from the nearest station.
4 I'm renting a room in **a shared flat** with four other students. It's nice, but it's cold. The central heating needs fixing.
5 I live on the fifth floor of an old block of flats. The whole place is quite **run-down**. It needs a lot of work done on it.
6 It's very **spacious**. It's the biggest place I've ever lived in.
7 It's very **affordable**. My rent is quite low. I only pay fifty pounds a week.
8 I live in a **newly built** block of flats. It's great. It's all very modern.
9 It's very **central**. I can walk into town in ten minutes.
10 It's not very big, but it's big enough. It's nice and **compact**.

D Work in pairs. Discuss which of the words above describe your home.

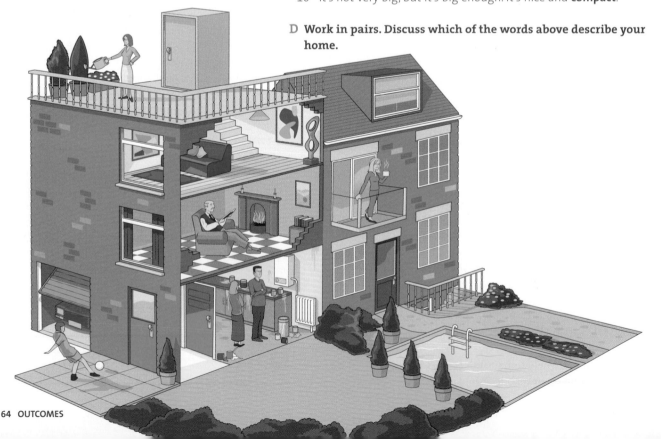

LANGUAGE PATTERNS

Write the sentences in your language. Translate them back into English. Compare your English to the original.
The flat needs a lot of work (to be) done on it.
It needs a lot of money (to be) spent on it.
The oven needs a good clean. It's really dirty.
It needs a new coat of paint.
The roof needs fixing. It leaks in heavy rain!
It does work. The batteries just need replacing.

LISTENING

You are going to hear two people, Gavin and Lynn, talking about their friends' new flat.

A ◐ 9.1 **Listen and answer the questions.**
1 Why did Nick and Carol move?
2 What is nice about their new place?
3 What are the problems with the new place?
4 In what way was their old place better?

B **Look at the sentence beginnings from the conversation you listened to. Discuss in pairs how each sentence ended. Then listen to the conversation again and check.**
1 Did I tell you I went ...
2 I haven't seen them ...
3 They said to say ...
4 It's quite a lot ...
5 That must be ...
6 That's the main reason ...
7 I must go ...
8 The only problem is, though, it's not ...

C **In groups, discuss these questions.**
- Do you like the sound of Nick and Carol's new place?
- How many times have you moved in your life? Why?
- Have you ever done any work on your place? What?
- Have you ever shared a room? How was it?

PRONUNCIATION
Adding emphasis with auxiliaries

In the conversation, Gavin said that Nick and Carol's flat '*does* need a bit of work done on it, but they've actually bought it'.

We can add emphasis to sentences by either adding the auxiliaries *do, does* or *did* – or by stressing the auxiliary verb already there.

A **Work with a partner. Which auxiliaries in the sentences below do you expect to be stressed?**
1 'I do like Paris. I just don't want to live there.'
2 'The kitchen's lovely, but it does need a good clean!'
3 'I did visit their flat once, but it was a long time ago.'
4 'They did send me their new address, but I've lost it.'
5 'It isn't very central, but it is very affordable.'
6 'I have been there. I've just forgotten the way.'
7 'They've got a huge flat, but it is a bit dark inside.'
8 'It's quite run-down, but it has got potential.'

B ◐ 9.2 **Listen and practise saying the sentences.**

DEVELOPING CONVERSATIONS
Making comparisons

We often describe how large places are by making comparisons with places that the listener knows.

The lounge is *huge – it's twice the size of* this room.
It's got a *great* kitchen – *it's a similar size to* yours, maybe a bit bigger.
Her garden's *nice – it's about the same size as* mine.

A **Correct the mistakes in these sentences. You may need to add extra words.**
1 His bedroom's tiny. It's about half-size of mine.
2 The kitchen is enormous. It's three times the size of my.
3 The bathroom's OK. It's about same size as yours – maybe a little bit bigger.
4 They've got a huge garden. It's twice the size of your.
5 They've got a small basement. It's a similar size of this room – maybe a little bit smaller.
6 They've got a lovely front room. It's twice as wide as this room and maybe a little bit more long.

B **Tell a partner how big the rooms are where you live.**

CONVERSATION PRACTICE

Think of the flat or house of someone you know and have similar conversations to the one you heard in *Listening.* **Start the conversation like this:**
A: Did I tell you I went round to see X the other day?
B: No, you didn't. How is she / he? I haven't seen her / him for ages.

VOCABULARY Describing changes

We often talk about changes using verbs in the present perfect. We add adverbs to describe the degree of change. Look at these examples.

	risen	dramatically	over the past few months.
Unemployment has House prices have	increased gone up	a lot steadily slightly	over the last few years. over the past ten years. since last year.
	gone down dropped fallen	a bit by 15%	

A **Decide how the things in the box have changed in your country from the past to now. Choose adverbs and time expressions to add more details.**

Unemployment	Food prices
House prices	The crime rate
The average wage	Interest rates
Petrol prices	The birth rate
The divorce rate	Taxes

B **Look at the comments below. Which changes in exercise A could the speakers be discussing?**

It's because there's an election next year.
I think it's happened because of problems in the economy.
I guess it might be because there aren't enough homes.
It's probably a result of having more police on the street.
It has something to do with rising oil prices.
I think it has something to do with the fact that people have to work long hours.

C **Work in pairs. Ask and answer questions about changes in your country using the language in exercises A and B. For example:**

A: *Why do you think the crime rate has fallen over the last few years?*
B: *I'm not sure. I guess it might be because people are richer.*

READING

You are going to read an article entitled *Priced out of the market*. It is about different solutions to the current shortage of housing in many countries.

A **Look at the pictures in the article. How do you think each one is connected to the title?**

B **Read the article and see if you were right. When do you think it was written? Why?**

C **Decide if these sentences about the article are true or false. Read again and check.**

1 Jim Wynand pays a lot of rent for his flat.
2 The development he's living in is temporary.
3 House prices in London have more than doubled over the last decade.
4 In recent years, it has become cheaper for house buyers to borrow money from banks.
5 More people want to sell houses than buy them.
6 Some houses are built specifically for people in jobs which are important for society.
7 The number of people adding extra rooms to their houses has increased slightly over recent years.
8 It is becoming more normal for people to leave home later than they had perhaps planned to.

D **Work in groups of three. Discuss these questions:**

1 Do you have any of the same problems in your country?
2 What do you think of the different ideas for dealing with the housing problem? What's the best solution? Can you think of any others?
3 How much do house prices vary in your town / city / country? Where is the best place to buy?
4 If you could live anywhere you wanted, where would you choose? Why?

E **Without looking at the article, complete the sentences.**

1 More and more young people are now .... advantage of the new housing developments.
2 Prices used to be so low it was inevitable that there would be dramatic price ....
3 By limiting new developments to inner city areas, the government aims to .... the environment.
4 Lots of people buy second homes as .... They keep them for a few years then sell them at a profit.
5 It's the main going out area, so it .... very noisy in the evenings.
6 There has been a huge .... in the number of people adding extra rooms to their properties.
7 More and more banks now offer mortgages .... very low interest rates.
8 They need to find some new ways of .... the problem.

PRICED OUT OF THE MARKET

around the world have risen dramatically. In London, for example, the price of an average house has increased by 240% over the past ten years, whilst prices in the Romanian capital, Bucharest, recently rose a terrifying 27% in just a few months!

The roots of the problem

There are several reasons for this. Firstly, banks have offered more **mortgages at low interest rates**, which has lead to more people borrowing enough to buy property. Demand has, therefore, increased faster than supply, which has pushed prices up. Also, prices in many countries started low, meaning **dramatic price rises** were inevitable. Finally, the number of people **buying second homes – as investments** or for use as holiday homes – has increased steadily.

Top-down solutions

Governments are constantly suggesting new ways of **tackling the problem**. As well as innovative ideas like the Amsterdam developments, these include building more social housing, particularly in inner cities, and making sure that plenty of this housing is kept for key workers such as nurses and teachers. There has also been more building on land previously used for commercial or industrial purposes. Such projects **protect the environment** and stop cities getting ever larger.

And bottom-up ones

While governments look for answers, families who can't afford to move are having to develop their existing properties instead. There has been a **huge increase in** the number of people building extensions in their gardens or adding basements, thus creating that extra space they so desperately want.

And one of the reasons why space is needed is that many young people are living at home longer than they might want. Indeed, in some parts of Europe the average age that children leave home has reached 34! It appears to be part of a broader trend where people today are doing everything later in life – especially getting married and having children, events which traditionally led to house purchases.

No place like home

Jim Wynand sits in his flat in Amsterdam, enjoying a cup of coffee before classes begin. "It's not my ideal home, and I wouldn't want to spend the rest of my life here", he admits. "It's a bit cramped inside, and **it gets** fairly **noisy** here with all the other students around, but for now this place is just right for me. For starters, it's very affordable. I mean, if it wasn't for places like this, I'd still be living at home with my parents! On top of that, it's very central, which is great."

Mr Wynand is one of many young people in Holland **taking advantage of** new developments aimed at tackling the country's housing shortage. He is renting a flat made from a recycled shipping container. The flats are compact, come with Internet, plumbing, gas and electricity fitted and can be placed one on top of another.

At present, the housing development only has permission to stay where it is for the next five years, but developers hope they will be given longer.

The shape of things to come?

It is quite possible that more and more people will soon find themselves living in similar kinds of developments, as they end up priced out of the housing market. Over the last decade, house prices

VOCABULARY Describing areas

| convenient | noisy | rough | lively | dirty |
| residential | dead | green | isolated | posh |

A Match the words in the box with sentences 1–10.
1 There's absolutely nothing to do round there in the evenings and it's fairly quiet during the day too!
2 We live on a main road and lots of lorries go past.
3 The nightlife's good. There's always something happening.
4 It's quite run-down and there's quite a lot of crime and social problems.
5 There are lots of parks and trees, which is nice.
6 It's incredibly expensive round there. All you see are beautiful houses with perfect gardens. I could never afford to live there.
7 It's in the middle of nowhere. You need a car to get anywhere.
8 There's a lot of litter – the streets are filthy and there's graffiti everywhere.
9 There are plenty of shops and it's well connected for transport.
10 There are lots of families living there, so it's nice for the kids, but we could do with more shops nearby.

B Write a list of areas you know. Work in pairs. Swap your paper and ask *What's … like?* Your partner should answer the questions using language from exercise A.

LISTENING

You are going to hear two people talking about the area they live in.

A 9.3 Listen and answer the questions about each conversation.
1 Do they like it?
2 What's nice about the area?
3 What's bad about the area?
4 How has the area changed?
5 What caused the change?

GRAMMAR
Comparing the past with now

A Try and complete the sentences from *Listening*. They compare things between the past and now. Check your answers in the audioscript on p. 168.
1 There are still bad things about it, but it's .... than .... before.
2 There's .... much crime as .... five years ago.
3 It's .... quiet as ....
4 There were .... flights than .... now.
5 One of the budget airlines started using the airport and over the past few years it .... bigger and ....

B Translate the sentences in exercise A into your language.

▶ Need help? Read the grammar reference on p. 148

C Complete these sentences so they are true about your town, country or society. Work in pairs. Explain your ideas. Some of the pictures may help.
1 .... is / are much worse than .... was / were before.
2 .... isn't / aren't as bad as it / they used to be.
3 There is much less .... than there was a few years ago.
4 There is / are more .... than there was / were in the past.
5 It's far easier to .... than it used to be.
6 .... is more touristy than it used to be.
7 .... is / are getting better and better.
8 Over the past few years, they've built more and more .... in ....

D Work in groups of three. Discuss how the world is better than before, and how it is worse.

SPEAKING

A Read adverts for six host families for foreign students studying in the centre of Berlin. Prices are per week. Give each a mark 1–5 (1=bad, 5=great).

B Work in pairs. Discuss whether you would like to stay in each one and why / why not.

RENTAL

Close to U-bahn underground station. 8km from the city centre – near airport and Tegeler See, lake and woodlands. Huge and beautifully decorated house. This very friendly family offers half board (€260) or self-catering (€190) accommodation.

This cheerful household consists of a young couple, two-year-old boy and baby. Breakfast and evening meal included. Lovely, spacious room in a flat in wealthy residential area near Tiergarten park and embassies. (€290)

Bright, cheerful apartment in the multi-cultural, working class area of Wedding. Self catering rooms for two single students sharing with a friendly lady owner. Very relaxed atmosphere. Within walking distance of lively nightlife. (€150)

Beautiful country house in village 35km from Berlin. Very green! Young and friendly homeowner. Internet access. 15 minutes to train station. (€160 with breakfast)

Compact room with access to own kitchen facilities in a large old house owned by a charming elderly couple offering quiet, comfortable accommodation. Very central. (€200)

Good-sized room in lovely big apartment.

A 45-minute bus ride from the centre. A very pleasant family of four (children 16 and 20). The flat is beautifully decorated. Half board (very good cuisine). 2 dogs. Non-smoking girls only. (€200)

DEVELOPING CONVERSATIONS
Asking about rules

A student is asking some questions to a new host family.

A Match the student's questions 1–6 with the host family's replies a–f. Notice the expressions in **bold**, which set limits to the answers.

1 Would it be OK if I have friends to visit?
2 Would you mind if I cooked for myself sometimes?
3 Do I have to be home before a certain time?
4 Can I use the washing machine whenever I like?
5 Would it be possible to get web access in my room?
6 Is it OK if I play music in my room?

a No, not at all – **as long as** you're quiet if you're back late.
b **I'm afraid not**, but there is an Internet café nearby.
c Not at all – **as long as** you clean up after yourself.
d **It depends how** long for. It's fine if it's just a few days.
e Of course, **within reason**. Obviously, you shouldn't play it too loud.
f **Within reason**. Obviously, I don't want you washing clothes in the middle of the night.

B Underline the different ways of making a request in the questions in exercise A.

C Work in pairs. Imagine you are going to stay with one of the host families in *Speaking* below. Write down six more questions you would ask and the replies you might get. Use the language from exercise A.

SPEAKING

A Role-play a phone call between a student and a host family. Use as much new language from this unit as you can. Ask questions about:

- the house
- rules
- the area
- any special requests

That's your room there.

10 GOING OUT

In this unit you learn how to:
- ask and answer questions about arts events
- give directions
- talk about a night out
- say why you don't want to do things

Grammar
- The future in the past

Vocabulary
- Films, exhibitions and plays
- Describing what's on
- Describing an event

Reading
- What's on in Buenos Aires?

Listening
- Arranging a night out
- How was it?

VOCABULARY Films, exhibitions and plays

A Decide which is the odd one out in each group and explain your decision.
1 a horror film / a thriller / a romantic comedy / an installation
2 landscapes / a trailer / portraits / a still life / abstract
3 the painting / the special effects / the soundtrack / the plot / the photography
4 a painter / a video artist / a director / a sculptor / an audience
5 a drama / a gig / a tragedy / a historical play / a comedy
6 the scenery / the lighting / the costumes / sculpture / the acting

B Work in pairs. Discuss these questions:
- How often do you go to the cinema / art exhibitions / the theatre?
- What kind of films / art / theatre do you like?
- Are there any films / exhibitions / plays on at the moment that you would like to see?

C Match the questions 1–6 with the pairs of possible answers a–f.
1 What's on in town at the moment?
2 What kind of exhibition is it?
3 What's it about?
4 Where's it on?
5 When's it on?
6 Who's in it?

a They've got showings at 6, 8.50 and 11.05.
It's on till next week and the gallery's open between 10 and 8.
b It's some kind of romantic comedy.
It's a drama about life in a rural community.
c Nobody I know.
Penelope Cruz and Charlize Theron.
d At the Hermitage gallery.
At the ABC Park cinema.
e It's a collection of still-life paintings.
It's an installation by the Mexican artist Gabriel Orozco.
f There's the new film by Lee Myung-se.
Not much really. There's a musical on at the theatre that might be OK.

D Work in pairs. Ask each other the questions in exercise C, but give your own answers about things that are on in your town.

LISTENING

You are going to hear two friends, Dan and Jason, making plans for the evening.

A 🎧 **10.1 Listen to the first part of the conversation and answer the questions.**
1 What's on?
2 What's it about?
3 When's it on?
4 Where's it on?

B 🎧 **10.2 Listen to the rest of the conversation and answer the questions.**
1 Where is the cinema? Mark it on the map below.
2 What time do they arrange to meet? Why?

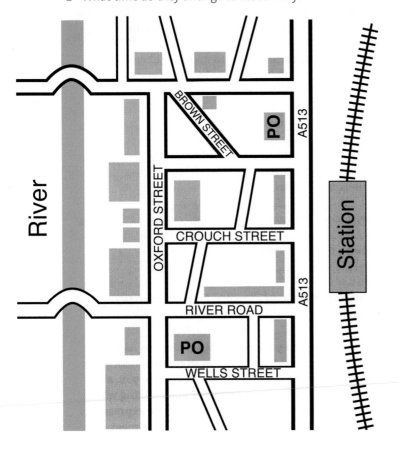

DEVELOPING CONVERSATIONS
Explaining where things are

A Complete the sentences with the words in the boxes.

halfway	front	off	next	at

1 You know Columbus Avenue? Well, it's about .... down there.
2 You know the cathedral? Well, it's right in .... of the main entrance.
3 You know the post office? Well, it's the .... turning down from there, on the other side of the road.
4 You know the cinema? Well, there's a car park .... the back.
5 You know the main square? Well, Hope Close is one of the streets .... there. I think it's the little pedestrianised one.

coming	back	towards	out	facing

6 If you've got your .... to the station, you turn left.
7 If you're .... the station, it's on your left.
8 If you're .... down the road away from the station, it's the second turning on the left.
9 If you're going up the road .... the station and away from the river, it's second on the right.
10 When you come .... of the building, you'll see it right opposite.

B Work in pairs. Take turns to draw maps to illustrate each of the descriptions in exercise A. Explain what you are drawing. Do you agree the map is accurate?

NATIVE SPEAKER ENGLISH

We use *right* before prepositional phrases to mean *exactly*.
It's right in front of the main entrance.
It's right behind you.
George Clooney was sitting right next to me!
We got to the theatre right on time.

CONVERSATION PRACTICE

A Work in pairs. You are going to have a conversation similar to the one in *Listening*.
Student A: invite your friend out tonight. Start by asking: *Do you fancy going to the cinema / an exhibition / the theatre?*
Think about what you want to do and some details about it. Suggest where and when to meet.

Student B: find out more about what your friend wants to do by asking *What's on?* and other questions. Agree to go. Ask where it is exactly. Do not accept the first meeting time your partner suggests.

VOCABULARY
Describing what's on

A Decide if the words in the box are positive, negative or could be both, depending on the context. Work in pairs to discuss your ideas.

spectacular	trendy	marvellous
touristy	dull	incredible
terrible	weird	terrific
dreadful	amazing	brilliant

B Think of some films, plays, musicals, exhibitions, books, CDs or places that you do not personally know, but that you could describe using some of the words in exercise A. Write sentences about them using the patterns in the box.

> **I haven't seen** the new David Lynch movie, **but it's supposed to be** quite weird.
> **I haven't heard** the new Snow Patrol CD, **but it's supposed to be** quite dull.
> **I haven't been to** the Julie Freeman installation yet, **but it's supposed to be** amazing.

C Work in small groups. Tell the other students your ideas from exercise B. See if they have heard similar things – or if they know the things / places and have different opinions about them.

READING

You are going to read a page from a website about what is on in Buenos Aires, the capital of Argentina.

A Before you read, work in pairs. Discuss what you know about the city and the country. You might need to use *It's supposed to ... / There's supposed to be ...*

B Now read the text quickly. Find seven adjectives from *Vocabulary* exercise A. What do they describe?

C Read the page again more slowly. Then, work in pairs. Discuss what you remember about the dates, times, people and things in the box below.

1908	trainers and jeans
Luana DeVol	décor
the 19th century	steak
Broadway	midnight
artists	street performers
Diego Maradona	

D Work in pairs. Discuss what you think the words in **bold** in the text mean.

E Now use the words in **bold** to complete these sentences.
1 It's a very .... club. It's members only.
2 They serve really .... Mexican food there.
3 My uncle is really fit. He's a very .... runner.
4 Mississippi is the .... of the blues, country music, and rock & roll.
5 I don't think Real Madrid will win the league this year. Their .... isn't strong enough.
6 It's a lovely evening. Let's go out for a .... around town.
7 If you ever get the chance to .... him playing live, don't miss it! He's just incredible.
8 It's got an amazing ...., but it's an awful film.
9 His music is a clever .... of jazz and hip-hop.
10 It's a nice club, but it does attract a very young ....

SPEAKING

A Work in pairs. Discuss these questions:
- From what you have read, how do you think the nightlife in your city / town compares to Buenos Aires?
- Can you think of any places in your city / town that are similar to the places you read about? Do you ever go to any of them?

DEVELOPING CONVERSATIONS
Why you do not want to do things

> When we are trying to arrange what to do and we are given different options, we usually explain why we don't like certain ideas. We use several common expressions to do this.

A Put the words in the correct order to make eight common expressions.
1 it's my thing really kind not of.
....
2 don't like really I feel it.
....
3 that mood I'm kind not for really in of the thing.
....
4 me sounds trendy it for a bit too.
....
5 touristy it looks me too for a bit.
....
6 too weird a bit me sounds for it.
....

B 🔊 10.3 Listen to check your answers. Then practise saying the expressions.

C Work in pairs. Imagine you are staying in Buenos Aires for a couple of days. Look at the *What's on in Buenos Aires* guide again. Decide which of the options sound good to you, and which do not. Then role-play a conversation deciding what you want to do. Reject options using some of the expressions from exercise A. Then discuss where and when to meet.

What's on in Buenos Aires?

1 / Teatro Colón /

The opera *Elektra* by Richard Strauss / 20.30 / Tickets from $25

Built in 1908, Teatro Colón is one of the most famous opera houses in the world. It has recently re-opened following a period of redecoration and is proud to present one of the major operas of the twentieth century – '*Elektra*'. The spectacular scenery, costumes and lighting have to be seen to be believed, whilst the excellent **cast** is headed by American soprano Luana DeVol.

2 / Señor Tango /

$25 including dinner and transport to and from your hotel

Buenos Aires is the **birthplace** of the tango, which was created in the 19th century as a **fusion** of European and African music. There is no better place to catch the magic of this incredible dance than Señor Tango. Very popular with tourists, this show features more than 40 dancers, singers and musicians, and is easily as good as any of the musicals on Broadway in New York.

3 / La Boca /

La Boca is one of the oldest and most **authentic** neighbourhoods in Buenos Aires. The area was built by Italian immigrants and today is home to both a large community of artists and also many normal working-class people.
Few tourists are adventurous enough to leave the main street, Caminito, because they have been put off by the area's negative reputation. However, La Boca is a great place to come and experience the city's café and bar culture.

4 / Boca Juniors vs. Independiete /

Kick-off 21.10 / Tickets $4-$15

Boca Juniors are one of the most famous football teams in the world. Former players include Diego Maradona and Carlos Tévez and the club have fans all over the world. This is your chance to **catch** the current **squad** play in their legendary stadium, the Bombonera.

5 / Opera Bay /

$10-$15 (includes one free drink)

The city's most **exclusive** disco attracts a posh after-office **crowd** – especially on Wednesdays, when there is a strict dress code: trainers and jeans are not welcome! Opera Bay plays no Latin music at all, preferring electronic music.

6 / Mundo Bizarro /

A trendy bar for the more adventurous tourist! Terrific cocktails, weird and wonderful décor and a great mix of music make this place very popular with those looking for something slightly different.

7 / La Chacra steakhouse /

Argentineans eat more meat per person than any other nationality in the world. This should come as no surprise, for when you get a good steak here, it is the best on earth!
La Chacra is a classic steakhouse and is unmissable for any **keen** meat-eater. The locals eat late – it is not uncommon to arrive at a restaurant at ten and to finish around midnight. The steaks are not the only thing worth coming for, however, as the salads are also delicious.

8 / Avenida Florida /

Avenida Florida is a great place to go for a **stroll** in the evening – and to maybe do some shopping too. As one of the main shopping streets in the city, it can be a bit touristy so don't accept the first price you are offered. You can usually negotiate a much better deal.
As well as offering great shopping opportunities, Av. Florida also has amazing street life. Dancers, singers, and all kinds of other street performers come here to earn money.

SPEAKING

A Work in pairs. Discuss these questions:
- Have you been out anywhere recently?
- Where did you go?
- How was it?

VOCABULARY Describing an event

A Match 1–8 with a–h.
1 It was really good, but they were quite weird paintings.
2 It's OK – a bit overrated, though.
3 It was really moving.
4 It was boiling hot.
5 It was completely sold out.
6 It's very trendy – full of young, beautiful people.
7 They were rubbish – just very dull.
8 Amazing. There was such a great atmosphere.

a It wasn't as brilliant as everyone's been saying.
b I can't really describe them or say why I like them!
c I was sweating like crazy.
d It was absolutely packed.
e I was in tears by the end.
f The music, the people, everything.
g I felt a bit out of place.
h We actually left halfway through.

B Decide if the answers could refer to a film, club, play, exhibition or gig. More than one answer may be possible.

C Work in pairs. Try to remember as much of the language in exercise A as you can.
Student A: ask *How was the ...?*
Student B: close your book and give an appropriate answer from exercise A.

D Tell each other about some films / clubs / plays / exhibitions you think are: *great / overrated / moving / trendy / rubbish / weird.*

PRONUNCIATION Intonation and lists

When we give our opinion about things we have seen, we often list what we liked or disliked. As we say a list of words, the intonation goes up on each word until the last one, when it goes down. We often finish these lists by adding *everything*.

A 🔊 10.4 Listen to these lists and repeat them.
It was great. The special effects, the soundtrack, everything!
It was awful. The music, the venue, everything!
It was terrific. The acting, the scenery, everything!

B Work in pairs. Take turns saying these sentences.
Student A: ask *What was so good / bad about it?*
Student B: give the answer.

1 The food, the service, everything. It was fantastic.
2 The people, the music, everything. It was just brilliant.
3 The story, the acting, everything. It was one of the worst things I've seen in a long time.
4 The music, the dancing, everything. It was dreadful.
5 The hotel, the countryside, everything. It was great.
6 The weather, the place, everything. We had a great time.
7 The special effects, the soundtrack, everything. It was one of the best things I've seen in ages.
8 The scenery, the direction, everything. It was really bad.

C Work in pairs. What do you think the sentences in exercise B are describing?

D Tell your partner about a great / terrible time you had on holiday / at a cinema / theatre / restaurant / hotel / party, etc. Use the patterns in exercise B. Add some more details with other language you have learned in this unit.

LANGUAGE PATTERNS

Write the sentences in your language. Translate them back into English. Compare your English to the original.
It was one of the worst things I've seen in a long time.
It was one of the best things I've seen in ages.
It's one of the worst clubs I've ever been to.
He's one of nicest people I've ever met.
It's the nicest thing anyone's ever done for me.
It's the best book I've read in ages.

LISTENING

You are going to hear three conversations about what people did the previous night.

A 🔊 **10.5** Listen and decide what kind of event each person went to.

1 .... 2 .... 3 ....

B **Work in pairs. Discuss these questions about each of the conversations.**

1 Did they change their plans? Why?
2 Did they enjoy the night? Why? / Why not?
3 Did their experience match what other people had said about the event?

C **Listen and check.**

GRAMMAR The future in the past

> There are several ways of referring to future plans, promises or predictions that we made in the past. Usually, *am going to* becomes *was going to* and *will* becomes *would*.
> ....
> *I was going to stay in, but a friend called me and so I ended up going out to see a play.*
> *The film was much better than I thought it would be.*

A **Look at these sentences from the three conversations in *Listening*. Work in pairs. Discuss what you think the original plan, promise, or prediction was.**

1 Brilliant – it was much better than I thought it would be.
   The original prediction was probably 'I don't think it will be very good'
2 Hans had promised me he'd pick me up at 7.
3 We decided we weren't going to get in.
4 I thought you said you were going to stay in.
5 I said I'd go with her.

B **Complete the sentences with one word in each gap.**

1 A: Did you go and see *The Bridge* last night?
   B: No, I was going ...., but I had an essay to hand in and it took longer than I thought it ...., so by the time I'd finished, it .... too late.
2 A: What did you do at the weekend?
   B: Nothing much. We .... going to go to the beach, but the weather was so awful, we just stayed at home.
   A: I know. It was terrible – and on the forecast they said it .... be sunny!
3 A: Is Keira coming?
   B: She wasn't sure. She said she .... meet us at the cinema if she finished work on time. Oh, and she promised she .... ask James to come as well.

C **Make sentences using the ideas in 1–6 and linking them with *but* and *so*.**

1 I / go out / feel exhausted / just stay in and go to bed early
   I was going to go out but I felt exhausted so I just stayed in and went to bed early.
2 They / have a barbecue / start pouring with rain / have to cook indoors instead
3 We / go to the beach for the day / miss the train / end up going to the park instead
4 She / give me a lift / car not start / get a taxi instead
5 I / drive here / start pouring with rain / have to drive
6 I / stay in and study / a friend call me / go out / meet him

▶ **Need help? Read the grammar reference on p. 149**

SPEAKING

A **Check you understand the words in bold.**

1 Have you ever been **pleasantly surprised by** something? Why?
2 Have you ever been very **disappointed by** something? Why?
3 Can you think of a time you had **a last-minute change** of plan? What happened? Did it **turn out well / badly**?
4 Can you think of any predictions that have **failed to come true**?
5 Have you ever **failed to keep a promise**? What happened?
6 Have your parents ever **promised to** do something and then not done it? How did you feel about it?
7 Has the government / local council in your country **broken** any of its **promises**? What did they say they would do?

B **Work in groups. Discuss the questions and explain your answers using future forms in the past.**

In this unit you learn how to:
· talk about different animals
· help people to tell stories
· ask and answer questions about pets
· stress adverbs to show emphasis

Grammar
· *-ing* clauses
· Passives

Vocabulary
· Animals
· Keeping pets
· Forming words

Reading
· Animals and the environment

Listening
· Unusual animal experiences
· Pets

VOCABULARY Animals

A Work in pairs. Look at the pictures in File 10 on p. 159 and discuss these questions:
· Which of these animals do you like? Why?
· Are you scared of any of these animals? Why?

B Close your books. How many of the animals can you remember?

C Which animals might you:
· see lying on a rock?
· see circling in the sky?
· see running across a road?
· see swimming and jumping around off the coast?
· see disappearing into long grass?
· hear making a dreadful noise?
· hear in the bushes?
· hear in the distance?
· find crawling around a dirty kitchen?
· find hiding in your shoe?
· find sitting in a tree?

LISTENING

You are going to hear three conversations about animals that people have seen.

A 🔊 11.1 Listen. Answer the questions.
1 Which animals did each person see?
2 What were they were doing?
3 How did each speaker feel?

B Listen again and decide in which conversation someone:
a nearly killed one of the animals.
b saved an animal's life.
c was too frightened to shout for help at one point.
d sounded quite adventurous.
e confused one of the animals for something else.
f was distracted from some work.
g had a lucky escape.
h kept the animal and looked after it.
i saw an animal eating.

SPEAKING

A Work in pairs. Discuss these questions.
· Have you heard any stories about animals escaping from anywhere?
· Would you ever save or kill an animal? In what situation?
· Do you like the idea of going trekking through the jungle? Why? / Why not?

DEVELOPING CONVERSATIONS
Helping to tell stories

> **Good listeners ask questions when people tell stories.**
>
> A: I really thought they were going to eat me.
> B: God! That sounds terrifying! *So what happened?*
> A: Well, luckily, the guides managed to stop the lizards.

A Complete the conversations below by adding the questions in the box.

What was that doing there?	Seriously?
What was that?	What?
So what happened in the end?	

1 A: You'll never guess what happened last night.
   B: Go on. ....
   A: Well, I was walking home from the bus stop when I suddenly saw a horse standing there in the street.

2 C: I saw something really strange while we were away.
   D: Oh yeah? ....
   C: We saw this whale stuck on the beach.
   D: ....? Still alive?
   C: Yeah! It was actually quite upsetting! We phoned the police to see if they could organise help.

3 E: I was just about to put my shoes on when I found a scorpion hiding in one of the shoes!
   F: Really? God! ....
   E: I don't know. I guess it was just looking for somewhere to sleep.

4 G: We spent hours trying to persuade the cat to come down from the tree, but it refused to come.
   H: Oh no. That's awful! ....
   G: Well, eventually, we gave up, but an hour later it walked into the kitchen, looking for its dinner!

B 🔊 **11.2 Listen and check your answers.**

GRAMMAR *-ing* clauses

> We can add clauses that begin with a verb in the ***-ing*** form to a sentence. It explains what someone / something is, or was, doing at a particular time.
>
> *I suddenly noticed a group of crows looking quite excited.*
> (= I suddenly noticed a group of crows. ~~They were~~ looking quite excited).
>
> *I suddenly saw this huge snake lying across the road.*
> (= I suddenly saw this huge snake. ~~It was~~ lying across the road.)

A Turn the pairs of sentences into single sentences by crossing out the words that are not needed.

1 I saw a fox in the street. It was eating an old kebab.
2 I could hear a large animal of some kind. It was moving around in the bushes.
3 As we were walking along, I saw an eagle. It was circling right above us.
4 I couldn't sleep because of my grandmother's parrot. It was making a dreadful noise all night.
5 When we were camping, I saw a huge lizard. It was lying on a rock in the sun.
6 The bear was lying beneath a tree. It was sleeping.
7 I once saw a wolf. It was disappearing into a forest.
8 I went into the bathroom and there was a snake in the corner. It was hissing at me.

B Work in pairs. Complete these sentences by adding *-ing* clauses.

1 This deer was standing about three metres away from us ....
2 When we were on the ferry to Greece, we saw some dolphins ....
3 Outside my window this morning, there was this squirrel ....
4 I didn't sleep very well last night. I could hear a dog somewhere ....

▶ Need help? Read the grammar reference on p. 150

CONVERSATION PRACTICE

A Think of any strange or unusual animals you have seen – or any animals you have seen doing something strange. Think about where they were and what they were doing when you saw them. Think about how you felt and what happened. Then work in groups. Tell some other students about your experiences. When one person finishes their story, another should try to tell a similar story. Use these expressions to connect the stories:
It reminds me of something I once saw …
It actually reminds me of something that happened to me …

READING

You are going to read four newspaper articles about animals and the environment.

A Look at the headlines below. Work in pairs. Discuss what you think each article might be about.

> **Illegal animal trade moves into cyberspace**

> **Back from the point of extinction**

> **Mass extinction predicted**

> Man arrested for smuggling animal skulls

B All of the words in the box appear in the four articles. Work in pairs. Discuss which words you think might appear in which article, and why.

bred	destroyed by global warming
skeleton	endangered species
tiger skins	hunting and trading
reintroduced	organised criminal gangs

C Read the four articles quickly and match them with the correct headline from exercise A. Then complete the gaps with the words from exercise B.

D Answer the questions about the four articles.
1. a In article A, what four threats to animals are mentioned?
   b Which sounds like the most serious?
2. a In article B, what do you think was the purpose of the IFAW investigation?
   b Why do you think organised gangs use the Internet?
3. a In article C, what did the man claim his smuggled goods were for?
   b What do you think the police thought he was doing?
4. a In article D, why do you think Mongolia is called 'the land of the horse'?
   b What saved the *takhi* from extinction?

LANGUAGE PATTERNS

Write the sentences in your language. Translate them back into English. Compare your English to the original.
Mongolia is known as 'the land of the horse'.
Shanghai is known as 'the Paris of the East'.
Aubergines are also known as eggplants.
The area is known for its oysters.
This rare species of shark is known to inhabit fresh water.
Very few details are known about this rare species.

A ....

Scientists have warned that up to 50% of all animal species could be 1....................... if action is not taken soon. Over the past five hundred years, 820 species have become extinct, whilst more than 16,000 plant and animals species are currently threatened with extinction, including the polar bear, the hippopotamus, sharks, tigers and rhinos. Anywhere between twenty and two hundred species are already dying out every week because of the destruction of habitats and because the 2....................... of rare species continues. However, if temperatures continue to rise, there could well be a massive increase in these figures. Indeed, some are predicting that 23% of all mammals could become extinct within the next fifty years!

B ....

Some of the world's most 3....................... are being bought and sold over the Internet, according to a new report. An investigation by the IFAW– the International Fund for Animal Welfare – found over nine thousand live animals for sale in one week on online trading sites. These included a live gorilla for sale in London as well as a rare Siberian tiger and four baby chimpanzees on US websites. All of the items were being offered for sale illegally. On top of this, animal body parts were also found online, with many websites offering illegal items. The IFAW are worried that 4....................... are using the Internet as a relatively safe way of selling illegal goods on to rich collectors. Since the report was released, several auction sites have promised to do more to stop the trade in live animals.

C

A man from the west of England has been arrested at Gatwick Airport for bringing bones from a range of protected animals into the country in his luggage. The man's shop was then searched and various other illegal items were found. These included the ⁵......................... of a dolphin, the skull of an ape, ⁶........................., and a bottle of wine with a dead snake in it. After he had been questioned by the officers, the man claimed that he had bought the illegal objects as a hobby.

D

Mongolia is known as 'the land of the horse', yet it is only very recently that the world's only truly wild horse, the *takhi*, has been ⁷.......................... into the country. Horses have played an important role in the country's history, and even today most Mongolian children learn to ride at the age of four or five. Indeed, the obsession with horses and horse riding is so great that the annual race for young riders is shown on national TV. Last seen in the wild in the 1960s, the *takhi* very nearly became extinct. However, *takhi* kept in zoos have been ⁸......................... and their numbers have increased. These are now being released back into the wild, where scientists hope they will soon adapt to their new way of life.

GRAMMAR Passives

> We use passives when it is not clear who does an action (or it is unimportant). Passives are formed using the correct form of the verb *to be* + the past participle.

Scientists have warned that up to 50% of all animal species *could be destroyed* by global warming if action *is not taken* soon.

A Complete these sentences from the articles in *Reading* by putting the verbs into a passive form.

1 More than 16,000 plant and animal species .... (currently threaten) with extinction.
2 All of the items .... for sale illegally. (offer)
3 A man from the west of England .... at Gatwick Airport. (arrest)
4 The man's shop .... then .... and various other illegal items .... (search, find)
5 The annual race for young riders .... on national TV. (show)

B Which past participle in the box goes with each of the groups of words (1–6)?

arrested	searched	smuggled
kept	released	taken

1 I was ... at the airport / His house was ... after the arrest / I was stopped and ... on my way to work
2 He was ... out of the country / The guns were ... across the border / Drugs are being ... into prisons
3 These photos were ... in Spain / Action really must be ... soon / He was ... to hospital late last night
4 The lions have been ... back into the wild / He is due to be ... from prison / The report was ... last week
5 She was ... for speeding / He has been ... for murder / No one has been ... yet
6 The dog's ... outside / The animals were being ... in awful conditions / The boss makes sure we're ... busy

▶ Need help? Read the grammar reference on p. 150

SPEAKING

A Work in groups. Discuss these questions:
- Are there any endangered species in your country? Is anything being done about it?
- Has global warming affected your country? How?
- Have you ever heard any other stories about animals being smuggled, traded, or cruelly treated (think about hunting, over fishing, fur, exotic pets and animal fighting for 'sport')?
- What else are organised criminal gangs involved in?
- Have you heard of anyone being arrested recently?
- Do you know any environmental groups? What do they do? Would you consider joining them?

VOCABULARY Keeping pets

A **Complete 1–10 with the words in the box.**

lick	tank
stroke	kittens
mess	size
the litter tray	dry food
aggressive	looking after

1 I keep it *outside / in a cage / in a* ....
2 They're quite *demanding / poisonous /* .... */ playful / smelly.*
3 She had six *babies /* .... */ puppies / eggs.*
4 You can't *hold /* .... */ play with* them.
5 They need *a lot of* .... */ exercise / food / attention.*
6 You can feed them *tinned food / leftovers /* .... */ mice.*
7 You have to clean *them /* .... */ the cage* regularly.
8 They grow *big / to about a metre / to an enormous* ....
9 They often *scratch / jump on /* .... you.
10 They can make an awful *noise /* ....

B **Work in pairs.**
Student A: compare and contrast photos 1 and 2 and say which animal you think makes the best pet.
Student B: do the same with photos 3 and 4. Use as much of the language from exercise A as you can.

1 dog

2 cat

LISTENING

You are going to hear two friends, Suzie and Al, talking about pets.

A 🔊 **11.3 Listen. Decide if these sentences about the conversation are true or false.**
1 Al is going to keep the puppies.
2 Suzie prefers cats to dogs.
3 Suzie's previous pet died.
4 The snake is not dangerous.
5 The snake eats tinned food.
6 Al wants to have his picture taken with the snake.
7 The snake once escaped into the kitchen.

B **Work in pairs. Discuss these questions. Listen again if you need to.**
1 What reasons do they give for not having these pets?
 - dogs   - cats   - snakes
2 Do you agree with the reasons they give?
3 What happened when the snake escaped?
4 Do you know anyone whose pet escaped / was lost?

NATIVE SPEAKER ENGLISH

We often describe ourselves in terms of things we like – or do not like – by saying we are *a dog / morning / film person*.
I'm actually more of a cat person.
I'm not really a people person. I don't like to socialise much.
I'm a night person. I often don't go to bed till three or later.
He's not a music person. He'd much rather sit and watch TV.

3 snake

4 ferret

PRONUNCIATION
Stress and intonation for emphasis

> In *Listening*, Suzie says *They're so cute*. We often put an extra stress on adverbs like *so* to emphasise how we feel. Notice how the vowel sound is also lengthened.

A 🔊 **11.4 Listen and repeat the sentences.**
1 Oh, they're <u>so</u> cute!
2 He's <u>so</u> lovely.
3 He's <u>so</u> annoying!
4 Their dog is just <u>real</u>ly out of control!
5 It <u>real</u>ly stinks!
6 It's just in<u>cred</u>ibly noisy!
7 He <u>e</u>ven lets the cat walk on the kitchen surfaces!
8 He <u>e</u>ven lets the dog <u>ac</u>tually lick his face!

B 🔊 **11.5 Work in pairs. Underline the adverbs below that you think carry an extra stress. Then listen and see if you were right.**

I don't really like dogs, but I really hate some dog owners. They can be so annoying – the way they talk about their pets like they were actually human beings! They say things like, "Oh, my little baby. You're so beautiful! Yes, you are. Yes, you are." It's so stupid. What really annoys me, though, is the way they let their dogs run out of control. They even let their dogs jump on top of you. Then, if the dog bites you, they actually blame you. They say you scared the dog!

C Work in small groups. Take turns reading the text in exercise B. Who does it the best?

D Think about things you really like or find really annoying about animals, pet owners or other aspects of modern life. Use some of the sentence starters below.
I really love …
They're so cute, the way they … / when they …
It's so annoying how …
What really annoys me is the way that / the fact that …

E Work in pairs. Tell your partner your ideas. Use extra stress to emphasise how you feel. Does your partner agree with you?

VOCABULARY Forming words

In *Listening*, Suzie said she liked cats' independence. The noun *independence* comes from the adjective *independent*.

A Complete 1–6 with noun forms of the underlined words.
1 The animals were set <u>free</u> after being bred in the zoo.
   Kids don't have as much .... as they had in the past.
2 Thousand of hectares of forest are <u>destroyed</u> every hour.
   The bears are struggling to survive because of the .... of their habitats.
3 Mount Elgon, like Kilimanjaro, is an <u>extinct</u> volcano.
   Many of the animal species in this country are in danger of ....
4 I <u>warned</u> them not to touch the plants, but they still did.
   Farmers ignored repeated .... that they were damaging the environment.
5 The gang <u>threatened</u> to kill anyone who got in their way.
   The construction of the road is a serious .... to wildlife.
6 Scientists are <u>investigating</u> the cause of the disease which is killing the trees.
   The crime is currently under ....

B Underline any collocations which go with the nouns in exercise A. Can you think of any other collocations?

SPEAKING

A Put the words in the correct order to make questions about pets.
1 poisonous is it?
2 it breed what is?
3 it do where keep you?
4 I him stroke can?
5 it if is pick I up him OK?
6 it long you have had how?
7 you do it what feed?
8 long how for they do live?

B Work in pairs. Describe a pet that you or someone you know has. Show a picture if you have one. Then talk about your pet, answering the questions from exercise A.

12 PEOPLE I KNOW

In this unit you learn how to
- describe character
- talk about your family
- ask about friends and family
- use synonyms

Grammar
- *used to* and *would*
- Expressing regrets (*wish*)

Vocabulary
- Describing character
- Synonyms

Reading
- Give me my space!

Listening
- Do you get on?
- How do you know Nicolas?

SPEAKING

A **Work in groups. Find out who has the biggest family. Ask about:**
- brothers and sisters
- nieces and nephews
- aunts and uncles
- great-grandparents
- grandparents
- cousins

Does anyone have a half-brother / half-sister or a stepbrother / stepsister?

VOCABULARY Describing character

A **Complete the sentences with the adjectives in the boxes.**

shy	outgoing	competitive
naughty	bright	easy-going

chatty	spoilt	generous
intense	lazy	stubborn

1 He's very clever – just really ....
2 She's really friendly – really .... She's really good at making new friends.
3 She's quite quiet – quite ....
4 They're very relaxed – just very ....
5 He's very sporty, and very .... He always wants to win!
6 He's very sweet and affectionate, but he can be quite .... sometimes.

7 He's quite serious – quite ....
8 He's a bit of a dropout – just very ....
9 She's very determined. In fact, she can be very ....
10 They're strict, but they can also be very kind and ....
11 He's very indulgent with his daughter. He gives her whatever she asks for, so she's very ....
12 He can seem quite quiet when you first meet him, but he's actually quite .... and funny once you get to know him.

B **Work in pairs. Discuss these questions:**
- Which adjectives could you use to describe the people in the pictures on these pages? Use these verbs:
  He looks ...   *They look like they could be ...*
- Which adjectives would you use to describe yourself?

LANGUAGE PATTERNS

Write the sentences in your language. Translate them back into English. Compare your English to the original.
He's very sweet and affectionate, but he can be quite naughty sometimes.
She's nice, but she can be really rude sometimes.
You can be such an idiot sometimes!
You can be so stubborn sometimes!
He can be very nice when he wants to be.
She can be very generous when she wants to be.

DEVELOPING CONVERSATIONS

That's like ...

When we talk about the character of someone we know, we often compare the person to someone with a similar character. To introduce these comments, we often use *That's like ...*

A Match sentences 1–5 with the comments a–e.
1 He never does anything around the house.
2 When he sees me, he always runs up and gives me a big hug. It's so sweet.
3 He's so serious. He's always talking about politics. You can never just have a good laugh with him.
4 He lets her do whatever she wants – really spoils her.
5 She really hates losing at whatever sport she does.

a That's like my cousin. He's really competitive as well. He always plays to win. He can never just play for fun.
b That's like my brother-in-law. He's very intense.
c Ah! That's like my niece. She's really affectionate too.
d That's like a friend of mine. He's very indulgent too and his kid's a nightmare – just really naughty.
e That's like my sister. She's really lazy too.

B Work in pairs.
Student A: read out 1–5.
Student B: say a–e, but change the people so the sentences are true for you.

LISTENING

You are going to hear a man called Lewis talking to a woman called Jessica about her family.

A 🔊 12.1 Listen and answer the questions.
1 Why does Lewis start asking about Jessica's brother, Noel?
2 In what way is Lewis's mum similar to Noel?
3 What is Noel like?
4 What is Jessica's younger brother like?
5 How has her relationship with him changed?

B Choose the words that you heard. Then listen again to check your answers.
1 Where did you *dissolve / disappear* to?
2 Maybe I am *excited / exaggerating* a bit.
3 Do you and your brother get *in / on* well?
4 He *awarded / won* a scholarship to study Physics.
5 We used to be quite *closed / close*.
6 He's always going on *manifestations / demonstrations* and complaining about me using the car too much.
7 Maybe it's just a *phase / phrase* he's going through.
8 He might grow *out of / up* it.

C Work in pairs. Discuss these questions:
• As a child, which is worst: being the oldest, the youngest or in the middle?
• Do you know anyone who has won a scholarship?
• Do you know anyone who went through a phase of being or doing something different?

CONVERSATION PRACTICE

A Have conversations about your family. Start by saying things like:
I'm going to my cousin's on Saturday.
Sorry, that was my sister (on the phone).

Continue the conversations by asking questions such as:
What's she like? Do you get on well?
Are you close? Do you see her / him a lot?
What does he / she do?
Where do they live? Is it near here?
Have you got any other brothers and sisters, etc.?

Make comparisons with friends and family when you can.
That sounds like my dad. He's always ...

GRAMMAR *Used to and would*

A 🔊 **12.2 Complete the sentences from *Listening* on p. 83. Then listen and check.**

We .... (be) quite close. We .... (be) both quite sporty – we .... (go) to the beach a lot, we .... (play) tennis together and that kind of thing – but he's not interested now.

> ***Used to** or the past simple can be used to describe someone's character in the past, especially when there has been a change since then. **Used to** and **would** and the past simple can all describe regular activities / habits in the past. We tend to start with **used to** and then use **would** or the past simple to give details.*

B **Complete the sentences with ONE word in each space.**

1   My brother used to [1] .... really naughty when he [2] .... younger. He [3] .... write all over the walls and he [4] .... never do what my parents told him. He sometimes [5] .... into fights at school too.

2   We used [1] .... go camping a lot when I [2] .... a kid. We usually [3] .... by the beach. We'd [4] .... swimming every day and do lots of sunbathing. One year, we [5] .... to Slovakia and [6] .... a week there, which was great.

3   I [1] .... to go to the gym all the time. I'd [2] .... every day after work and I [3] .... usually spend two or three hours a day there. Eventually, though, I just [4] .... fed up with it.

C **Make sentences like those in exercises A and B using *used to, would* and the past simple. For example:**

be close – my brother – play together – go fishing a lot
I used to be close to my brother. We'd play / we played together and we'd go / we went fishing together a lot.

1   my gran – very religious – go to church – Sunday – always make us say a prayer before dinner

2   my grandfather – be very indulgent – always buy us sweets – let us watch TV all day

3   when – I – a kid, we – go to mountains every summer – go walking – dive and swim in the river – be fantastic

4   I – play basketball a lot – train twice a week – have a match every Sunday – we – win the league once

5   we – sit together at school – always talk to each other – pass notes – teacher – tell us off

D **Work in pairs. Tell your partner about two of the things below. Use *used to* and *would* to explain character and habits.**

•   someone you know whose character has changed
•   your memories of a grandparent
•   your memories of summer holidays with family
•   the lunch break when you were at primary school
•   a free-time activity you no longer do

▶ **Need help? Read the grammar reference on p. 151**

LISTENING

You are going to hear five people talking about how they became friends with a Belgian man called Nicolas.

A Before you listen, work in groups. Talk about how you got to know your closest friend, girlfriend / boyfriend or partner.

B 🔊 12.3 Now listen and write the number of the speaker against the correct statement a–f. There is one statement you do not need to use.

a   They met while travelling round a country.   ....
b   He / She shared a bad experience with Nicolas.   ....
c   They didn't like each other to begin with.   ....
d   He / She fell out with a friend of Nicolas's.   ....
e   She's an ex-girlfriend of Nicolas's.   ....
f   She's going out with Nicolas.   ....

C Work in pairs. Discuss these questions. Listen again if you need to.
 • What do you learn about Nicolas's life?
 • What is Nicolas like?

VOCABULARY Synonyms

A Look at these sentences from *Listening*. What meaning do the words in *italics* share?
a   It's difficult *maintaining* a long-distance relationship.
b   We've *remained* friends.
c   We *kept* in touch via e-mail.
d   I sometimes wish we'd *stayed* together.

B Decide which word in *italics* from exercise A completes each set of collocations 1–4 below. Then discuss these questions as a class.
 • Which two words share the most collocations?
 • Which word does not share any collocations with the other words?

1   ~ calm, ~ in touch, try and ~ fit, ~ warm ~ friends, ~ in bed all morning, ~ quiet
2   ~ calm, ~ in touch, try and ~ fit, ~ warm, ~ it warm, ~ it cold, ~ trying, ~ getting into trouble, ~ forgetting
3   ~ calm, ~ in control, ~ a serious problem, the economy ~s strong, ~ a big challenge, ~ in power
4   ~ a conversation, ~ a friendship, ~ contact with, ~ good relations

> Although synonyms share meanings and can share collocations, they are often not interchangeable. They will have different collocations or use a different grammar. If you want to understand the differences, you need to notice these contexts.

C Work in pairs. Discuss these questions:
 • Do you find it easy to stay calm under pressure?
 • Do you know anyone who keeps getting into trouble?
 • Can you think of anything that remains a serious problem / big challenge in your country?
 • Do you find it difficult to maintain a conversation in English?

GRAMMAR
Expressing regrets (*wish*)

A Look at the sentences from *Listening* and answer the questions.
I sometimes wish *we'd stayed* together.
I wish we *hadn't split up*.
We'd talk about the things we wished *we'd said* to him.

1   What tense follows *wish* here?
2   Is it referring to past or present situations?
3   Did the actions that follow *wish* happen or not?
4   How could you rewrite the following sentences from *Listening* using *wish*?
 • It's a shame it took so long to get together.
   I wish it ... .
 • I didn't want to be first to apologise. I regret that really.
   I wish I ... .

▶ Need help? Read the grammar reference on p. 151

B Decide why someone might say each sentence 1–10 and what actually happened.
1   I wish I'd known.
2   I wish I'd met him.
3   I wish I'd never asked.
4   I wish they'd told me earlier.
5   I wish I'd tried harder at school.
6   I really wish we hadn't moved house.
7   Honestly, I wish I hadn't said anything.
8   I wish I hadn't gone to the meeting.
9   I sometimes wish they'd given me a different name.
10 I think he sometimes wishes he'd studied something else.

C 🔊 12.4 Listen and repeat the sentences. Notice how we often do not pronounce the *'d* in *I'd* – or the *t* in *hadn't*.

D Write three sentences about things you wish you *had / had not done*. Work in pairs. Say as much as you can about your regrets.

READING

A Read the article about the Internet and maintaining friendships. Choose the correct answer to these questions. Underline the part of the article that tells you the answer.

1 Which sentence best describes how the writer feels about the Internet?
   a He can't stand it.
   b He's got serious reservations about it.
   c He's got mixed feelings about it.

2 How does the writer feel when he gets invited to join social networking sites?
   a It drives him mad.
   b He's pleased to be asked to join.
   c He feels quite guilty.

3 How does the writer explain the fact that some people have so many online friends?
   a They must be really popular.
   b It helps them feel more important.
   c Communicating online is better than talking face-to-face.

4 What worry about social networking sites does he have?
   a There could be unexpected consequences to publishing information online.
   b Terrible pictures of parents could be posted online.
   c People can already read private information about him online.

5 He doesn't want to see old school friends again because …
   a it's too much effort to find out where they are now.
   b he feels they wouldn't have much to talk about.
   c they might be different now to when they last met.

6 The writer thinks he might shock some people because …
   a he doesn't know how to use Instant Messenger.
   b he doesn't use the Web to organise his social life.
   c he's so talkative.

B Mark the text with a ✓ where you agree with what is said, a ✗ where you disagree, and a **?** where you do not understand something. Discuss your ideas in pairs.

C Complete the definitions with these words from the text.

come across	struggle with	paranoid
drift apart	distant friend	track down
endlessly	ego trip	

1 If something continues for a long time in an unpleasant way, it happens ....
2 A .... is one you don't see very often anymore and aren't close to.
3 If you believe people want to hurt you, even though you don't have any proof of this, you're ....
4 If you find something by accident, you .... it.
5 If two friends slowly stop being close, they ....
6 If you manage to .... a person, you find them after a long search in lots of different places.
7 If you do something just to make yourself feel important – and to show others how important you are – it's an ....
8 If you find something very difficult and have to make a big effort to do it, you .... it.

GIVE ME

First things first

To begin, let me just say that I DON'T hate the Internet. Honestly, I really don't! It's important to make this clear from the start, because I don't want you to get the wrong impression. I use the Internet every day – at work and in my free time. I have plenty of favourite websites and I also write lots of emails. Generally speaking, I see the Internet as a good thing.

However, there are also lots of things about it that worry me – scare me even – and the biggest concern I have is the way it has affected how people maintain their friendships these days. You'll soon see what I mean.

Social networking sites

If one more person asks me if I'm on a particular social networking site, I'll scream! I'm **endlessly** getting invited to join and I have had a look at friends' profiles, but to be honest, the whole thing just depresses me. To begin with, there's too much information there. Why should I care which online group some **distant friend** has joined? Or who has become 'friends' with who? And what does 'friend' mean in cyberspace anyway? I know one guy who **struggles with** face-to-face conversations, yet who has over 500 'friends' online. I should add, though, that one of them is his mum! It's not right. If you ask me, people only want you to join these sites to make them look even more popular! It's just an **ego trip**.

Added to this is the fact that I believe in privacy. I don't want every aspect of my private life stuck on the Web for everyone to see. I've seen photos on some networking sites that would give those girls' parents heart attacks if they ever **came across** them! Also – and I know this makes me sound **paranoid** – I worry about what all the private information these sites collect could be used for in the future.

MY SPACE

Turning back the clock

Then, of course, there are all the sites that help you **track down** people you went to school with. Hasn't anyone realised that there's a reason why people lose touch? People **drift apart** because they don't have enough in common to make it worth staying in touch! I don't know about you, but personally I have no desire to relive my school days. There weren't great and I don't miss anyone from my old class. I don't see why I should get back in touch with someone I last saw twenty years ago, when I could go out and make new friends. At least they would be in the same city as me, rather than still living in the town where I grew up!

Keeping it simple

Now, you might think I'm a little bit old-fashioned, but I actually already have the mobile numbers and email addresses of my closest friends. I don't need to go through a third-party site to contact them all or to arrange when to go out. I know this might shock you, but I actually like talking to my friends – and yes, really TALKING, not 'chatting' or 'Instant Messaging'! I like the sound of other humans – and I'd rather meet people in the real world than in cyberspace any day!

SPEAKING

A **Put the sentences in the correct order to make a short story about a friendship. The first one is done for you.**

a Eventually, we lost touch completely.   ......

b when he suddenly got back in touch again after   ......

c After we left school, ...

d tracking me down via the Internet.   ......

e but we slowly drifted apart.   ......

f I hadn't heard from him for ages, ...

g We used to be really close when we were at school.   *1*

h We'd play together all the time and we'd go round to each other's houses.   ......

i we stayed in touch for a while, ...

j Since then, we've seen each other quite regularly.   ......

B **Work in pairs. Discuss these questions:**

- Do you have the same best friend as you did ten years ago? Why? / Why not?
- Do you stay in touch with friends from primary or secondary school / university?
- Have you ever been close to someone, but then drifted apart? Do you regret it?
- Is there anyone you would like to get back in touch with?
- Have you ever tracked anyone down via the Internet?
- Do you have any online friends? Have you met them face-to-face? How was it?

"I don't want to be alone when I'm old, either, so when we're old let's get back in touch."

LEARNER TRAINING

Work in groups of three. Read the statements. Then discuss these questions:
- Which statements do you agree with? Why?
- Are you happy with your accent in English? Why? / Why not?
- Which aspects of your pronunciation do you want to work on?

When you look up words in the dictionary, write the pronunciation in phonetic script.

I want to keep my accent so people can hear where I am from.

It is important to practise saying individual sounds.

I prefer American accents to British accents.

It is best to practise saying words together.

GAME

Work in pairs. Student A use *only* the green squares; student B use *only* the yellow squares. Spend 5 minutes looking at your questions and revising the answers. Then take turns tossing a coin: Heads = move one of your squares; Tails = move two of your squares. When you land on a square, your partner looks at the relevant page in the book to check your answers, but *you don't*! If you are right, move forward one space (but don't answer the question until your next turn). If you aren't right, your partner tells you the right answer, and you miss a go. When you've finished the game, change colours and play again.

Start

1
Developing Conversations p. 65: compare the room you're in to two different rooms you know using the patterns.

2
Vocabulary p. 66: say four things that have changed in your country using the patterns in the box.

3
Vocabulary p. 68: say eight adjectives for describing areas.

4
Developing Conversations p. 69: your partner will ask the six questions. Answer using three of the forms in **bold**.

5
Vocabulary p. 70: say ten words about films, plays and exhibitions.

6
Native English note, p. 71: if you can say what the *Native English* note was, throw again.

7
Developing Conversations p. 72: use five of the expressions to say why you don't want to do things.

8
Miss a go!

9
Pronunciation p. 74: your partner will ask five questions: *what was so go / bad about the film / etc.* Answer with the patterns.

10
Vocabulary p. 76 (file 10): say twelve of the animals.

11
Miss a go!

12
Grammar p. 79: your partner will read six verbs. Say one passive sentence for each one.

13
Native English note, p. 80: if you can say what the *Native English* note was, throw again.

14
Speaking p. 81: can you remember six questions about pets?

15
Vocabulary p. 82: say eight of the adjectives for describing character.

16
Grammar p. 84: talk about how you spent your free time using three different structures.

17
Grammar p. 85: say four regrets about the past using wish.

18
Native English note, p. 87: if you can say what the *Native English* note was, throw again.

Finish

For each of the activities below, work in groups of three. Use the Vocabulary Builder if you want to.

CONVERSATION PRACTICE

Choose one of these *Conversation Practice* activities:
Houses p. 65
Going out p. 71
The natural world p. 77
People I know p. 83

Two of you should do the task. The third person should listen and give a mark of between 1 and 10. Explain your decision. Then change roles.

ACT OR DRAW

One person should act or draw as many of these words as you can in three minutes. Your partners should try to guess the words. Do not speak while you are acting or drawing!

halfway down	graffiti	a cage
an open fire	dull	shy
an installation	a gig	a patio
crawl around	a squirrel	in tears
sweat like crazy	a cockroach	hiss
smelly	stroke	a nest
a demonstration	stay calm	aggressive

QUIZ

Answer as many of the questions as possible.
1 What is the opposite of a **cramped** flat?
2 Say three things that can **drop dramatically**.
3 What kind of things happen in a **rough** area?
4 Say three different kinds of **play**.
5 If a film is **terrific**, is it good?
6 Why might you feel **out of place**?
7 What is the opposite of **breaking** a promise?
8 What might you see **circling in the sky**?
9 Say three **endangered species**.
10 Why might the police **search** a building?
11 Say two things people **exaggerate** about.
12 What might kids do if they are **naughty**?
13 Say three things people **grow out of**.
14 Why might two friends **fall out**?
15 How could you **track** someone **down**?

COLLOCATIONS

Take turns to read out collocation lists from Unit 9 of the Vocabulary Builder. Where there is a '~', say '*blah*' instead. Your partner should guess as many words as they can. Each time you change roles, move on to the next unit.

PRONUNCIATION Diphthongs

A ◈ R 3.1 Listen and repeat the sounds and words

/ɪə/	/eə/	/ʊə/	/eɪ/
w<u>ei</u>rd	sp<u>a</u>re	r<u>u</u>ral	s<u>a</u>fe
....	....	....	....
/aɪ/	/ɔɪ/	/əʊ/	/aʊ/
t<u>i</u>ger	destr<u>oy</u>	cr<u>ow</u>	p<u>ow</u>er
....	....	....	....

B Add the words below to the appropriate box, according to the way the underlined sounds are pronounced.

loc<u>a</u>ted	wh<u>a</u>le	now<u>a</u>days	sp<u>oi</u>lt
sh<u>a</u>red	t<u>ou</u>rist	disapp<u>ea</u>r	h<u>i</u>de

Which sounds do you find hardest to pronounce?

SPEAKING

A Work in pairs. Look at the pictures below. Discuss what you think the two people in each picture are talking about.

B Role-play the two conversations. Decide which roles you are each going to take. Spend five minutes planning what you are going to say. Look back at Unit 9 p. 69 and Unit 12 p. 84 for ideas if you need to. Then have the conversations.

C When was the last time you had conversations like these? Who with? What did you talk about?

LISTENING

A 🔊 R 3.2 **Listen to four people talking and decide what each person is talking about. There is one extra topic below that you do not need.**
a ...... A night out at the theatre
b ...... A trip to the zoo
c ...... A family pet
d ...... A film they went to see
e ...... An adventure holiday

B **Listen again and decide which extract the sentences describe. There is one extra sentence that you do not need.**
a ...... It has caused a few problems.
b ...... It was better than the speaker was expecting.
c ...... It was a very rewarding experience.
d ...... There was a big argument.
e ...... It wasn't as good as the speaker was expecting.

[... / 8]

GRAMMAR
Comparing the past with now

Complete each sentence by adding the adjectives in the box in the correct form.

touristy	expensive	good	bad
big	polluted	dead	noisy

1 I watched *Star Wars* again the other day, for the first time in ages. It was great – just .... it was the last time I saw it.
2 The town is still fairly quiet in the evenings, but it's not .... it used to be. At least there's a bit of nightlife now.
3 The online market is growing at an incredibly fast rate. It's getting .... and .... every day.
4 Property in the city is much .... than it was a few years ago. Prices have gone up a lot.
5 Crime is much .... than it used to be. I don't feel safe on the streets anymore.
6 They've dealt with the problem really well, and so the rivers are much .... than they used to be, which is great.
7 In the 1970s, Lombok wasn't nearly .... it is now. I sometimes felt like I was the only foreigner on the island.
8 They built a road around the city last year and since then it's nowhere near .... as it used to be.

[... / 8]

▶ **Find this difficult? Look back at grammar reference p. 148.**

EXPRESSING REGRETS

Complete the second sentences so that they mean the same as the first ones.
1 My grandfather died before I was born, so I never had the chance to meet him.
  I wish .... my grandfather.
2 She got really upset when I told her how I felt.
  I wish I .... her how I felt.
3 It's my own fault I'm in this class. I didn't study that much at school.
  I sometimes wish .... harder when I was at school.
4 I really regret not asking her out for a drink.
  I wish .... her out for a drink.
5 It's a shame we didn't have time to visit you when we were in Milan.
  I wish we .... time to visit you when we were in Milan.

[... / 5]

▶ **Find this difficult? Look back at grammar reference p. 151.**

PREPOSITIONS

Choose the correct preposition.
1 The crime rate has fallen quite a lot *over / from* the past few years.
2 Banks are now offering more mortgages *on / at* lower rates.
3 They're building a new shopping mall *on / in* the outskirts of town.
4 It's the second turning *from / on* the left.
5 I just saw a deer running *across / through* the road.
6 We could hear wolves *in / at* the distance.
7 They live *in / on* the eighth floor, I think.
8 She was rushed *in / to* hospital late last night.
9 The group is a serious threat *for / to* the government.
10 What's your sister like? Is she similar *to / with* you?

[... / 10]

LANGUAGE PATTERNS

Correct the mistake in each of the sentences.
1 It still needs to discuss more at the next meeting.
2 The whole place is need a good clean.
3 It's one of the bad films I've ever seen in my life.
4 It's the nicest thing nobody's ever done for me.
5 Suzhou is sometimes known the Venice of the East.
6 She's nice, but she can quite intense sometimes.
7 You can be so idiot sometimes!

[... / 7]

PASSIVES

Correct the mistake in each of the sentences.

1 Police fear that drugs and guns are still been smuggled across the border.
2 I'm afraid my flight has delay, so don't wait for me. Go home and I'll get a taxi to the hotel.
3 I just worry that all sorts of private details could be post online.
4 The mosque build in the twelfth century.
5 I had a horrible feeling I was following, so I started to run.
6 Some of the most beautiful parts of the country are slowly being destroyed from global warming.

[... / 6]

▶ **Find this difficult? Look back at grammar reference p. 150.**

DEVELOPING CONVERSATIONS

Complete the dialogues with one word in each gap.

1 Their garden's huge. It's about twice the .... of mine!
2 Would it be .... to move the appointment to a later date?
3 Would you .... if I invited friends over?
4 You can come back late if you want to – as .... as you don't make too much noise.
5 Where are you? I'm waiting outside the college. I'm right in .... of the main entrance.
6 A: Do you fancy going rollerblading later?
   B: No, thanks. I'm not really in the .... for that kind of thing.
7 A: Are your grandparents still ....?
   B: Three of them are, yes, but one died last year.

[... / 7]

COLLOCATIONS

Match the verbs with the words they go with.

1	take out	a	my appetite
2	tighten	b	a phase
3	protect	c	in power
4	kill	d	trying
5	go through	e	my mind at rest
6	remain	f	a mortgage
7	keep	g	the law
8	put	h	the environment

[... / 8]

▶ **Find this difficult? Re-read units 9–12 in the Vocabulary Builder for more information on collocation.**

FORMING WORDS

Complete the sentences with the noun forms of the words in CAPITALS.

1 We needed more space, so we decided to build an .... EXTEND
2 It used to be quite run-down, but there's been a lot of .... in the area recently. INVEST
3 There's a .... of affordable housing. SHORT
4 Many species are currently threatened with .... EXTINCT
5 The real problem is that much of the animal's natural .... has been destroyed. INHABIT
6 The country gained .... in 1962. INDEPENDENT

[... / 6]

VOCABULARY

Complete the words in the three short texts. The first letter(s) are given.

Affordable property in central location. Walking ¹d........................... from main park and shopping district. Has three bedrooms, gas central heating and roof ²te........................... . Needs a bit of painting and ³de..........................., but is generally in good condition and has real ⁴po........................... for improvement.

Nasrul Roesli has been called one of the greatest artists of our time. His work ranges from landscapes and ⁵po........................... to video installations and ⁶sc........................... . His new ⁷ex........................... opened last week at The Yahong ⁸G........................... and is one of the best things I have seen in ages. I have never been a great fan, but was very ⁹pl........................... surprised both by the work on display and also by the ¹⁰ve........................... itself.

Let me tell you a bit about myself. I like to think of myself as a fairly easy-going, ¹¹r........................... kind of person. I'm quite sporty, but I don't see myself as being ¹²co........................... . I just play for fun. I like meeting new people, and my friends tell me I am quite ¹³ch........................... and easy to talk to. I work hard and am ¹⁴de........................... to do well in my job. However, I realise that sometimes I might come across as being fairly ¹⁵st........................... too because I like doing things my own way.

[... / 15]

 [Total ... /80]

13 TRAVEL

In this unit you learn how to:
- talk about journeys
- explain travel problems
- use phrasal verbs
- use strong adjectives
- talk about whose fault problems are

Grammar
- Third conditionals
- *should have*

Vocabulary
- Ways of travelling and travel problems
- Phrasal verbs
- Strong adjectives

Reading
- Journey to a new nation

Listening
- How was your journey?
- Travel experiences

SPEAKING

A Work in pairs. Discuss what you think the words in bold mean.
1. When was the last time you went on **a day trip**? Where did you go?
2. Does anyone you know ever go on **business trips**?
3. Have you ever been on **a shopping trip**, **a school trip** or **a hunting trip**? Where to? What was it like?
4. Do you usually **travel light**?
5. Do you know anyone who has **been travelling** for a few months? Where did they go?
6. What's the longest **journey** you've ever taken?

B Now answer the questions in groups.

VOCABULARY
Ways of travelling and travel problems

A Match the words in the box with a way of travelling. Put the words under the correct heading in the table.

security	line	crossing	take-off
carriage	deck	platform	traffic lights
bend	tyre	harbour	check-in desk

By train	By ferry	By car	By plane

B Work in pairs. Add two more words under each heading in the table.

C Complete the sentences below with nouns from exercise A.
1. I was waiting on the wrong .... and so I ended up missing my train!
2. The sea was really rough. It was pouring with rain and very windy, so we couldn't go out on ....
3. We got a flat .... on the motorway and had to stop and change it.
4. I hate flying. I get really anxious – especially during .... and landing.
5. Last time we came over it was quite rough, but this time we had a very smooth .... It was lovely.
6. There'd been a terrible storm and there were trees on the ...., so the train was delayed for ages.
7. I got stopped going through .... and they confiscated a little penknife that I'd forgotten to take out of my bag.
8. It was terrifying. The taxi driver overtook another car on quite a tight .... You couldn't see if anyone was coming in the opposite direction.

D Work in pairs. Look at the pictures. Discuss what is good and what is bad about each way of travelling. Which way do you prefer? Why?

VOCABULARY Phrasal verbs

A phrasal verb is a verb – *put, throw, take*, etc. – plus a particle like *up, off, out, down*, etc. Sometimes they are used instead of single word verbs. Phrasal verbs are more colloquial and informal than single word verbs.

A Look at the extracts from *Listening*. Can you remember the phrasal verbs that were used in place of the words in *italics*? Compare your ideas with the audioscript on p. 171–172.

1 Andre didn't want to spend too long *sitting, waiting and not doing much* at the airport.
2 I don't want to *experience something unpleasant like* that again, I can tell you!
3 Do you want to go to the office, or do you want to *sign and get your room* at the hotel first?
4 Well, to begin with, it was still dark when we *started our journey.*
5 And then it immediately started to *rain very heavily,* so the roads were really slippery.
6 I couldn't *find an answer to the problem of* where I was or where I was going!
7 When I finally *returned* onto the right road, I almost had an accident.
8 I did have to stop and park the car for a few minutes to *stop feeling so angry and upset.*

B Complete the sentences with the missing particle.

1 We set at 5 in the morning, so I'm exhausted.
2 We didn't have to queue because we checked online.
3 We had to hang at the station for an hour because my mum couldn't pick us up till 4.
4 I was exhausted. I left home at 6 in the morning and I didn't get till ten at night.
5 My child got into a panic and she wouldn't calm.
6 We went absolute hell to get here, I can tell you!
7 I was totally lost. I couldn't work where I was.
8 It started to pour halfway there. We were absolutely soaked by the time we arrived.

C Write your own sentences using the phrasal verbs.

LISTENING

You are going to hear two conversations about journeys.

A 🔊 13.1 Listen and answer the questions.
1 How did the people in each conversation travel?
2 What three problems did each have?

B Can you remember what nouns in the listening texts these adjectives were used to describe? Work in pairs to compare your ideas. Then listen again to check.

1 huge	bumpy	terrifying	
2 slippery	wrong	stupid	hurt

C Work in pairs. Discuss these questions:
- How long before your flight do you usually get to the airport? Why?
- Have you ever missed a flight? Why?
- Has anything strange or scary ever happened to you while flying / driving?
- Can you drive? What are your strong points and weak points as a driver?
- Do you agree with Lara's comments about male drivers?

CONVERSATION PRACTICE

A Work in pairs. You are going to have a conversation about a terrible journey Student A has had. Student B: begin by asking, 'So how was your journey?' Then change roles.

SPEAKING

A Check you understand the words in **bold**. Then work in pairs. Discuss these questions:
- Who would **stamp** your passport and why?
- Have you ever had to get a **visa** to visit another country?
- What **restrictions on immigration** might a country have?
- Is there much **bureaucracy** in your country?
- Why do people **emigrate**?
- Why might someone become a **refugee**?

READING

A Read part 1 of an article about immigration below and then answer the questions in pairs.
1 What does the author say has changed about immigration? Do you agree?
2 Why does he think building fences can be hypocritical and useless? Do you agree?
3 What reasons does he give for emigration? Can you think of any examples of these reasons?

B Before you read part 2 of the article, look at the pictures on page 95 and discuss in pairs.
1 where you think the people were from.
2 why you think they were escaping.
3 what dangers you think they faced.
4 what happened to them in the end.

C Now read and find out the answers to 1–4 in exercise B for Mai Ho.

D All the words in *italics* in 1–7 were used in the article. Can you remember how they were used?
1 I *invested* all my savings to set up the business.
2 The teacher *confiscated* my mobile phone.
3 The teacher *bribed* the kids with sweets to calm them down.
4 A lot of women still face sexual *discrimination*.
5 I've *set up* my own website.
6 She was *elected* president last year.
7 He got the job *thanks* to the school he went to.

E Who are the most famous immigrants into / emigrants from your country? What difference have they made?

1

JOURNEY TO A NEW NATION
Martin O'Neill celebrates international migrants day and his own special anniversary.

Forty years ago, I arrived in New Zealand. I handed the immigration official my passport.

"Are you here on holiday or here to live?" he asked.

"To live," I replied, expecting a long interrogation.

"Good on you, mate!" he said and stamped my passport.

Things aren't so easy these days. Many countries are increasing bureaucracy or building physical walls to keep immigrants out. These measures are often both hypocritical and useless: not so long ago a Californian company was fined for employing illegal immigrants. And what does the company do? Well, among other things, it has had a contract to build a fence to stop immigrants entering the United States! The needs of rich countries and the poverty of others will always mean that people will try to find a better life abroad.

Of course, it's not just lack of money which drives people to emigrate and nor is emigration anything new. People have always moved countries – maybe out of curiosity or for love, or weather or land. Stories of people escaping war, persecution or famine feature in the Bible and in the Koran. The sadness is that these last reasons still exist today. However, these stories can also be incredibly uplifting. Take the story of Mai Ho.

GRAMMAR Third conditionals

A Complete the explanation with one word in each space.

> At the end of the article in *Reading*, Martin O'Neill, the author, says:
>
> If she hadn't .... so determined, she would .... have made it to Australia.
>
> I would probably .... ended up in trouble if I .... stayed there.
> ....
>
> These are examples of a third conditional. The *if* part of the sentences uses the .... perfect to talk about imagined situations in the past. The second part of the sentence uses .... / *might* + *have* + the past .... to talk about the results of the imagined situation.

B Match 1–6 with a–f.

1 Our country would have been in a worse situation
2 If it hadn't been for the war,
3 They wouldn't have crashed
4 If I hadn't had that teacher,
5 If we'd left a bit earlier,
6 The team might have won

a I probably would never have gone to university.
b if they had been driving more slowly.
c if all the players had been fit.
d if we hadn't had immigration.
e we would've stayed in our country.
f we might not have missed the beginning of the film.

C Write an alternative ending to the second half of each sentence in exercise B.

▶ Need help? Read the grammar reference on p. 152

Born in Saigon, Mai Ho grew up during the Vietnam War. When the war ended in 1975, her life and business were made impossible because her father had been an anti-communist journalist and she'd married into a rich family. In 1978, the two families invested nearly all their savings to buy a boat to escape, but a few months later it was confiscated by the government. Over the next three years, Mai Ho had to befriend and bribe government officials in order to get the boat back and then get a trading permit so that the boat could travel out of Vietnam.

In 1981, Mai Ho finally set off with 160 friends, family and neighbours. They had to hide in the tiny space below deck. They avoided the government ships to reach international

waters, but then got caught in a storm. Mai Ho still remembers her fear and how everyone was seasick. They survived and, despite being threatened by pirates, continued for another three days before finally coming across a friendly ship. The ship's captain agreed to take the refugees to the safety of Malaysia, but Mai Ho had to agree to sink her boat. It was her last possession: she didn't even have clothes.

After three months in a refugee camp, where they again suffered cramped conditions and lack of food, she was finally given a visa to go to Australia.

Arriving in a new country brings great hope and another journey: the one to rebuild your life. Unfortunately, for some refugees that journey includes suffering racial discrimination: When

Mai Ho studied business, she felt hurt when her fellow students ignored her or refused to work in pairs with her. But she is obviously very strong – if she hadn't been so determined, she would never have made it to Australia. She completed her courses and then set up two successful businesses. In 1993, she was even elected the mayor of her town! Mai Ho loves Australia and it seems many Australians appreciate her too.

Indeed, what would the world be like without immigration? Personally speaking, I had no hope of work in Northern Ireland when I left. I didn't really get on with my parents, and I would probably have ended up in trouble if I'd stayed there. My life changed for the better when I became a New Zealander. But it's not just individuals that mature and grow thanks to immigration – nations do too.

VOCABULARY Strong adjectives

> A small group of adjectives contain the idea of *very*. For example, *terrified* means *very scared*. To make them stronger, we use *really* or *absolutely*, not *very*.

A Match the questions 1–6 to the responses a–f.

1 What was the weather like in Greece? Was it hot?
2 What was the weather like in Finland? Was it cold?
3 What was Istanbul like? It's quite a big city, isn't it?
4 What was the food like in Italy? Was it good?
5 So what was your trip like? Was it good?
6 How was the journey back? Did you get wet in that storm?

a Great, really delicious. They really know how to eat.
b We got absolutely soaked! I didn't have an umbrella or anything.
c Yeah, it was fantastic! We had a great time.
d Yeah, it was boiling – over 40 degrees most days.
e Yeah, it's huge. The population's around 12 million.
f Yeah, it was freezing – around minus 10 most days.

Now match the comments in 7–12 to the responses g–l.

7   You must be angry about them losing your luggage.
8   You must be tired after such a long journey.
9   You must be hungry after such a long journey.
10 It's supposed to be quite a dirty city, isn't it?
11 It's supposed to be quite crowded, isn't it?
12 Tabriz is supposed to be quite an interesting city.

g Yes, it was really filthy! I couldn't believe it.
h Yeah, I am. I'm exhausted. I'm ready for bed.
i Yeah, it was. It was absolutely packed when we went!
j Yeah, it's fascinating. It dates back over a thousand years.
k I am. I'm absolutely furious!
l I am. I'm starving. Have you got anything to eat?

B 🔊 13.2 **Listen and check your answers.**

C Listen again. Mark the main stress in each of the adjectives in a–l.

D Try to remember responses a–l. Test each other in pairs.
Student A: read out 1–6.
Student B: close your book and say the responses. Then change roles.
Student B: read out 7–12.
Student A: close your book and say the responses.

E Tell your partner as much as you can about any places you have been to that were: *boiling / freezing / filthy / huge / fascinating / packed*.

LISTENING

You are going to hear four conversations about travel experiences.

A 🔊 13.3 Listen and answer the questions.
1 Which strong adjectives do the speakers use?
2 What are they describing?

B Listen again. Complete the phrases about the mistakes each person made. Why did they do / not do these things?
1 It was stupid – I should've .... about what to pack.
2 We were silly. We should've ....
3 Oh, it was my own fault. I shouldn't have .... for so long, especially with my skin! I should've at least ....!
4 I told you we should've ....

NATIVE SPEAKER ENGLISH

I bet
We often use *I bet* to respond to what people have told us. It means *I'm sure*.
A: It was boiling.
B: Lucky you! I bet that was nice.

A: The town was absolutely dead at night.
B: I bet you're glad you were only there for a day.

GRAMMAR *Should have*

> We use *should have / should not have* + past participle to talk about things that went wrong in the past. *Should have* explains good things you failed to do or that you were unable to do. *Should not have* explains things you did that were a bad idea.

A Work in pairs. Decide what actually happened in 1–8. Then use a third conditional to explain what would have been a better idea and why.

1 I knew we should've taken the plane instead of the ferry.
2 I should've worn something lighter.
3 He shouldn't have been driving so fast in the rain.
4 You should've read the instructions more carefully.
5 I knew we should've booked the tickets in advance.
6 They should've told you about the party sooner.
7 His parents shouldn't have left him on his own at home.
8 I shouldn't have left my bag hanging from the back of my seat.

▶ Need help? Read the grammar reference on p. 152

SPEAKING

A Work in pairs. Discuss the situations below and decide who is to blame. Use *should have* or third conditionals to explain why.

SITUATION 1
You get distracted doing some shopping at the airport after checking in. There is a queue to transfer to the terminal and extra security. The boarding gate is closed when you arrive and they won't let you board. They had not called your name or given you any other warning. The airline says you will have to pay for a new ticket.

SITUATION 2
You hired a car. The first problem was you had to ask for roadside assistance because you got a flat tyre and there wasn't a spare one. You hadn't bought insurance for this. Later you put petrol in the car with a diesel engine. You were not told this when you hired it, although it says so on the form you filled in. The car company wants to charge you for both problems.

SITUATION 3
You have reserved seats on trains to attend an important meeting. The first train arrived five minutes late so you missed the connection. You had been warned this might happen. The next train was full and you had to stand for an hour and a half during the journey. You arrive at your meeting tired, late and angry. You telephone to ask for compensation from the train company, but they refuse.

SITUATION 4
You and a friend have hired a car to go to a wedding. Your friend has been to the place once before so tells you he doesn't want to pay extra for a GPS. You leave the motorway at one point to avoid a traffic jam. You try and follow your sense of direction (which is normally very good) and then get completely lost. When you get back on the motorway, you try to make up for lost time, but are caught speeding. You argue with your friend about who should pay the speeding fine.

DEVELOPING CONVERSATIONS
Blaming people

> We use *it's my / his fault* or *I blame myself / him* to say who caused a problem. We often use *should have* and the third conditional as well.

A Complete the sentences with one word in each gap.

1 Don't .... me. You ....'ve read the small print.
2 It's not .... fault we're late. If you hadn't .... so long to get ready, we would .... caught the train.
3 It's not his fault – it's ....! You were the one who was driving. You should've .... more careful.
4 If you ask me, it's the airline's .... They .... have waited for us for one more minute.
5 I blame .... I should've listened to my dad. If I .... done what he said, none of this would've happened.
6 The problem could .... happened to anyone. It's nobody's .... It's just one of those things that happen.

B Work in pairs. Choose one of the situations. You are going to role-play the conversation. Before you start, decide who will take which role and think about how you will try and blame the other person.

14 TECHNOLOGY

In this unit you learn how to:
- talk about computers
- respond to advice
- talk about markets
- describe technology
- discuss things that affect the environment

Grammar
- *-ing* forms and *to*-infinitives

Vocabulary
- Computers
- Talking about markets
- Technology, programs and gadgets

Reading
- Here today, gone tomorrow!

Listening
- A computer problem
- Gadgets and technology

SPEAKING

A Work in pairs. Discuss these questions:
- What kind of computer do you have?
- Why did you choose that make? Are you happy with it?
- Are you good with computers? What kind of things do you know how to do?
- Is there anything you would still like to learn how to do?

VOCABULARY Computers

A Label the picture with the words in the box.

1 cable	2 hard drive	3 mouse
4 scanner	5 cursor	6 keyboard
7 plug	8 screen	9 file
10 menu	11 printer	12 socket

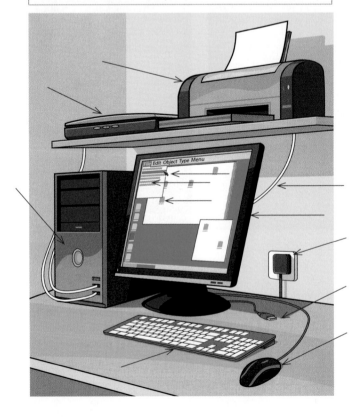

B Complete the sentences with the nouns from exercise A.
1 Have you got a ....? OK. Good. Then just scan the images in, save them as JPEGs, and email them to me.
2 Can you just make sure you've plugged the microphone into the right ....?
3 If you click on the icon at the top left-hand side, that should display the drop-down ....
4 Move the .... over the image and wait for the instructions to come up.
5 You won't be able to use that laptop in Spain. It's got a three-pin .... on it and they don't work over there.
6 In future, you really should make back-up copies of all your work on the external .... – just to be safe.
7 I deleted a really important .... by accident.
8 Every time I tried to play a DVD, the .... kept freezing and I kept having to restart the computer.
9 I tripped over a .... on the floor and knocked the whole computer over.
10 I had to hand in an important essay at university ASAP, but the .... ran out of ink after the first three pages!
11 I spilled coffee all over the .... Half the keys stopped working after that.
12 Right-click on the .... and select 'hyperlink'.

C Underline the words that collocate with the twelve gapped nouns in exercise B. Translate these collocations into your language.

D Work in pairs. Discuss these questions:
- Have you ever had any of the problems described in 7–12 in exercise B? When? What happened?
- What do you usually do when you have computer problems?

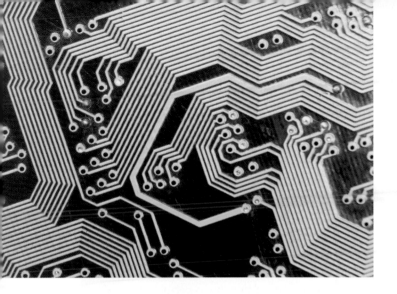

PRONUNCIATION Abbreviations

> Abbreviations are formed using the first letters of each word in the name of something. For example, *USA* is an abbreviation for the *United States of America*. When we say abbreviations, we usually stress each individual letter. However, occasionally we say them as one word.

A Work in pairs. Do you know what these abbreviations are?

IT	USB	PC	URL	RTF
PDF	DVD	FAQs	ASAP	GPS
JPEG	WiFi	RAM	CD-ROM	AIDS

B 🔊 14.1 Now listen and practise saying them.

LISTENING

You are going to hear a telephone call between Ella, a marketing manager for a large design firm, and Jirka, who works in the IT department.

A 🔊 14.2 Listen and answer the questions.
1 What is the main problem with Ella's computer?
2 What other problem had she been having with it?
3 What two suggestions does Jirka make?
4 How does Ella respond to each of them?
5 What does Jirka suggest Ella should do in the end?

LANGUAGE PATTERNS

Write the sentences in your language. Translate them back into English. Compare your English to the original.
Have you tried re-booting it at all?
Have you talked to anyone in IT about it at all?
I didn't learn anything at all on that course!
I don't have any plans at all for the holidays.
He hardly ate anything at all.
I hardly know her at all, to be honest.

SPEAKING

A Work in pairs. Discuss these questions:
- What do you think of the advice Jirka gives Ella?
- Do you know anyone who works in IT? Do they enjoy it? Would you like to do that kind of work?
- Do you think men tend to be better with technology than women? Why? / Why not?

DEVELOPING CONVERSATIONS
Responding to advice

A Translate the phrases in the boxes into your language.

A: Have you	tried rebooting?
	checked the connection?
B: Yeah,	but it didn't work.
	but it made no difference.
	but it didn't do any good.
	but I didn't have any success.

A: Have you	tried rebooting?
	checked the connection?
B: No,	I haven't.
	not yet.
A: Well, try that.	Otherwise, I can't really help.
	Otherwise, you're best taking it to a shop.
	Otherwise, you'll have to get a new one.
	Otherwise, I don't know what else you can do.

B Look at the situations in 1–5. Take turns to give advice and respond to it.
1 The attachment won't open.
2 The printer's not working.
3 The computer crashed and I can't find the file I was working on.
4 I can't log on to the network.
5 I left the power cable for my laptop on the train.

CONVERSATION PRACTICE

A Work in pairs. Make a list of as many problems you could have with a computer as you can. Compare your list with another pair. Did they have any ideas you had not thought of?

B Now role-play four telephone calls between someone who works on a help desk and someone with computer problems. Change roles after each conversation. Use as much language from these pages as possible.

READING

A The things in these photographs are all connected to the theme of an article you are going to read. Work in pairs. Discuss what you think the article might be about, and how the things could be connected.

a canal

a floppy disc

videotapes

the Sinclair C5

B Read the article quickly and see if your ideas were correct. Work in pairs. Compare what you remember about the things in the photos.

C Decide if these sentences about the article are true or false, according to the author. Then look back and underline the parts of the text that showed you the answer.
1 The floppy discs the writer found were extremely old.
2 Canals played an important role in the development of some countries.
3 Canals have started becoming more popular again.
4 VHS videotapes became more popular than Betamax videos because they were better quality.
5 VHS videotapes dominated the market for a long time.
6 The Sinclair C5 was designed to be environmentally friendly.
7 You needed a driving licence to drive the C5.
8 The writer mentions the C5 in order to suggest that it is not worth buying the latest gadgets and inventions.

D Work in pairs. Discuss these questions:
*   Can you think of any other examples of technology that soon became out of date and were replaced by something else?
*   Can you think of anything that has enjoyed a revival recently?
*   What are the hot new pieces of technology at the moment? Have you bought any of them?
*   The writer mentioned the videotape format war and the Mac / PC debate. Can you think of any other similar examples?

NATIVE SPEAKER ENGLISH

hot

When we describe something as *hot*, it means we think it is very exciting and interesting – because it is so new.
That hot new piece of technology you queued all day to buy.
Their new web phone is the hot new thing this winter.
She's one of the hottest young directors in Hollywood.
It's a great site. They have all the hot news and gossip!

E Work in pairs. Discuss what you think the words in **bold** in the article mean.

VOCABULARY Talking about markets

In *Reading*, you read about the bitter fight between Sony and JVC for *market share*.

A Decide which of the two possible endings for each sentence below best describes the situation in your country. Then work in pairs to compare your ideas. Explain your choices.
1 The beauty salon market is *almost saturated / growing steadily.*
2 The English language market is *huge / tiny.*
3 The hat market is *bigger / smaller* than it used to be.
4 The mobile phone market is *completely saturated / booming.*
5 The computer game market is *in decline / still growing.*
6 The bottled water market is *big business / dead.*
7 The DVD market is *in decline / fairly steady.*
8 The package holiday market is *bigger / smaller* than it was twenty years ago.

B Which endings in *italics* in exercise A best describe these markets in your country?

the housing market
the cigarette market
the DIY market
the tourist market
the fast food market

the organic food market
the coffee shop market
the online market
the black market
the digital camera market

HERE TODAY, GONE TOMORROW!

I was cleaning the other day when I came across a box of floppy discs. I pulled them out, cleaned them and then just couldn't stop staring at them. How was it possible that something that had seemed so modern a little over ten years ago could now seem so ancient? They looked like something from a different age, but the date on them clearly said 'October 1998'!

We are now so used to Broadband and memory sticks that it's easy to forget how things used to be. However, a look at the history of technological innovation **reveals** a long list of once great inventions that soon became out of date – as well as plenty of **non-starters**! Here are some examples:

CANALS

Canals nowadays are strange, deserted places, yet only 200 years ago they were an essential part of the industrial revolution. As Britain, the United States and Canada became industrial powers during the second half of the eighteenth century, a network of canals was developed to transport goods and raw materials. However, from the 1830s onwards, railways started taking over. Not only were they faster, but they could also carry more than boats. By the 1900s, most canals had **fallen out of use** and it is only very recently that they have enjoyed a revival as a holiday destination.

VIDEO CASSETTES

Anyone who grew up in the 1970s or 80s will remember the great videotape format war, a war fought between Sony's Betamax tapes and JVC's VHS versions. This **bitter** fight for **market share** was eventually won by VHS, despite the fact that many believed it was inferior. The victory was short-lived, though, for within 20 years, VHS tapes were more or less replaced by DVDs!

There are many modern versions of this story, with public opinion perhaps being most divided on the Mac / PC debate.

THE SINCLAIR C5

The C5 was an interesting idea, but very unsuccessful. This battery-operated electric **vehicle** was launched in 1985 and I still remember laughing as I watched its inventor, Clive Sinclair, getting into one of his tiny machines on the news and driving around. Intended to be a green alternative to the motor car, the C5 ended up being a financial disaster. It sold less than 20,000 and cost its **creator** several million pounds!

One of its many disadvantages was the fact that it had a top speed of only 24 kilometers per hour. This was because with vehicles that could go over that speed, you had to have a driving licence in the UK. On top of that, the battery did not last very

long, especially in the cold – not very helpful in Britain! Finally, it was very low and close to the ground, **thus** dangerous in traffic.

It all just goes to show. That hot new piece of technology you queued all day to buy could well be out of date before too long – or, even worse, could have all of your friends laughing at you next year!

VOCABULARY
Technology, programs and gadgets

design + cool	100GB + store
saves + automatically	allows + formats
runs + greener	lighter + carry
warns + dangerous	upgrade + powerful
set + switches	screen + picture
save + efficient	use + straightforward

A Complete the sentences with the pairs of words.

1 I wanted to .... to something which was more
....

2 It's .... so I can .... a lot of games and
videos on it.

3 It has a bigger .... and so the .... is a lot
clearer.

4 They .... on electricity bills because they're more
energy-........................... .

5 It .... a lot of time because it does it all
....

6 It's just a very nice .... It looks really ....

7 You can just .... the timer and it .... itself
on.

8 It .... you when you're about to visit a ....
website.

9 It .... you to change videos into different
....

10 It's .... and easier to .... around.

11 Even my mum finds it easy to .... It's so
....

12 It .... off solar power, so it's a lot ....

**B Work in pairs. What kind of things do you think are being
described in 1–12 in exercise A?**

HE STILL REFUSES TO UPGRADE

SPEAKING

A Work in pairs. Discuss these questions:
- Do you know anyone who always buys the latest gadgets, technology or computer programs?
- Do you know anyone who is a bit of a technophobe? In what way?
- Have you bought any new electronic items, gadgets or software recently? What? Why did you get them?

LISTENING

You are going to hear three conversations about gadgets or technology.

A 🎧 14.3 Listen and answer the questions.
1 What items are they talking about?
2 Do all of the speakers think the items are good?

**B Now answer these questions. Listen again if
you need to.**
1a Why is using solar energy so common in Germany?
1b Is it accessible even to poor people?
2a Why do they start talking about the GPS?
2b What reasons does she give for not getting one?
3a What are the advantages of the egg cooker?
3b What does the woman see as a better invention? Why?

C Work in pairs. Discuss these questions:
- Does your government subsidise anything? Do you think it is good?
- Is there any gadget or piece of technology that you could happily do without?
- Can you think of any other gadgets which are environmentally friendly?
- Is there anything that you would like to be invented – but that has not been invented yet?

"I'm sorry, Jason. I don't date anyone new until
I've googled them."

GRAMMAR -ing forms and to-infinitives

A **Match the examples 1–5 from *Listening* to the rules a–e.**

1 What's wrong with just putting them in some water?
2 You still need the cash to install the panels.
3 I did consider getting one.
4 If you want to have the perfect boiled egg, ...
5 Using this is more energy-efficient than boiling eggs.

a -*ing* forms are often used after a preposition such as *in, on* and *from*
b -*ing* forms follow certain verbs such as *avoid, miss,* and *mind*
c -*ing* forms are used when they're the subject of a clause
d *to*-infinitives are used to explain the reason or purpose for something
e *to*-infinitives are used after certain verbs such as *learn, ask* and *plan*

B **Work in pairs. Discuss these questions:**
- Does your language have an equivalent of the -*ing* form and *to*-infinitive?
- Are they used in the same way as the examples in exercise A?

C **Decide if the following sentences are correct or incorrect.**

1 My computer keeps to crash.
2 You should take it somewhere to get it looked at.
3 To make your own films is much easier with MDirector.
4 I became much greener after to see *An Inconvenient Truth.*
5 I use them for saving energy.
6 We're all guilty of to damage the planet in some way.
7 People need to get used to not drive everywhere. They should walk more.
8 I took the laptop back to the shop and luckily they agreed to exchange it.

▶ Need help? Read the grammar reference on p. 153

D **Complete the sentences so they are true for you. Use a verb phrase with an -*ing* form or a *to*-infinitive. Then work in pairs to compare your ideas.**

1 I keep ....
2 I wish they'd invented a machine ....
3 I think .... is OK for women, but not for men.
4 I'm hoping .... sometime in the future.
5 I could never get used to ....
6 I think .... is better for you than ....
7 I spend most of my weekends ....
8 I've arranged .... at the weekend.

SPEAKING

A **Work in groups. Explain why each of the following things may be good or bad for the environment. Which is the most important thing to do? Use these sentence starters:**

I think X is bad for the environment because ... .
...-ing is more important than ...-ing because ... .
I think it has something to do with ...-ing.

- Leaving your TV on standby overnight.
- Eating regularly at a fast food / hamburger place.
- Planting a tall tree near your house.
- Closing curtains at night.
- Using a ceiling fan in the summer and winter.
- Taking a plastic bag from every shop you buy from.
- Eating a lot of rice.
- Going on holiday abroad.
- Wearing a hat in the house if it is cold.
- Cycling and walking everywhere.
- Using energy-efficient light bulbs.
- Using biofuels: fuels made from biological materials such as sugar cane or palm oil.

B **Write your own ideas about things you have heard are good / bad for the environment. Has anyone in your group heard the same?**

... is supposed to be bad.
... is supposed to cause / create / be a good way of ...-ing.

C **Work in pairs. Discuss these questions:**
- Which of the things in exercises A and B do you do? Why?
- Which do you avoid doing?
- Which would you consider doing or stopping?
- Which could you never get used to doing?

In this unit you learn how to:
- talk with a doctor about injuries and illness
- explain causes and results
- tell stories about accidents

Grammar
- Reported speech
- Reporting verbs

Vocabulary
- Injuries and illness
- Forming words
- Explaining causes and results
- Accidents and problems

Reading
- Fact or myth?

Listening
- At the doctor's
- A big help

A bandage

B elasticated support

C painkillers

SPEAKING

A Work in pairs. Discuss these questions:
- How often do you go to the doctor's?
- When was the last time you felt unwell? What symptoms did you have?
- Do you have a healthy lifestyle? Why? / Why not?

VOCABULARY Injuries and illness

A Use the extra information in sentences 1–10 to guess the meanings of the words in bold. Translate the sentences.

1 He says he's got the *flu*, but it's really just a *cold*. He's **coughing** a lot at night.
2 He's developed an *allergy* to cats. He starts **sneezing** as soon as he comes near one.
3 It's not really a **stomach ache** – it doesn't really hurt. It's just an *upset stomach* – I've got diarrhoea and I feel sick.
4 I think I've **sprained** my ankle. I don't think it's *broken*.
5 She's got a **stiff** neck. She can hardly turn it.
6 My gran's got *arthritis*. The joints in her hands and her wrists are really **swollen**. She can't hold things.
7 I sometimes feel really **dizzy** and have to sit down. The doctor says it might be because of **high blood pressure**.
8 I've developed this nasty **rash** on the back of my hand. It's all red and it's really **itchy**.
9 I've been getting **migraines** – just very painful *headaches* – and I sometimes feel quite sick.
10 I hit my head and got a nasty *cut* and a big **bump** appeared.

B How many of the problems in bold and *italics* have you had in the last five years? Are there any you have never had?

C Why might you need the things in the pictures?

D thermometer

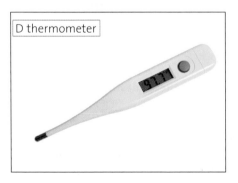

E cream

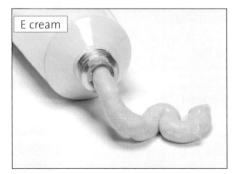

F medicine

D Match the patients' and doctors' comments.

1. My ankle's quite swollen. I can hardly walk on it.
2. I've done something to my back. It really hurts.
3. I hit my head and got this nasty bump.
4. I've had this nasty cough for weeks.
5. I've got this nasty rash. It's really itchy.
6. It's quite a nasty cut.
7. You've broken your leg, I'm afraid.
8. You've got very high blood pressure.

a. It's a chest infection. It should clear up with antibiotics.
b. Don't scratch it. I'll give you some cream for the itchiness.
c. It's probably just sprained, but we should have it X-rayed.
d. Well, I have been under a lot of stress recently.
e. Oh no! How long will I have to have it in plaster?
f. Did you feel dizzy or lose consciousness at all?
g. Will it need some stitches?
h. I'll get the nurse to give you some painkillers, but you'll need to rest it. Don't do any lifting.

E Spend two minutes memorising a–h in exercise D. Work in pairs.
Student A: say 1–8.
Student B: close your book and say as much as you can from a–h.

LANGUAGE PATTERNS

Write the sentences in your language. Translate them back into English. Compare your English to the original.
I'll get the nurse to give you some painkillers.
If it rains, I'll get my dad to drive us there.
As I was off sick for a week, I got the doctor to write a note.
I got a friend to help me carry stuff because of my bad back.

LISTENING

You are going to hear two conversations between a doctor and a patient.

A 🔊 15.1 Look at the questions that are asked and discuss what you think is wrong with the patients. Then listen and check if you were right.

Conversation 1	Conversation 2
Does this hurt?	What seems to be the problem?
Can you put any weight on it at all?	How long have you been like this?
How did you do it?	Any diarrhoea?
How long will I have to wait for the X-ray?	And has he been able to drink anything?
Are you on any medication?	Does this hurt at all?
Any allergies?	And here?
You've never had any adverse reactions to any drugs?	

B Listen again. Note down the answers to the questions.

C Work in pairs. Role-play the two conversations.

DEVELOPING CONVERSATIONS
Short questions with *any*

We often shorten questions to *any* + plural / uncountable noun, especially when they follow other related questions.

Are you allergic to anything? = *Any allergies?*
Have you had any diarrhoea? = *Any diarrhoea?*

A Re-write the questions with *any*.

1. Do you have any other symptoms?
2. Are you on any medication?
3. Does it feel itchy?
4. Have you felt dizzy at all?
5. Does it feel stiff?
6. Did you vomit at all?
7. Do you want to ask me anything?
8. Does it hurt at all?

CONVERSATION PRACTICE

A You are going to have a similar conversation to the ones you heard in *Listening*. Work in pairs. Decide on a medical problem.
Student A: plan what questions to ask the doctor – and think of details of your problem.
Student B: decide what advice to give

B Role-play the conversation. Try to use as much new language from these pages as possible.

READING Fact or myth?

You are going to read a medical website which discusses whether certain beliefs about health are true or are myths.

A Work in pairs. Look at the following statements. Discuss if you think they are true. Explain your ideas.
1 You can catch a cold if you go out with wet hair.
2 Antibiotics can cure a cold.
3 Eating chocolate can cause acne.
4 Cracking the joints in your fingers can cause arthritis.
5 The less cholesterol you have, the better.
6 Swallowing chewing gum is bad for you.
7 Coffee is a drug.

B Now read the website. Decide if the statements in exercise A are true or if they are myths, according to the writer. Why?

C From the website, can you remember:
1 what mothers often tell their children?
2 the best way to avoid catching a cold?
3 when you may need antibiotics?
4 the best way to deal with a cold?
5 what makes acne worse?
6 what other factors can cause heart attacks?
7 what people think happens when they eat chewing gum?
8 what can happen when people give up coffee?

Look again at the website. Did you remember the exact words?

NATIVE SPEAKER ENGLISH

a bug

A bug is often used to talk about a disease such as a virus.
The best way to avoid viruses like these is to wash your hands regularly when there's a bug going around.

I picked up a bug while I was away. I was in bed for two days.

A: Are you feeling better?
B: Much better. I think it was just one of those twenty-four-hour bugs.

Fact or myth?

It's difficult to ignore your mother when she tells you to "wrap up warm" or "dry your hair or you'll get a cold" – but colds are not caused by the cold: they are caused by viruses! Walking around with wet hair or a T-shirt in winter may look silly, and will make you feel cold, but you will only get a cold or the flu, if you come into contact with an infected person. The best way to avoid viruses like these is to wash your hands regularly when there's a bug going around.

Despite the huge medical advances that have been made over the last century, the common cold is still incurable and medicine does little for the symptoms either. Antibiotics won't help as your cold is caused by one of over 200 viruses. The only time you may need them is if you develop a throat or ear infection. Otherwise, go to bed and drink lots of fluids and wait till you get better.

Acne is a hormonal condition which **causes** the skin to produce too much oil. Eating a lot of fatty foods may be bad for you in other ways, but research has failed to find any connection between diet and acne. Incidentally, washing too much can **make** the condition worse. It's best just to wash gently twice a day and don't rub the skin too hard.

Doctors have several ideas about what **leads** to arthritis including bacterial or viral infections and jobs which involve an overuse of your joints. Some types of arthritis can even affect children. However, no types are **caused** by cracking your finger joints.

! Remember this is for information only. If you have any worries about your health, you should always consult your doctor.

5

In many countries you can buy foods which are advertised as being low in cholesterol or actually able to reduce how much you have. You might think therefore cholesterol is an entirely bad thing, but you'd be wrong. Cholesterol is produced naturally in the body and is essential for life, which **means** it is difficult to reduce it through diet. As such, a few doctors have questioned if there is a link between cholesterol and heart disease. Of course a balanced diet may have other benefits, but don't forget that factors such as smoking, stress and high blood pressure also **lead** to heart attacks.

6

Don't worry. Chewing gum won't stay in your stomach forever or block your insides. It'll just pass through you and come out the other end!

7

The caffeine in coffee is a stimulant which **makes** your body speed up: your heart rate increases and it wakes you up. You may see these things as benefits, but caffeine also has a number of negative side effects. It's addictive. People who suddenly stop drinking coffee may suffer withdrawal symptoms such as headaches, irritability and restlessness.

Caffeine has also been **linked** to other problems but, like most things, coffee is fine if you don't drink too much.

VOCABULARY Forming words

A **Find words in the text in the same family as the words in the box.**

virus	infectious	cure	medicine
fat	natural	addicted	irritable

B **Correct the words in the wrong form in sentences 1–8.**
1 Apparently, the virus is quite infected, so I don't want to visit him in case I catch it.
2 She's got some kind of medicine condition which means she can only work part-time.
3 Unfortunately, the condition is not cure, so he'll have to live with it for the rest of his life.
4 The drugs can be quite addicted, so you have to be careful how long you take them for.
5 You shouldn't eat too many fat foods.
6 He's been very irritability recently. I don't know why.
7 The body produces vitamin D natural when exposed to sun.
8 He picked up this really nasty viral when he was on holiday.

SPEAKING

A **Work in pairs. Discuss these questions:**
- Was there anything in the text that surprised you?
- Why do you think these myths have come about?
- Have you heard any stories about health issues? What do you think about them?

VOCABULARY Explaining causes and results

A **Look at the verbs in bold in the text. They all connect causes or reasons with results. Which prepositions or verb patterns go with the words?**

B **Complete the sentences with one word in each gap.**
1 He's got a genetic condition which .... he has to see the doctor regularly.
2 A poor diet in childhood can .... to health problems in later life.
3 Depression has been .... to a lack of vitamin C in the diet.
4 The changes the government have introduced to the health service have .... things worse.
5 The main side effect of the medication is that it .... you feel tired and sleepy.
6 The disease is .... by a virus that attacks the brain.

C **Work in pairs. Use the patterns in exercise B to talk about the causes / results of these medical problems:**

asthma	migraines	diabetes	rashes
malaria	sneezing	insomnia	stress
HIV	upset stomach		

D **Do you know anyone who suffers from the problems in exercise C? How does it affect their life?**

VOCABULARY Accidents and problems

A Choose the correct words.

1 I was grilling some meat and I caught my hand on the grill and *burned / bruised* it quite badly.
2 I was jogging and I *tripped over / slipped* a rock and hurt my knee really badly.
3 I was out riding and the horse got scared by a bang and I *fell off / fell down* the horse and broke my collar bone.
4 I was walking down the street and this dog suddenly attacked me and *bit / stung* me on the leg.
5 I was cycling and a bus drove across me. I *crashed into / fell into* the side and sprained my wrist.
6 I had some food at a street market and I think I got food *infection / poisoning* from there. It was awful.
7 I spent the whole day on the beach and ended up with terrible *suntan / sunburn*.
8 It was really hot on the underground and I felt dizzy and then just *fainted / disappeared*.
9 I broke my arm when I *tripped / slipped* on some ice.
10 This bee *stung / bit* me on the arm and my whole arm swelled up.

B Look at the pictures. Choose one and imagine you are the person in it. Decide how to describe what happened to you. Add as many extra details as you want to. Then work in pairs. Tell your stories.

LISTENING

You are going to hear a Swedish woman, Anna, talking to her colleague, Dan, about his holiday. In the conversation, Dan describes an accident that his friend James had.

A ⏺ 15.2 **Listen and answer the questions.**
1 What kind of holiday was it?
2 How did the accident happen?
3 Was James badly injured?
4 How did they get him to a hospital?
5 What did the doctors tell him?

B **Work in pairs. Put the events from the conversation in order. Listen again to check your answers.**
a He had quite a few cuts and bruises.
b It spoilt his holiday, really.
c James went off the road into some bushes and fell off.
d He had to have a few stitches in the cuts.
e She took him to hospital, which was really kind of her.
f We were going back to the hotel down a steep road.
g He's now found out his bike frame's broken.
h A woman came past in her car a minute or two later.

C **Work in pairs. Discuss these questions:**
• When was the last time someone was very kind to you?
• Did Dan's story about James remind you of any other stories you have heard?

GRAMMAR Reported speech

> When we tell people about things that happened to us, we often report things using *said / told me (that)* + clause.

A **Look at the examples 1–4 from *Listening* and answer the questions.**
• What structures are the forms in *italics*?
• Why are they used? What did the people actually say?

1 He kept saying he*'d* be OK.
2 After a couple of hours, they rang and told me they*'d given* James an X-ray and there *was* nothing broken.
3 They said he *needed* to stay there a bit longer, though, as he *was waiting* to have a few stitches in the cuts.
4 He said he*'s going to* have to buy a new bike now.

▶ **Need help? Read the grammar reference on p. 154**

B **Complete the sentences with the correct past forms.**
1 The doctor told me I .... a chest infection and .... me some antibiotics. It cleared up after a week. (have, give)
2 The doctor said he .... too much and he .... to go on a diet, but he refused. (eat, need)
3 The doctors said she .... some problems in the future, but she .... incredibly lucky to survive the crash. (have, be)
4 The doctor told me the injection ...., but it .... really painful! (not hurt, be)
5 They said the surgeon .... everything she .... to keep him alive. (do, can)
6 She told me they .... several tests already, but they still didn't know what .... the problem, so they had to do more. (do, cause)

C **Work in pairs. Take turns to ask each other *What did the doctor say?* Report something different each time.**

GRAMMAR Reporting verbs

> We also use other reporting verbs to summarise the content of what was said.

A **Can you remember how the following reporting verbs were used in *Listening*? Underline the verb patterns in the audioscript on pp. 173–174.**

offered   insisted   persuaded
promised   told him not

B **Work in pairs. Discuss these questions. When was the last time someone you know:**
• offered to do something for you?
• promised to do something?
• insisted on doing something?
• persuaded you (not) to do something?
• told you (not) to do something?

▶ **Need help? Read the grammar reference on p. 154**

SPEAKING

A **Work in pairs. Talk about a time when you had an accident – or were ill. Describe what happened. Use reported speech and some reporting verbs.**

16 NEWS AND EVENTS

In this unit you learn how to:
- describe different sections of a newspaper
- talk about stories in the news
- respond to news
- explain who people are

Grammar
- Defining relative clauses

Vocabulary
- Newspapers
- Explaining who people are

Reading
- Seeking fame and fortune

Listening
- Stories in the news
- Famous people

VOCABULARY Newspapers

A Look at these different parts of a newspaper. Tick ✓ the parts you usually look at and put a cross ✗ by any you never look at.

national news
the business pages
the letters page
the reviews

international news
the sports pages
the gossip pages
the horoscopes

B Work in pairs. Compare your ideas and explain your decisions. Which part do you usually read first?

C Check you understand the words and expressions in **bold**. Then discuss which part of the newspaper each question refers to.
1 How many **marks out of ten** did they give it?
2 What's the **exchange rate** at the moment?
3 Did you see what she was wearing at the **premiere**?
4 What was **the score** in the game last night?
5 So have they agreed a **ceasefire** yet?
6 What **star sign** are you?

LISTENING

You are going to hear five conversations about different news stories.

A The words below come from the conversations: two from each. Work in pairs. Discuss which pairs of words go together, and what kind of story they might come from.

close down
get divorced
stab
pass away
sign

funeral
have an affair
midfielder
made redundant
victim

B 🔊 **16.1 Now listen and check your ideas. Take notes on:**
- which of the words in exercise A appear in which conversation.
- what story is being discussed in each case.

C Work in pairs. Can you remember the whole sentences that each of the words in exercise A appeared in? Compare your ideas. Then listen again and read the audioscript on p. 174 to check your answers.

D Work in pairs. Practise reading the conversations. Continue each conversation for as long as you can by adding your own ideas and comments.

LANGUAGE PATTERNS

Write the sentences in your language. Translate them back into English. Compare your English to the original.

Did you see that thing on TV about the mobile phone factory closing down?

Did you see that thing in the papers about Moscow being the most expensive city in the world now?

Did you read about Paris Simpson getting arrested?

Did you read about Inter Milan signing that young Irish kid?

Did you hear about Laura losing her job?

Did you hear about Lee getting promoted?

DEVELOPING CONVERSATIONS
Apparently

We often introduce sentences about things in the news with *apparently*. This shows we are not 100% certain these facts are true – we are just reporting what we have heard.

Apparently, she found out her husband was having an affair with another Hollywood actress.

Apparently, they think his attackers might have been even younger than him.

A Complete the dialogues below with your own ideas.

1 A: Did you see that thing in the paper about the murder in town last night?
   B: Yeah, it was awful, wasn't it? Apparently, ...

2 A: Did you see that thing on TV about the new shopping mall they're going to build?
   B: Yeah, it's great, isn't it? Apparently, ...

3 A: Did you see that politician on TV last night trying to dance to hip-hop?
   B: Yeah, it was really funny, wasn't it? Apparently, ...

4 A: Did you see that thing in the paper about that tennis player, James Jenkins?
   B: No. What was that?
   A: Well, apparently, ...

5 A: Did you see that thing on the news about Shaynee Wilson and her boyfriend getting arrested?
   B: No. What was that?
   A: Well, apparently, ...

B Have you heard any gossip or stories you aren't sure are true? Tell a partner using *apparently*.

PRONUNCIATION Responding to news

When we comment on things people tell us, we often add the question tags *wasn't it? / isn't it?* As we expect people to agree with us in these situations, our voice goes down on the tag.

E: Did you see that thing on TV about the murder last night?

F: Yeah. It was shocking, *wasn't it?*

A 🔊 16.2 Listen to ten sentences. Repeat them.

B Work in pairs. Take turns saying the sentences below. Respond with a comment + question tag.
1 Did you hear about Jay and Selma splitting up?
2 Did you hear about John getting food poisoning from his own cooking?
3 Did you read about Angelina booking a special hotel room for her dog?
4 Did you read that the ceasefire has ended already?
5 Did you read that she paid $5,000 for that dress?
6 Did you hear that Jay and Selma are back together?

CONVERSATION PRACTICE

A Think of two news stories you have read or heard about recently. Write one question for each story, using the ones in *Language patterns* as a model.

B Work in groups. Discuss the stories. Start your conversations with your questions from exercise A.

SPEAKING

A Work in groups. Do you know who any of the people in the photos below are? Discuss them. Use some of these expressions:

I haven't got a clue!   He looks really familiar, but I can't remember who he is.
Isn't that that American politician? What's his name?   I'm fairly sure that's ...

VOCABULARY Explaining who people are

artist	activist	scientist	athlete	dictator	founder	doctor	mathematician

A The descriptions 1–8 describe some of the people in the pictures. Complete the sentences with the words in the box.

1   Marie Curie was a Polish .... who *studied radiation* and *discovered* the radioactive substance polonium.
2   Martin Luther King was a human rights .... who *campaigned for the rights of* black people in the United States.
3   Pol Pot was a .... in Cambodia who *was responsible for the deaths of* over a million people.
4   Kemal Atatürk *led the liberation struggle* in Turkey and was the .... of the republic.
5   Sergey Bubka is a Ukrainian pole-vaulter. He's perhaps the greatest .... of all time. He *set the world record* in 1994 and he still holds it. No one's come close to beating it.
6   Euclid was a Greek .... who *is considered the father of* geometry.
7   Pedro Alonso is a Spanish .... He led a team which has *developed a vaccine against* malaria.
8   Gustav Klimt is an Austrian .... whose *most famous work is* probably 'The Kiss'.

B Translate the parts of the sentences in exercise A in *italics*.

C Can you use the words in *italics* to describe any other famous people from now or in the past?

Ceci n'est pas une pipe.

LISTENING

You are going to hear three short conversations about four more famous or important people.

A 🔊 **16.3 Listen and answer the questions for each conversation.**
1 Why do they start talking about Garibaldi / Comenius / Eddy Merckx / Magritte?
2 What is each person famous for?
3 Where is each person from?
4 What else do you learn about each one?

B Work in pairs.
1 Can you think of a place:
 • which is *named after* a famous person?
 • which is decorated with *memorabilia*?
2 Can you think of someone:
 • who is a national hero?
 • who was ahead of his / her time?

GRAMMAR Defining relative clauses

> **We often use relative clauses to add information after a noun:**
> He was a Czech writer *who wrote about education*.
> ··
> **You can also use *that* instead of *who* in the sentence above.**
> To add information about things, use *that* or *which*.
> To add information about times, use *that* or *when*.
> To add information about possessions, use *whose*.
> To add information about places, use *where*.

A Cross out the word or words that are not correct in sentences 1–8.
1 He was a military leader in the nineteenth century *who / that / which* helped unify Italy.
2 It's a European Union scheme *that / who / which* provides grants to teachers.
3 It's *who / when / where* they have Rembrandt's most famous paintings.
4 He set up a charity *that / which / where* has helped thousands of poor children.
5 He's a composer *who / that / whose* most famous work is probably the Rites of Spring.
6 At the time *that / who / when* he was writing, his ideas were very radical.
7 It's supposed to be the house *when / where / that* Shakespeare was born.
8 She was a writer *whose / who / which* ideas were very influential.

▶ Need help? Read the grammar reference on p. 155

SPEAKING

A Work in pairs. Role-play a conversation.
Student A: You are visiting the town / country where **Student B** lives. Ask about statues, monuments and streets named after people, dates or places, to find out their significance. For example:
Who's that statue of in the main square?
Why's it called The Darwin Institute?
Student B: Explain.

B Make the following lists:
 • the four greatest living people in your country.
 • the four most important people who have ever lived in your country.

Write the list individually. Then work in pairs. Compare your list with a partner and try to agree on the same lists.

If your partner does not know any of the people you have chosen, explain who they are / were.
Use these sentence frames:
He's the man who …
She's the woman who …

READING

A **Read the short article about a survey. Then work in pairs. Discuss these questions:**
- Why do you think so many people want to be famous?
- What kind of problems do you think these ambitions might cause?
- Can you think of any celebrities who have found fame hard to cope with?
- Which six different ways of becoming rich and famous do you expect the article to mention?

SEEKING FAME AND FORTUNE

In a recent survey, over 80% of 18-to-25-year-olds said getting rich was their first or second most important life goal, whilst 51% said the same about becoming famous.

Of course, being a celebrity can be problematic. We have all seen stories about stars turning to drink or drugs as they find themselves unable to cope with the emotional stress of life in the public eye. However, this doesn't seem to discourage anyone. The main problem for many seems to be how to actually become rich and famous – especially if you have no real talent! Given this, here's our six-point guide on how to go about it.

B **In which of the six sections of the article were the following mentioned?**

a a popular talent show
b retired people
c an act of great generosity
d an act of great bravery
e viral emails
f physical attraction

C **Read the rest of the article. Then work in pairs. Discuss why the people and things below were mentioned. Check your ideas by looking at the article again if you need to.**

the gossip magazines
an advertising company
The Guinness Book of Records
Kurt Nilsen
Paris Hilton
Kim Sing and Bee Lian Man
Golda Bechal
Mahir Cagri
karaoke
Kuldeep Singh
The Zimmers
The Who

D **Complete the sentences with the correct form of the words from the article. Underline the words that collocate with them in each sentence.**

barrier	control	footsteps	option	will

1 We would love to buy a house and move in together, but on our wages that .... isn't available to us.
2 My dad wants me to follow in his .... and join the army, but it's just not what I want to do with my life.
3 Physical disability is no .... to a successful career.
4 My spending just got out of .... If you ask me, it's the bank's fault for lending me so much money.
5 My aunt left me a house in her ....

catch	come into	forward	repay	save

6 You .... my life! How can I ever thank you enough? I would've died if you hadn't rescued me.
7 Could you .... the email from Head Office to me?
8 There were some really good-looking guys at the party, but one in particular .... my eye.
9 Thanks again for everything you did for us. I hope that one day we can .... your kindness. All the best, Omar.
10 She .... a lot of money when her father died.

E **Work in pairs. Use three of the collocations from exercise D to say something about your life. For example:**
I'd like to follow in my father's footsteps and become a surgeon.

NATIVE SPEAKER ENGLISH

easier said than done
When we think someone's advice or suggestion sounds good, but is actually very difficult to do, we often say it is *easier said than done.*
Obviously, finding a famous partner is easier said than done.
I know I should stop smoking, but it's easier said than done.
People keep telling me to forget her, but that's easier said than done.

SPEAKING

A **Work in pairs. Discuss these questions:**
- Can you think of any other people who have become famous in the six ways mentioned in the article?
- Would you like to be famous? Why? / Why not?
- What do you think is the best way to become famous?
- Can you think of any bad ways of becoming famous?

1 DATE SOMEONE WHO'S ALREADY FAMOUS

Obviously, finding a famous partner is easier said than done. However, anyone who can manage to catch the eye of a top footballer or movie star can expect to find themselves on the front page of the gossip magazines before too long. This might then be enough to get a TV or advertising company interested and you can end up becoming a star yourself.

2 GO ON A REALITY TV SHOW

The kind of out-of-tune singing that was once reserved for the privacy of a karaoke room has now become prime-time Saturday night TV – and shows such as *Pop Idol* have brought instant fame and fortune to hundreds around the world. Take Norwegian Kurt Nilsen, for example. His versions of well-known songs were so popular that he was able to give up his job as a plumber! He then went on to win *World Idol* and became a huge star in his native country. If you can sing, you could follow in Kurt's footsteps. If this option isn't available to you, then why not just try to appear on any of the reality TV shows which require no talent at all from their contestants?

3 INHERIT A FORTUNE

Obviously, if you want to come into a lot of money when one of your loved ones dies, it helps if you have incredibly rich parents – like Paris Hilton's. Alternatively, you just need to be lucky when choosing your friends, like Chinese restaurant owners Kim Sing and Bee Lian Man were. They befriended an elderly widow, Golda Bechal, who then repaid their kindness by leaving the couple £10 million in her will when she died.

4 START A BLOG OR SET UP A WEBSITE

The Internet has given many their fifteen minutes of fame. An email arrives from a friend containing a link to an online video, a blog or a new site. You have a look, forward the link, and before long, a million people have seen it!

Perhaps the first Internet superstar was a Turkish teacher called Mahir Cagri, who, in 1999, asked a friend to set up a simple website for him. It contained some photos, some personal information and began with the words "Welcome to my home page! I kiss you!!" Things soon got out of control and Cagri found himself in *The Guinness Book of Records* after over 12 million people visited

5 Become a hero

One good way of getting yourself in the papers is to save someone's life or catch a wanted criminal. Kuldeep Singh for instance, became a national hero in India when he removed a bomb from a bus he was driving in Delhi. Mr Singh, who was injured when the bomb later exploded, was widely praised for his courage.

6 DON'T GIVE UP!

Age is no barrier to becoming famous either, as plenty of old-age pensioners have proved. The Zimmers are among recent examples: a group of around 40 British pensioners, put together by a documentary film maker who was interested in the experiences of the elderly, the band's singer was 90 – and the oldest member was 101! They had a hit with a cover version of The Who's *M Generation* – and went on to appear on TV and travel to America.

LEARNER TRAINING

Work in groups of three. Read these ideas about different ways of improving your English outside of class. Then discuss the questions.

- What do you think are the advantages and disadvantages of each idea?
- How are you planning to improve your English once your course has finished?

> Go and live in an English-speaking country for a while. Try and stay with a local family.

> Listen to audio books, and if you can, read the books at the same time as you listen.

> Buy a good grammar book and work through it.

> Do a language exchange with a student learning your language.

GAME

Work in pairs. Student A use *only* the green squares; student B use *only* the yellow squares. Spend 5 minutes looking at your questions and revising the answers. Then take turns tossing a coin: Heads = move one of your squares; Tails = move two of your squares. When you land on a square, your partner looks at the relevant page in the book to check your answers, but *you don't*! If you are right, move forward one space (but don't answer the question until your next turn). If you aren't right, your partner tells you the right answer, and you miss a go. When you've finished the game, change colours and play again.

Start

1
Vocabulary p. 93
your partner will say 1–8 in part A. You say the phrasal verbs.

2
Grammar p. 95: your partner will read 1–6. You complete each sentence with the correct forms.

3
Native English note, p. 96: if you can say what the *Native English* note was, throw again.

4
Vocabulary p. 96: your partner will ask 8 of the questions. Say *yes* + a strong adjective.

5
Pronunciation p. 99: can you remember ten of the acronyms?

6
Language Patterns p. 99: say two questions and two negative sentences that end in *at all*.

7
Miss a go!

8
Native English note, p. 100: if you can say what the *Native English* note was, throw again.

9
Vocabulary p. 100: use five different words to describe various markets in your country.

10
Miss a go!

11
Vocabulary p. 104: say eight health problems.

12
Developing Conversations p. 105: say six of the short questions with *any*.

13
Native English note, p. 106: if you can say what the *Native English* note was, throw again.

14
Grammar Reference p. 154: your partner will say 6 of the reporting verbs. Say a sentence for each using the right pattern.

15
Vocabulary p. 110: your partner will say the questions in C. You say the section of the newspaper the questions refer to (in part A).

16
Vocabulary p. 112: your partner will say five names from 1–8. You describe who they were.

17
Native English note, p. 114: if you can say what the *Native English* note was, throw again.

18
Reading p. 115: can you remember the six ways of becoming famous?

Finish

For each of the activities below, work in groups of three. Use the Vocabulary Builder if you want to.

CONVERSATION PRACTICE

Choose one of these *Conversation Practice* activities:
Travel p. 93
Technology p. 99
Injuries and Illness p. 105
News and Events p. 111

Two of you should do the task. The third person should listen and then give a mark of between 1 and 10 for the performance. Explain your decision. Then change roles.

ACT OR DRAW

One person should act or draw as many of these words as you can in three minutes. Your partners should try to guess the words. Do not speak while you are acting or drawing!

a flat tyre	solar power	stitches
slippery	socket	celebrity
bumpy	a temperature	karaoke
freezing	dizzy	a blog
filthy	a bump	robbery
pour down	itchy	athlete
a scanner	sneeze	dictator
GPS	insomnia	
a cable	a talent show	

QUIZ

Answer as many of the questions as possible.
1 Say four different kinds of **trip** you can go on.
2 When might people have to deal with **bureaucracy**?
3 What kind of things happen when you **suffer discrimination**?
4 When might you **get distracted**? By what?
5 If a market is **saturated**, is it good?
6 What kind of things can **enjoy a revival**?
7 Say three things the government might **subsidise**.
8 Say three things you can **run out of**.
9 What is the difference between having **a cold** and having **the flu**?
10 How could you **sprain** your wrist?
11 What should you do if you get **a rash**?
12 Say three things that can be **addictive**.
13 Who might **agree a ceasefire**? Why?
14 How many **star signs** can you name?
15 Why do people get **made redundant**?

COLLOCATIONS

Take turns to read out collocation lists from Unit 13 of the Vocabulary Builder. Where there is a '~', say '*blah*' instead. Your partner should guess as many words as they can. Each time you change roles, move on to the next unit.

PRONUNCIATION Phonetic symbols

A Write the correct spelling for the words in phonetic script below.

1 / ˈhɑːbə / ....
2 / refjuˈdʒiː / ....
3 / ɪgˈzɔːstɪd / ....
4 / ˈkɜːsə / ....
5 / inˈfɪərɪə / ....
6 / ɔːtəˈmætɪkli / ....
7 / daɪəˈriːə / ....
8 / daɪəˈbiːtiːz / ....
9 / ˈhɒrəskəʊps / ....
10 / ˈdredfʊl / ....

B 🔊 R 4.1 Listen to the words from exercise A. Practise saying them.

SPEAKING

Work in pairs. Look at the pictures below. Discuss the different roles that animals play in our lives. How do you feel about each one?

LISTENING

You are going to hear five people talking about things connected with technology.

A 🔊 R 4.2 **Listen. Which of the things in the box does each person do?**

computer programmer	pilot
engineer	writer
flight attendant	doctor
teacher	surgeon
businessman	bus driver

Speaker 1 ....
Speaker 2 ....
Speaker 3 ....
Speaker 4 ....
Speaker 5 ....

B **Listen again and decide which speaker:**
a has to deal with a lot of paperwork.
b lost their job.
c thinks technology has made things safer.
d is setting up a website.
e worries about being clear.

[... / 10]

GRAMMAR Conditionals

Complete the sentences with one word in each gap. Contractions such as *didn't, can't,* etc. count as one word.
1 We wouldn't have got lost if I'd .... driving.
2 If I'd known my ex-boyfriend was going to be here, I .... have come to this party!
3 If you'd been more careful, it wouldn't .... happened!
4 I don't regret moving here. If I ...., who knows what might have happened to me?
5 If you .... told me earlier, I could have helped you.
6 Without her help, I would never have had enough money to buy a flat. I .... probably still be living at home!

[... / 6]

▶ **Find this difficult? Look back at grammar reference p. 152.**

EXPRESSING REGRETS

Complete the sentences using *should've / shouldn't have* and the correct form of the verbs in the box.

book	eat	post	say	tell	work

1 It's your birthday? You .... me.
2 She was really upset afterwards! I .... anything about her haircut!
3 My parents were furious when they saw the photos! I knew I .... them on the Web!
4 They're completely full! We .... in advance.
5 I feel really sick. I .... so much earlier.
6 He's so lazy! I saw him chatting on the phone earlier – when he ....

[... / 6]

▶ **Find this difficult? Look back at grammar reference p. 152.**

-*ing* FORMS AND *to*-INFINITIVES

Choose the correct form.
1 I'm really glad I gave up *smoking / to smoke.*
2 We're hoping *moving / to move* into a bigger place.
3 I tried to explain, but he refused *listening / to listen.*
4 I look forward to *hear / hearing* from you soon.
5 The government promised *to cut / cutting* taxes if they were re-elected, but they haven't done it yet!
6 I seem to spend my whole life *to work / working*!
7 I was caught *cheating / to cheat* in an exam!
8 Research has failed *finding / to find* any link between mobile phones and memory loss.

[... / 8]

▶ **Find this difficult? Look back at grammar reference p. 153.**

DEFINING RELATIVE CLAUSES

Correct the mistake in each of the sentences.
1 He's someone who music was ahead of its time.
2 Yalta is which they held a big meeting after the war.
3 She was a nurse which set up her own hospital.
4 She was an activist campaigned for women's rights.
5 The story was written around 500BC, during the time which Persia and Greece were at war.
6 We started living together – and that's I realised how different we were!
7 That's the house where my mum used to live in.

[... / 7]

▶ **Find this difficult? Look back at grammar reference p. 154.**

REPORTING VERBS

Complete the sentences with the correct form of the verbs in the box.

apologise	deny	threaten	insist on
offer	persuade	recommend	warn

1 I tried to .... him to go and see a doctor about it, but he didn't listen!
2 I .... you not to trust him, but you didn't listen!
3 The doctor .... that I take a week off work.
4 After I complained, they .... to refund me in full.
5 She's so stubborn. She always .... doing things her own way!
6 Now we've split up, my ex-boyfriend .... to post personal pictures of me on the web. It's horrible.
7 I'm sure he's having an affair, but whenever I ask him about it, he just .... everything.
8 If she really wants to make up, she'll have to .... first. She's the one in the wrong – not me!

[... / 8]

▶ Find this difficult? Look back at grammar reference p. 154.

FORMING WORDS

Complete the sentences with the correct forms of the words in CAPITALS.

1 He was .... president last year. ELECTION
2 My son has developed an .... to eggs. ALLERGIC
3 He's got a rare skin disease. It doesn't hurt or itch, but it is .... CURE
4 It's an amazing gadget – and it made its .... a millionaire. CREATE
5 Have you checked the ....? Maybe it's not plugged in properly. CONNECT
6 I got terrible food .... while I was backpacking. POISONOUS
7 I chose this car because it's more .... friendly than my old one. ENVIRONMENT
8 He lost his first big boxing match, but he's still only young and he showed real .... BRAVE
9 Bird Flu is incredibly .... – but only for birds! INFECTION
10 Thank you so much for all your .... GENEROUS

[... / 10]

COLLOCATIONS

Match the verbs with the words they go with.

1	develop	a	the computer
2	feel	b	a day trip
3	stamp	c	a horse
4	bribe	d	a vaccine
5	restart	e	your passport
6	fall off	f	trees
7	save	g	the crash
8	survive	h	the officials
9	go on	i	someone's life
10	plant	j	sick

[... / 10]

▶ Find this difficult? Re-read units 13–16 in the Vocabulary Builder for more information on collocation.

VOCABULARY

Complete the texts by choosing the correct words.

We had an awful journey. We ¹m...... the first train from the main station because we were waiting on the wrong ²p...... . Then the next train was ³de...... for ages! We heard it was because of some kind of animal on the ⁴l...... . Because of that, we ended up missing our flight. We then had to spend ages ⁵ha...... around at the airport. Oh, and Lawrence got stopped going through ⁶se......, which was horrible as well.

After growing ⁷st...... for several years, the market for hi-tech gadgets is now in ⁸de...... . However, the latest mobile from Korea will surely change all that and will have people rushing to ⁹up...... their phones. The G999 is greener and more ¹⁰en...... - efficient, but still very ¹¹str...... and easy to use. Plus, it has a very cool design.

Patient complains that she has been feeling ¹²di...... lately and has also been getting terrible ¹³mig...... . Seems to be ¹⁴u...... a lot of stress at work. Also suffers from high blood ¹⁵p...... .

[... / 15]

 [Total ... /80]

01 WRITING
INTRODUCING YOURSELF

SPEAKING

Work in pairs. Discuss these questions:
- Have you ever had a pen friend or have you ever written to anybody in a different country?
- How did you get in touch?
- What can you remember about them?

VOCABULARY Free-time activities

A Match the words in the box to the pictures.

aerobics	kick-boxing	waterskiing
trekking	karaoke	gardening

B Work in groups of three. Discuss these questions:
- Which of these activities have you done? When? Did you enjoy them?
- Are there any you would like to try sometime in the future?
- Are there any you really do not want to try? Why not?

WRITING Introducing yourself

A Read this Internet advert from a person looking for pen friends. Would you write to Kay. Why? / Why not?

Kay

I'm 22 and I'm from Malaysia. I can write in English, Malay and Mandarin. I'm really into sports and love swimming, surfing and kick-boxing. I'm quite keen on aerobics, dancing and karaoke as well.

B Below is a reply to Kay. Complete the message with the words in the box.

about	also	as well	in	on
quite	really	to	which	who

⬤⬤◯

To   kaykoolkaye@hotmail.ml

Subject   Re: Hello there

Dear Kay,

I saw your advert looking for a pen friend ¹......................... the Worldwide Pen Friends website and I would like to start writing ²......................... you. Let me tell you a bit about myself. My name is Fernanda. I am a 17-year-old student from Chile, ³......................... in case you didn't know is in South America, next to Argentina, Bolivia and Peru. I am from the capital, Santiago. I live with my parents and my sister, ⁴......................... is a year younger than me. I have one more year at school and then I'd like to become a fitness instructor. I ⁵......................... love surfing, swimming and waterskiing and I ⁶......................... like football as well. Apart from that, I like reading and watching movies. I ⁷......................... really like listening to music. I'm really into electronic music and I quite like jazz and hip-hop ⁸......................... . What kind of music are you into? Please write and tell me more ⁹......................... yourself. I'm sure we'll have a lot ¹⁰......................... common.

Fernanda

C Work in pairs. How much do you have in common with Fernanda?

KEY WORDS FOR WRITING
Too, also, as well, as well as

> **As *well*, *too* and *also* all mean the same thing. However, the way we use *as well* and *too* is different from the way we use *also*.**
>
> *I'm really into electronic music and I quite like jazz and hip-hop as well.*
> *I'm really into electronic music and I quite like jazz and hip-hop too.*
> *I'm really into electronic music and I also quite like jazz and hip-hop.*

A Which patterns can you see in the sentences above?

B Compete these sentences by putting the words in brackets into the correct place.
1 I'm really into computers, but I like going out and having fun. (too)
2 I like reading and writing and I do photography. (also)
3 I go to the theatre quite a lot, but I like staying in and reading. (as well)
4 I really love gardening and I'm into yoga. (also)
5 I do a lot of kick-boxing and I go running a lot. (as well)
6 I'm studying Art History and I'm doing a French course at the moment. (also)

> **As *well as* is sometimes used to join two ideas instead of using *and* or *but*. It is often used along with *as well*, *too* and *also*.**
>
> *As well as being really into electronic music, I quite like jazz and hip-hop too.*
> *As well as working long hours, I also like going out and having fun.*

C Rewrite 1–6 in exercise B so that each sentence starts with *As well as*.

GRAMMAR Common questions

A Put the words in the correct order to form questions people might ask when writing to pen friends for the first time.
1 do time usually free you do what your in?
....?
2 of what are into music you kind?
....?
3 favourite is your band who?
....?
4 saw was last what the you film?
....?
5 a favourite you do have writer?
....?
6 read was last what the you book?
....?
7 you do sport like?
....?
8 you got favourite have a team?
....?

B Work in pairs. Ask and answer the questions in exercise A.

PRACTICE

A You are going to a write a message to someone you would like to be pen friends with. The message should be around 150 words long. Before you start, underline any language from these pages you want to use. Try to remember it.

B Close your book and write the message. When you have finished, check that you remembered the underlined language correctly.

SPEAKING

Work in pairs. Discuss these questions:

- How often do you check your email?
- How many emails a day do you think you send?
- Who do you write to most often?
- Do you ever send emails in English? Who to? Why?

WRITING
Explaining why you are writing

> We generally begin emails with a line explaining why we are writing. To people we already know, we often begin with sentence starters like this:

Just a	quick short	one note email	to let you know to remind to ask to tell to say I'm sorry to say thank you to say congratulations

A **Complete each of the pairs of possible endings below with one sentence starter from the box.**

a ... you that next Monday is a public holiday.
  ... you to bring that book you said you'd lend me.
b ... I missed you while you were in Berlin.
  ... to hear you've been ill.
c ... for all your hard work organising the conference.
  ... for a lovely weekend.
d ... I arrived safely in Hong Kong.
  ... I'll be a bit late to the meeting tomorrow.
e ... if you could do me a big favour.
  ... if you could send me the photos you took at the party.
f ... you I can't make the meeting tomorrow.
  ... you how much we enjoyed the barbecue last night.
g ... on your exam results.
  ... to you both. The baby's beautiful.

B **Work in pairs. Write one more possible ending for each of the seven sentence starters in the box.**

C **Complete the three emails on the right by adding the correct whole sentences from exercise A.**

1

Hi Thorsten –

…………………………………………… . I'm planning to come to Germany next month on business and need to contact Matthias Einhoff before I arrive. I want to arrange a meeting with him to discuss a new project. The problem is, though, I've lost his contact details. Do you know anyone who might have them? I'd be really grateful if you could try and find out.

Anyway, I hope all is well – and hope to hear from you soon.

Many thanks,
Oliver

2

Hi Lars

…………………………………………… . I think you arrived the day after I had to go to Vienna for a friend's wedding. I was there for three days and had a great time, and then came back on the 27th and tried to call you, but I got a message saying the number wasn't available. Have you changed your mobile or lost it or something?

Anyway, I hope you had fun here and please let me know in advance next time you're planning to come here again. I would love to see you again. It's been a long time!

All the best,
Melanie

3

Hi Tatsu,

………………………………………… . I can't believe you got an A! You must be really pleased. Still, after all your hard work, you deserve it! I hope you're going to go out and celebrate. I've got my exams next month and am really worried about them. I just hope I do as well as you did.

Anyway, write to me when you have a free minute and tell me all your news.

Cheers for now,
Davorka

SPEAKING

Work in pairs. Discuss these questions:

• Have you ever lost anyone's contact details? How? Did you manage to get them back again?
• Have you ever been to a wedding? When? Whose?

GRAMMAR Leaving out words

> When we add information to a sentence using *and / or*, we often leave words out if they have already been used. We assume the missing words are understood by the reader.
>
> ....
>
> *I hope this is OK with you and (I hope this) won't cause too many problems.*

A **Decide which words have been left out of sentences 1–4.**

1 I'm planning to come to Germany next month on business and really need to contact Matthias Einhoff before I arrive.

2 I'll talk to Rose on Thursday and ask her what I missed, but please let me know if there's anything urgent I need to do or know about before then.

3 I've got my exams coming up next month and am already really worried about them.

4 Have you changed your mobile or lost it or something?

B **Rewrite each of the groups of sentences below as one sentence. Link your ideas using *and / or*. Leave out any words you think are unnecessary.**

1 We left Sydney on Friday night. We arrived in Hong Kong on Saturday morning.

....

2 I really want to send one of the photos to my mum. I want to burn some of the other photos onto a CD.

....

3 Don't worry about missing class tomorrow. Don't worry about taking time off if you need to.

....

4 Don't feel you have to wear a suit to the party tonight. Don't feel you have to bring a present.

....

5 I am going to Rome tomorrow. I am going to Pisa on Friday, so I won't be at the meeting on Thursday. I won't be at work for the rest of this week.

....

6 I thought the story was great. I thought the acting was really good, but I didn't really like the ending. I didn't really like some of the songs.

....

VOCABULARY Ending emails

> The way we end emails depends on who we are writing to. Some endings are more common for formal emails; some are more common for informal ones.

A **Look at these nine different ways of ending emails. Work in pairs. Discuss which endings you could use:**

• in business emails
• in emails to acquaintances
• in emails to close friends / family members

Kind regards
Yours faithfully
Many thanks
Love
All the best
Yours sincerely
Lots of love
Cheers for now
Yours

B **Work in pairs. Think of the letters and emails that you send. Which endings in exercise A could you use if you wrote them in English? Say as much as you can about who the emails are to, and which endings you would use.**

PRACTICE

Write four short emails. Begin each one with a sentence from *Writing: explaining why you are writing*. Try to write two informal emails, and two more formal ones. Use as much of the language from these pages as you can.

SPEAKING

You are going to read a short story written for an exam. It starts with the line: *It was dangerous, but I knew I had to do it.*

Work in pairs. Discuss these questions:
*   Based on this first line, think of four possible things that the writer was about to do.
*   How do you think each of these four stories might then develop?

WRITING A story

The four sentences a–d below all come from the story. Check you understand the words in **bold**. Then answer the questions.
1 What do you think is the connection between the sentences?
2 What order would you expect them to happen in?

a I could feel the wind **rushing** past me as I fell.
b I **floated** slowly down.
c I moved my feet closer to the **edge** and looked down!
b Eventually, I pulled the **cord**.

GRAMMAR Narrative tenses

A **Do you remember how to use the past simple, the past continuous and the past perfect? Look back at the grammar reference on pp. 136–137 to check.**

B **Now read the story and put the words in brackets into the correct form.**

It was dangerous, but I knew I had to do it. If there is one thing I love, it's a challenge. I moved my feet closer to the edge and looked down! I was just about to jump when it suddenly hit me! I was really going to do it! Nobody had believed me when I [1]........................... (say) I would do it, but there I was.

I took a few deep breaths, it was a very long way to the ground! Everyone else [2]........................... (seem) so relaxed, but my heart [3]........................... (beat) like crazy. Just as I [4]........................... (think) about maybe changing my mind, the voice behind me [5]........................... (scream), "Go! Go! Go!" - so I jumped. Suddenly, the panic and the fear just disappeared. I [6]........................... (really / fly)! I could feel the wind rushing past me as I fell.

Eventually, I pulled the cord on my parachute and it [7]........................... (open) - thank God! I floated slowly down, enjoying the incredible views. I [8]........................... (land) safely and knew at once that this was something I wanted to do again.

SPEAKING

Work in pairs. Discuss these questions:
*   Do you know anyone who has done a parachute jump?
*   Would you like to do one? Why? / Why not?
*   Would you like to any of these other dangerous things? Are there any you have done already?
    - go white-water rafting
    - go mountaineering
    - do a bungee-jump
    - go hang-gliding
    - hitch-hike round the world
    - explore caves

KEY WORDS FOR WRITING
Just about to, just as

> **Was / Were (just) about to + verb** is used to talk about something you were planning to do before something else happened. **When suddenly** often follows *just about to*.
> *I was just about to jump when it suddenly hit me!*
>
> ⋯⋯⋯⋯⋯⋯⋯⋯⋯⋯⋯⋯⋯⋯⋯⋯⋯⋯
>
> **Just as** is used to emphasise that two verbs happened at exactly the same time. It is more common to use the past continuous after *just as*, but the past simple is also possible.
> *Just as I was thinking about maybe changing my mind, the voice behind me screamed, 'Go! Go! Go!'*
> *Just as I turned on the computer, the lights went out.*

A Match the sentence halves.

1 I was just about to give up and stop looking
2 She was just about to go back to bed
3 We were just about to kiss
4 Just as we were all sitting down to eat dinner,
5 Just as the band appeared on the stage,
6 Just as I was walking out of the store,

a when she suddenly heard a strange noise downstairs.
b three men ran in, holding guns and pushed past me.
c when suddenly I saw something shiny in the dirt.
d there was a loud knock at the door.
e when my ex-boyfriend suddenly walked in.
f the woman next to me started screaming like crazy!

B Work in pairs. Think of one more possible ending for each sentence half in 1–6 in exercise A.

C Rewrite 1–5 as one sentence. Link your ideas using the words in brackets.

1 We were planning to leave. Then they gave us a table. (just about to)
   ....

2 I was planning to give up and go home. Then I saw him walking towards me. (just about to)
   ....

3 I was planning to go to bed. Then the doorbell rang. (just about to)
   ....

4 We were walking towards our car. A police car drove up and stopped right in front of us. (just as)
   ....

5 We were starting to think the holiday would be a disaster. At that moment, the sun came out. (just as)
   ....

VOCABULARY Ways of doing things

> Using descriptive verbs makes stories more exciting.
>
> ⋯⋯⋯⋯⋯⋯⋯⋯⋯⋯⋯⋯⋯⋯⋯⋯⋯⋯
>
> *The voice behind me screamed, 'Go! Go! Go!'*

A Match the descriptive verbs and definitions.

1 say very quietly   slam
2 move very quietly / slowly grab
3 look at something a long time shout
4 close / put something angrily / loudly stare
5 say very loudly   rush
6 run / go in a hurry   creep
7 take hold with your hand suddenly whisper

B Take turns acting the words in exercise A. Can your partner guess what you are doing?

C Complete the sentences with a word from exercise A.

1 The train was leaving in ten minutes, so we .... to the station.
2 He ran out and .... the door shut behind him.
3 I .... at the paper. I couldn't believe it!
4 Just as I was leaving, someone .... my bag and ran off.
5 It was chaos. Everyone was screaming and ....
6 I .... down the stairs trying not to make a noise.
7 I tried to .... the answer to my friend, but the teacher heard me.

PRACTICE

A Look at the exam questions below and choose one. Write a story that starts with one of the following lines:

• It was three in the morning when the phone rang.
• It was dangerous, but I knew I had to do it.

Or write a story that ends with one of the following lines:

• ... and that was the best day of my life.
• ... and that the worst day of my life.

B Spend five minutes planning your story. Then work in pairs to discuss your ideas. Can you think of any ways to make the story more exciting?

C Write a story of between 150 and 180 words.

SPEAKING

Check you understand the words in bold. Then discuss the questions in pairs:

- When was the last time you **did a friend a favour**? What was it?
- When was the last time you **asked a friend to do you a favour**? What was it? How did you ask? What did they say?
- Do you **owe** anyone **a favour** at the moment?

GRAMMAR Requests

When we ask people to do things for us, we use modal verbs like *can* and *could*. We also sometimes use past tenses to sound polite. However, we also make questions longer using typical sentence starters.

For example: *I was wondering if you could help me* is more polite than *I wonder if you can help me*. Less polite than either is *Can you help me?*

A Match the sentence beginnings and endings to make requests.

1 I was wondering …
2 Do you think you could …
3 Is there any way …
4 Could you do me a favour …

a and pay for it now and then I'll pay you back later?
b if you could possibly send me some information about the French courses you offer?
c you could translate this letter for me?
d give him a ring and speak to him about it?

B Work in pairs. Look at the four requests in exercise A and underline the parts of each that can be re-used in other questions. Then discuss these questions:

- Which of the four question starters is the most formal?
- What form of the verb follows each of the question starters?

C Write a different ending for each of the four question starters in exercise A.

WRITING

A Read the four short emails. Then work in pairs. Discuss these questions. Do not fill in the gaps yet.

- Do you think all the requests are reasonable?
- Are there any you would not ask? Why?

1

Dear Sir/Madam,

I have already a........................... a reservation under the name of Rosario for the 18th–20th January. Would it be possible to stay an extra night on Saturday 21st January? If not, do you b........................... you could inform me as c........................... as possible as I would then need to make other arrangements.

Many thanks.

Yours faithfully,
Sandra Rosario

2

Hi Zarina,

Just a quick one to a........................... thanks for the email. I love the photos! Is there any b........................... you could print them out, though, as my printer isn't very good and I'd c........................... to frame the photos and put them on my wall?

Michaele

3

Dear Margot,

Long time, no see. How are you? I've been very a........................... finishing my final dissertation for my degree, so I haven't been out much. I've attached it here. As your English is so good, could you do me a big b........................... and look through it carefully to check it's OK? I'd c........................... really grateful.

Cheers for now,
Olaf

4

Dear Mario,

Just a quick email to ᵃ.......................... you know when I'll be arriving in Milan. The flight gets in at 05.10 on Friday morning. Actually, I was ᵇ.......................... if you could possibly come and pick me up, if it's not too much trouble? I'd be really grateful as I'll have loads of luggage.

ᶜ.......................... the best,
Andre

B Complete the emails with one word in each gap.

KEYWORDS FOR WRITING *as*

We saw in *Writing 02* on pp. 122–123 that *as* is sometimes used to mean *while*. *As* is also commonly used to mean *because*:

As your English is so good, could you do me a big favour and look through it carefully to check it's OK? I'd be really grateful as I'll have loads of luggage.

Use the ideas below to write five requests and say thanks. Add reasons using *as* and then add your own ideas. For example:
look after the kids? / really grateful
Is there any way you could look after the kids tonight as we really need a night out together on our own? We'd be really grateful.

1 send me another copy of the invoice / Many
2 give me a lift? / really grateful
3 stay at your place for a few days? / really grateful
4 extend the deadline for my essay? / incredibly grateful
5 complete the work by Thursday / thanks

VOCABULARY *as ... as* expressions

As is also used in certain common expressions
....
Do you think you could inform me as soon as possible?

A **Put the words in the correct order to make six expressions.**
1 as as possible soon
2 as know far I as
3 can as quickly as you
4 you as soon as hear
5 arrive soon you as as
6 as the concerned as is far hotel

B **Complete the sentences with the expressions in exercise A.**
a Do you think you could email me .... any news as I'm a bit worried about him?
b When you arrive, you need to go .... to Terminal B as there isn't much time for the transfer between fights.
c Give me a call .... at the station and I'll come and pick you up. Just wait outside the main entrance.
d ...., it's all booked and confirmed. Is there any way you could sort out the car hire, though, as I don't have a driving licence?
e Could you let me know .... whether you can come or not as we need to make the booking?
f ...., the shuttle bus runs all night, but perhaps you should ring the tourist information office to check.

PRACTICE

A **Work in pairs. Write two short emails making requests. One should be to a hotel or company and the other should be to your partner. Use as much language from this writing unit as you can.**

B **Swap your emails with your partner. Write a reply to each one.**

SPEAKING

Work in groups. Discuss these questions:
- What things need doing when you organise the following?
  - a meeting
  - a surprise party
  - a wedding
  - a group excursion
  - a conference
- Which is the most difficult thing to organise? Why?
- Have you ever been involved in organising any of these things? How easy was it?
- Did you have to make any changes or compromises?

WRITING

Fourteen 15-year-old schoolchildren are going on an exchange visit to Valencia, Spain. One of them, Simon Holden, has written to the leader of the organisation that is arranging the trip (Ms Roberts) to ask for a change to the programme.

A Read the letter. If you were Ms Roberts, would you agree to the change? Why? / Why not?

B What ways does Simon Holden use to try and persuade Ms Roberts?

C Translate the words in **bold** into your language. Then write new example sentences using the words.

Dear Ms Roberts,

I am writing **on behalf of** the students who are going on the trip to Valencia in October.

Firstly, can we say thanks for all your hard work organising the trip. **On the whole**, it looks great and we are all really looking forward to it. However, we were wondering if we could possibly suggest one change. The Sunday after we arrive, there is a motorcycle Grand Prix in Cheste and ten of us would like to go.

At the moment, we **are scheduled** to go to the zoo that day and are free after lunch. Although we are sure the zoo is really nice, it seems a shame to miss such a big event while we are there and Cheste is supposed to have a very special atmosphere. The four who are not interested in the motorcycling said they do not mind missing the zoo either. **Alternatively**, we could visit the zoo on Wednesday afternoon, which is currently free for shopping.

We can get public transport to the Grand Prix as it is only 30km from Valencia. Obviously, we would pay for any extra cost, although we imagine you would have to come with us to supervise. We are **sorry if this causes any inconvenience**, but we are all really keen to go.

We really hope the change is possible and thanks again for all your work putting together the programme - we really appreciate it.

Yours sincerely,

Simon Holden

VOCABULARY *Programme*

In the letter the writer says thanks for *putting together the programme*. Complete the sentences with other collocations with *programme*.

include	swap
full	exciting
last-minute	

1 There's been a .... change to the programme.
2 We could .... some things round in the programme.
3 It is a very .... programme. Could we drop something and make room for some more free time?
4 It looks like a very .... programme of events.
5 In the end, we can't .... everything in the programme.

KEYWORDS FOR WRITING
However, although and *but*

However, although and *but* can all have a similar meaning, but they use different grammar.

A Look in the letter and find examples of the words. Then complete the rules 1–3. Did you notice how commas were used in the sentences?
1 .... and .... connect two parts of the same sentence. .... usually starts the sentence, but can come in the middle.
2 .... always connects to an idea in a previous sentence. It usually starts the second sentence, but it can come in the middle or at the end of the second sentence.

B Complete the sentences.
1 .... it would be nice to visit the museum, we don't have enough time.
2 It's a very full programme. ...., there is space for one more visit on Monday afternoon.
3 We would really like to go to the exhibition, ... we were wondering if we could go on Tuesday instead of Sunday.
4 Thanks again for your help. .... we realise these last minute changes are inconvenient, we are sure they will improve the programme.
5 On the whole, everything seems to be very clear. I do have couple of queries, ...

C Punctuate these sentences correctly.
1 Giving all the participants a souvenir is a nice idea but it might be a bit too expensive.
2 Although I personally like rock music some of the older people coming might prefer something different.
3 The menu for the dinner looks great however I think we should have a better option for vegetarians.

PRACTICE

A Work in pairs. Plan either a day trip round a city you know or a surprise party / event for a friend. Write out the programme of events and times.

B Swap your programme with another pair. Write a letter suggesting a change to their programme. Explain why you want to make the change and how it could be done. Use as much of the language from these pages as you can.

SPEAKING

Work in pairs. Discuss these questions:
- Look at the pictures below. What kind of age group do you think the activities / places are good for?
- What other

  3-6   7-11   12-15   16-18
- What facilities are there for young people where you live? Do you think there are enough facilities? Why? / Why not?

WRITING

A Read the report on the facilities for young people in a residential area called Rocafort. Work in pairs. Discuss the questions.
- Do you think the area is better or worse for young people than where you live? Why?
- Can you think of any other services or facilities that could be provided for the young people of Rocafort?

B Look at the report. Underline all the examples of the Passive that you can find. Then work in pairs. Discuss these questions.
- Why is the passive used in writing reports?
- Do you use the passive in this way in your language?

C Which three ways of giving advice / recommendations were used in the report?

Current provision
Currently, there are only a limited number of things for young people to do in Rocafort. As a result, the main free time activity is simply hanging out in the street.

Sports
There is a small outdoor sports centre, which has a football pitch, a basketball court and two tennis courts. In addition, there is a swimming pool, although this is only open from July till the first week in August. Nearby, there is a small park with a climbing frame and swings.

Other activities
The village has a social centre which runs classes in dance and capoeira two days a week. For younger children, there are painting classes. This centre also has a small cinema screen and auditorium. However, this is rarely used.

Recommendations
As far as classes are concerned, the council could provide a wider range for all age groups. For example, they could do drama or run music groups. More could be done with the cinema: why not show regular films on Friday evenings or Saturday mornings?

In terms of the sports facilities, the council could provide more organised teams and subsidise coaching sessions. Finally, the council should consider covering the swimming pool so it could be used in winter.

VOCABULARY Describing facilities

A Complete the sentences with words from the report in the correct form.

1 There is only a .... selection of classes you can go to.
2 The problem is that there's nowhere safe for kids to .... out with their friends.
3 There are several squash .... and table tennis tables.
4 The school .... a drama club in the evenings. Anyone can go.
5 There is a sauna at the sports centre, but for some reason it is .... used.
6 The cinema could put on a .... range of films.
7 More could be .... with the existing facilities: why not open them in the evenings?
8 The government should .... swimming pools so everyone can afford to use them.
9 The council should .... providing free sports equipment.

B Work in pairs. Discuss these questions.

- Where do kids hang out in your town / area? Is it a problem?
- Does the government subsidise anything in your area?
- Are there any places / facilities you know which are under used? How could more be done with them?
- Is there anything your local council should consider doing?

KEY WORDS FOR WRITING
Referring to things

We often refer to particular things in a report using *as far as X is / are concerned* or *in terms of X.*

As far as classes are concerned, the council could provide a wider range for all age groups.

In terms of the sports facilities, the council could provide more organised teams.

A Match 1–6 with the endings in a–f.

1 As far as public transport in the area was concerned,
2 In terms of the canteen,
3 As far as the hotel facilities are concerned,
4 In terms of security,
5 As far as the French classes are concerned,
6 In terms of the park,

a the number of students should be reduced.
b the owners should consider building a swimming pool.
c more could be done to stop robberies.
d most people are satisfied with the quality of food.
e there's a good range of play equipment for younger kids.
f many complained that the trains do not run late enough.

B Think of the area where you live. Write endings for these sentence starters explaining how people feel or how things could be different.

1 As far as public transport is concerned,
....
2 As far as schools are concerned,
....
3 In terms of sports facilities,
....
4 In terms of things for young people,
....

C Work in pairs. Discuss your sentences from exercise B. Does your partner agree?

PRACTICE

Write a short report on one of the following.
- Facilities for young people where you live
- Public transport where you live
- Your school / university / workplace

Talk about the current situation and make some recommendations about how things could be improved.

SPEAKING

You are going to read a short essay about cars. First, work in pairs. Discuss these questions:

- What kind of car do you / the people in your family have?
- Do you have a favourite kind of car?
- What is the traffic like where you live?
- Do you use the car much? To go where?

WRITING

A Look at the essay title below. Write three reasons why people might agree with the statement in the title, and three reasons why people might disagree.

> 'Cars are no longer the most effective means of transport.' How far do you agree with this statement?

Cars are good because...	Cars aren't good because...
1.	1.
2.	2.
3.	3.

B Work in pairs. Compare your ideas. Then discuss if you agree with the statements. Why? / Why not?

C Read the essay. Does the writer think the same as you?

D Complete the gaps with the words in the box.

obviously	However	Otherwise	Secondly
Firstly	thirdly	In conclusion	Personally

The number of cars on our roads has increased a lot over the last twenty years. Traffic is getting worse every year and we are slowly running out of oil. As such, it is worth asking if cars are still the most effective way to travel. [1]........................, I do not believe they are.

There are several reasons why cars are so popular. [2]........................, they allow one to get directly from A to B. [3]........................, people feel comfortable in their cars and [4]........................, the car industry is a large employer and has influence with the government.

[5]........................, in the long term, we [6]........................ need to find alternatives to the car. [7]........................, we will end up unable to move round our cities, road deaths will increase and there will be terrible environmental damage. It is time to limit car use and to encourage greater use of public transport and bicycles.

[8]........................, while car users may want to continue using their vehicles, other options must be explored more fully.

E The list below contains seven pieces of advice. Find examples in the essay of where the writer follows each piece.

DOS AND DON'TS IN ACADEMIC WRITING

1 Show you know why the question is being asked by giving examples of current trends or problems connected to it.
2 Make your own opinion clear in your introduction.
3 Allow space for points of view you disagree with.
4 Explain why you disagree with them.
5 Use paragraphs.
6 Avoid using *you*. Use impersonal forms like *people* or *one*.
7 Don't use contractions like *it'll* or *that'd*.

GRAMMAR Describing trends

> We usually begin introductions to essays by describing current trends (or problems) connected to the title. To describe a change that happened before now, but which has present results, use the present perfect simple.
> *The number of cars on our roads has increased a lot over the last twenty years.*

> To describe a trend that is not finished, we usually use the present continuous.
> *Traffic is getting worse every year and we are slowly running out of oil.*

A **Complete these sentences by putting the verbs in brackets into the correct form. Then underline the time expressions.**

1 Public transport .... (improve) dramatically over the last few years. Despite this, more and more people .... (drive) into the city centre to work every day.

2 Crime .... (get) worse and worse at the moment. The government .... (recently / increase) the amount of money available to the police, but this has not made much difference.

3 It is said that children's behaviour these days .... (got) worse and worse. Many parents today seem unconcerned about these problems, whilst society as a whole .... (stop) caring about the young.

4 The number of women working .... (increase) a lot in recent years and more and more women .... (now / become) bosses.

5 Over the last few years, there .... (be) several stories about people helping loved ones to die and euthanasia .... (become) a major issue. As such, several pressure groups .... (now / call) for a change in the law.

B **Work in pairs. Discuss which trends are the same in your country – or how they are different.**

C **Write similar introductions to those in exercise A for the two essay titles below.**

> 'We need the death penalty. It stops people from committing terrible crimes.' Discuss.

> 'Fast food is having a terrible effect on the health of the nation. As such, it should be banned.' Do you agree?

KEYWORDS *As such*

> To introduce results or conclusions, we often use *as such*. It means 'Because what has just been said is true.' It usually begins a sentence and is followed by a comma.

> *Traffic is getting worse and we are slowly running out of oil. As such, it is worth asking if cars are still the most effective way to travel.*

A **Match sentences 1–5 with the results / conclusions.**

1 Many people nowadays are too busy to meet potential partners in the traditional way.

2 The war had become one disaster after another.

3 Over the last few years, the company has decided to do a lot more e-marketing.

4 More and more people are suffering from depression.

5 The school had the best results in the country last year.

a As such, sales have grown dramatically.

b As such, it is important to learn from its success.

c As such, Internet dating is growing in popularity.

d As such, the decision was made to bring the army home.

e As such, research into the factors affecting happiness has become more and more important.

B **Work in pairs. Think of one more possible sentence you could follow 1–5 with. Start each one with *As such*.**

PRACTICE

A **You are going to write an essay of between 150 and 180 words based on the title below. Work in pairs. Discuss possible reasons why people might agree or disagree with the statement – and then discuss your own opinions.**

> 'Some sports and entertainment stars earn far too much money.' How far do you agree with this statement?

B **Plan the content of each of your paragraphs. Use the model text on the previous page to help you.**

C **Write the essay. Use as much language from this unit as you can.**

SPEAKING

Work in groups. Discuss these questions:
- Which do you prefer: watching films at the cinema, on DVD, on TV or downloaded from the internet? What is good / bad about each one?
- How do you decide what film you want to watch? Do you ever read review?
- Have you ever been given a recommendation which turned out to be a bad one?

VOCABULARY Describing films

A Match the words in the box to the descriptions 1–6.

moving	gripping	entertaining
uplifting	funny	scary

1 I couldn't stop laughing. It's great.
2 It's so sad! I was in tears at the end of the film.
3 Some scenes make you jump out of your seat and it could give you nightmares!
4 It has lots of action and a great soundtrack.
5 Although she has a difficult life, the film leaves you feeling really happy and positive. It's an inspiring story.
6 It's really exciting – you just don't know what's going to happen next.

B Complete the sentences with the adjectives in the box.

acted	chosen	directed	filmed	written

1 The soundtrack contains several well-.......................... songs, which really remind you of the time the film is set in.
2 The main character is superbly .... by Daniel Day-Lewis.
3 It has a very well-.......................... script, full of jokes.
4 The mountains and countryside are beautifully ....
5 The film is brilliantly .... by Steven Spielberg.

C Choose four adjectives from exercises A and B. Use them to tell a partner about films you know.

WRITING

You are going to read a short article recommending three films.

A Read the text and answer the questions.
1 Have you seen the films? Do you agree with the descriptions?
2 Would you like to see the films? Why? / Why not?
3 Does the choice of films offer 'something for everyone'?

B Work in pairs. Answer the questions.
1 What tense is used to describe the plot?
2 Are you told the whole plot? Why not?
3 When does the writer give opinions about the film?

KEY WORDS FOR WRITING
While and *during*

> **While** and **during** both introduce a period of time when something else happened. They have different grammar:
>
> ....
>
> **during** + noun
> *It tells the story of an Italian man and his son who are sent to a concentration camp during the Second World War.*
>
> ....
>
> **while** + clause
> *While they are there, the father distracts the boy from all the bad things that are happening.*

Complete the sentences using *while* or *during*.
1 The film takes place .... The Gulf War in 1990.
2 They fall in love .... she is planning his wedding!
3 .... he's not looking, he puts a drug in her drink.
4 .... the night, the toys come alive.
5 Lots of things happen .... the journey that bring the family closer together.
6 .... the parents are away, he has to defend the house against robbers.

Something for everyone!

Life is Beautiful
(La vita è bella)
★ ★ ★ ★ ★

This is a strangely uplifting film directed by and starring Roberto Benigni. It tells the story of an Italian man and his son who are sent to a concentration camp during the Second World War. While they are there, the father distracts the boy from all the bad things that are happening by turning their life into a game. The film has everything: it's funny, moving, superbly acted and beautifully filmed.

Spellbound
★ ★ ★ ★ ★

This is a marvellous documentary about the national spelling competition for children which takes place every year in America. The film follows the fortunes of eight of the contestants before and during the final in Washington. The kids come from a fascinating range of backgrounds and are often both funny and inspiring. The film is also quite gripping, as you really want to find out who will be the champion speller!

Batman Begins
★ ★ ★ ★ ★

If you want a thoroughly entertaining film that you don't have to think about too much, then try *Batman Begins*. It features a well-chosen cast and stars Christian Bale, Katie Holmes and Liam Neeson. It also stars Cillian Murphy, who is particularly brilliant as the scary villain, the Scarecrow. The film explores the origins of the Batman story and is incredibly well-written. A great plot and lots of action keeps you entertained throughout the whole film.

GRAMMAR
Adding information after the noun

A **Can you remember how 1–3 were written as one sentence in the articles?**
 1 This is a strangely uplifting film. It is directed by and stars Roberto Benigni.
 2 This is a marvellous documentary. It is about the national spelling competition
 3 It also stars Cillian Murphy. He is particularly brilliant as the scary villain, the Scarecrow.

> We often make a text shorter by adding information after a noun using an *-ed / -ing* participle, a prepositional phrase, or relative clause.

B **Rewrite 1–6 as one sentence using each method twice.**
 1 This a moving love story. It's about a disabled woman.

 ....

 2 This is a comedy action film. It stars Akshay Kumar.

 ....

 3 The film is directed by Lasse Hallstrom. He also directed *The Cider House Rules*.

 ....

 4 The film is set in a small town. The story happens during the mayoral election.

 ....

 5 The main character is a brilliant but lonely doctor. The part is superbly played by Jennifer Jenkins.

 ....

 6 The documentary follows the lives of four couples. The couples have recently emigrated to Australia.

 ....

PRACTICE

A film magazine has a competition inviting readers to send in review of three films. Each week they publish one winner. Write your entry for one of the choices below. It should be between 150 and 180 words.
Three best films of last year
Three films for a Sunday afternoon with the family
Three classics
Three films for three different moods

01 MY FIRST CLASS

QUESTION FORMATION

The present simple

Present simple questions ask about present states, habits and regular activities.

Do you enjoy your job?
How much *do they earn*?
How often *does he come* here?

Questions with *be* are followed by adjectives or nouns.

Am I right?
Whose *is this book*?
Is your sister married?
Are they ready to go?

Present continuous

Present continuous questions ask about unfinished, temporary things at the moment. They also ask about future arrangements.

Are you working or *studying*?
Which course *is he doing*?
What time *are we meeting*?
Where *are they living* now?

Past simple

Past simple questions ask about past states, habits and regular activities and events – often with past time expressions.

What time *did you leave* the party last Friday?
Why *did she leave* her last job?
How long *did they live* in Germany?

Questions followed by adjectives in the past use *was / were*.

Were you angry about it?
Was she upset?

Present perfect simple

Present perfect questions ask about general experiences before now. They also often go with the adverb *yet*.

Have you been here before?
Has he finished his degree yet?
Have your parents met your new boyfriend yet?

Present perfect continuous

Present perfect continuous questions ask about actions that started in the past and are still continuing.

How long *have you been working* there?
How long *has she been talking* on the phone now?
What *have they been doing* all day?

be going to

Be going to questions ask about future plans.
What *are you going to do* after you graduate?
When *is he going to arrive* back in England?

Exercise 1

Complete the questions with the correct question words.

1 .... are you working these days?
2 .... are you laughing?
3 .... are you going to do after the course?
4 ....'s going to look after your cats while you're away?
5 .... coat is this?
6 .... do you visit your grandparents?
7 .... did you go to bed last night?
8 .... did you pay for your car?
9 .... have you been playing the guitar?

Exercise 2

Match the questions 1–9 in exercise 1 with the answers a–i.

a I don't really know. I still haven't really decided yet.
b I can't remember, but I know it was late!
c I got it second-hand. It was £2,000.
d It's nothing. I just suddenly remembered something. Sorry!
e Oh, thanks. It's mine. I almost forgot that!
f A friend is going to come every day and feed them.
g Well, I started in 1990, so it's nearly 20 years now.
h Not as often as I should! Maybe twice a year.
i I'm still at the same place I was at last time, actually.

Exercise 3

Correct the mistakes in all the questions in 1–7.

1 A: What kind of films you like?
   B: Anything really. The only films I don't like are musicals and anything which is dubbed.
2 A: How's your part-time job go at the moment?
   B: Better thanks. I'm quite enjoying it now.
3 A: You're good at this. Did you play before?
   B: No, I haven't. It must just be beginners' luck!
4 A: Do you work on any projects at the moment?
   B: Not really. It's been quite boring at work recently.
5 A: Are you decided where you're going on holiday?
   B: Yes, Sicily.
6 A: How long is he learning Chinese, then?
   B: I think about 6 years. You'll have to ask him.
7 A: How did you and your wife first met?
   B: That's a long story!

Glossary

be away: if someone is away, they are in a different town or country on business or on holiday
second-hand: something which someone else owned before
feed: if you feed something, you give it food
dubbed: if an American film is dubbed, the actors speak in a different language to English. They are dubbed into French, etc

NARRATIVE TENSES

When we tell people about events that happened to us in the past, we use three main tenses: the past simple, the past continuous and the past perfect.

The past simple

Use the past simple to describe finished events that followed each other. These events are often linked together using the words *and, and then, after that, when, after, before*, etc.
I *heard* a noise and *turned* round to see what it *was* and then I just *tripped* and *fell* and *hurt* my knee.

On Friday, we *met* and *had* a coffee. After that, we *did* some shopping and then we *went* home.

You probably know the most useful irregular verbs already. It is best to learn any new ones when you learn a new verb. Use the list in the *Vocabulary Builder* to help you.

The past continuous

Use the past continuous to show an action or event was unfinished when another action happened. The verbs are often linked together using the words *and, when* or *while*.
I *was walking* down the street when I heard a noise behind me and I turned round and tripped and fell.
(= I fell before I got to the end of the street)

My parents met when *they were* both *working* in Nigeria. (= They continued to work there after they met)

While I made the dinner, *she was* just *sitting* around watching TV. (= I finished making dinner before she stopped watching TV)

The past perfect

Use the past perfect to emphasise that something finished before another past action, past event or time already mentioned. The past perfect is very common after the verbs *realise, find out, discover* and *remember*. The past perfect often goes with the words *by the time, before, after* and *already*.
I suddenly remembered I *hadn't turned* the cooker *off*, so I went back home, but by the time I got there, *the kitchen had already caught fire*.

She found out it wasn't the first time *he'd stolen* something from her.

When I unpacked my bag, I realised *I'd forgotten* to bring any underwear!

These are not the only uses of these tenses. You will meet some other examples later on in the course.

Exercise 1

Match sentence endings a–f to six of the sentence starters 1–12.
1 I was really surprised he failed the exam because
2 I asked them to turn the music down because
3 He didn't post the letter because
4 He didn't post the letter, even though
5 We were running out of petrol, so
6 We ran out of petrol, so
7 When she told us she was thinking of becoming a model,
8 I think she got upset because
9 By the time we got there, the show had already started, so
10 When we got there, the show was just starting, so
11 I met my girlfriend while
12 I met my girlfriend and then

a ...... we had to look for a garage.
b ...... he'd studied a lot.
c ...... we went to a friend's for dinner.
d ...... we didn't really miss much.
e ...... I'd reminded him at least three times.
f ...... we were laughing at her.

Exercise 2

Complete the stories by putting the verbs in the brackets into the correct tense.

1 This embarrassing thing [1]........................ (happen) to me last week. I [2]........................ (go) to the cinema with my best friend and her new boyfriend, who I [3]........................ (never/meet) before. Anyway, we [4]........................ (watch) a horror movie and my friend and I usually reach for each other's hands when a scary part comes on. At one point, I [5]........................ (try) to grab my friend's hand – but I [6]........................ (grab) her boyfriend's instead! I felt awful about it!

2 It was really stupid. I [7]........................ (walk) along the road, and I [8]........................ (see) a man arguing with a woman on the other side of the road, and I [9]........................ (stare) at them, not looking where [10]........................ (go) and I [11]........................ (walk) straight into a box which someone [12]........................ (left) in the street. I [13]........................ (fall over) and I [14]........................ (hit) my head really hard. The man and the woman [15]........................ (stop) arguing and [16]........................ (start) laughing at me. I felt like such an idiot!

> ### Glossary
>
> **run out of:** if you run out of something, you use it and so you have no more of it
> **get upset:** if you get upset, you get angry or sad
> **grab:** if you grab something, you take it in a quick, sudden way
> **stare:** if you stare at something, you look for a long time at it

02 EMOTIONS

be, look, seem, etc.

A few verbs, called linking verbs, can be followed by an adjective on its own. These verbs are: *be, feel, look, seem, sound, taste* and *smell*.

You *sound depressed*. What's up?
Mmm. That *smells delicious*. What is it?

These verbs are also followed by *like* + noun, which means *the same as*, or *similar to*.

She *looks like a model*!
It *tastes* a bit *like chicken*.

These verbs can also be followed by *as if* or *like* + clause. Using *like* here is very common, but some people say it is wrong. In exams and writing it may be better to use *as if*.

You look *like you're in a very good mood*. How come?
I feel guilty. *I feel as if it's my fault*.

All the examples are in the simple tense. These verbs are sometimes also used in continuous tenses. There is no difference in meaning.

You're looking well!   =   You look well.
I'm feeling a bit ill.   =   I feel a bit ill.

Exercise 1

Correct the sentences which are incorrect.

1. It's quite frustrating in the class. It sometimes seems as if I'm the only person who wants to study and learn.
2. He was in shock. Honestly, he looked as he'd seen a ghost!
3. She sounded like quite upset the last time I spoke to her.
4. I had to tell him the bad news. I felt as if terrible afterwards.
5. I've only met him once, but he really annoyed me with the way he spoke about women. He seemed like an idiot to me.
6. Don't eat that. It tastes like disgusting.
7. She said the flight would cost €50 and the hotel €30 a night, which sounds like a really good deal.
8. Do you think this dress makes me look like fat?

> ### Glossary
>
> **tapping the table:** if you tap the table or the door, you hit it lightly and quickly
> **drives me mad:** if something drives you mad or crazy, it really annoys you
> **halfway through:** if something happens halfway through a film or a meeting or a class, it happens in the middle

−ed / −ing adjectives

Here are some more adjectives with two forms.

He wasn't very *amused*. / It's an *amusing* story.
I was *frightened*. / It was a *frightening* story.
I'm quite *annoyed* about it. / It's *annoying*.
I'm *confused*. / It's *confusing*.
I feel quite *relaxed*. / I had a *relaxing* holiday.
He was very *disappointed*. / It was *disappointing*.
I was *shocked* by the news. / It's *shocking*.
I was a bit *embarrassed*. / My parents can be *embarrassing*.
I was *exhausted*. / I've had an *exhausting* week.
I'm *excited* about it. / It should be an *exciting* game.
I felt a bit *frustrated*. / It's *frustrating* learning to windsurf.
He's feeling *depressed*. / The news is *depressing*!

Here are some pairs of adjectives that do not use both −ed / −ing.

scared / scary   upset / upsetting
stressed / stressful   calm / calming

Exercise 1

Complete the pairs of sentences with the adjectives in the box.

annoyed / annoying	confused / confusing
frustrated / frustrating	scared / scary
bored / boring	depressed / depressing
surprised / surprising	worried / worrying

1a Can you explain it again? I'm still a bit ....
1b The instructions for this camera are really ....
2a He's got a really .... habit of tapping the table with his finger all the time.
2b I'm a bit .... that he hasn't phoned me! He promised he'd ring me tonight.
3a This weather is really ....! It's so wet.
3b He's been .... for a while, but he refuses to go and see someone about it.
4a That film was so .... I jumped out of my seat about five times!
4b I can't look down. I'm .... of heights!
5a I'm .... we'll miss our flight.
5b The news of all these terrorist attacks is a bit ....
6a I was really .... when I arrived here. I didn't expect to see people living on the streets.
6b I thought the ending was really .... I mean, I didn't expect him to really be a ghost!
7a I get really .... when I can't say what I want to say. It drives me mad!
7b It's quite .... working there, because sometimes you know you could a better job, but you just don't have time!
8a It was so .... that I fell asleep halfway through the film, so I didn't see the end.
8b I'm ....! Can't we do something else?

The present continuous

Use the present continuous to talk about temporary, unfinished actions.

This weather's depressing! It's raining again.
Can I call you back later? *We're having dinner.*
I feel sorry for him. *He's losing his hair.* He's only 21!

To emphasise that something is temporary, use expressions such as *at the moment, currently, this week* and *this month*.

I'm reading a great book *at the moment.* I'll lend you it when I've finished it.

Use the present continuous to talk about things in the future that are already organised or arranged with other people.

I'm going out for dinner with a client on Friday.
They're moving to Boston next month.

Present simple and present continuous

Use the present simple to talk about habits or more permanent things.

I usually *go swimming* every day.
I *live* in Budapest.

We explain how often using adverbs such as *usually, often, sometimes, hardly ever, never.*

I *usually play* football on Wednesdays.

Some verbs are normally used in simple tenses even when the situation is temporary.

You *sound* exhausted. Were you out late last night?
I still *owe* my brother €100. He's a bit fed up about it.
I *love* this soup! It *tastes* fantastic. How did you make it?
A: They're doing building work outside our office. The noise is driving me mad. I *hate* it!
B: I know what you mean! They're doing the same in front of my house. It's really annoying.

Other verbs like this are:

agree	believe	belong	depend	disagree	doubt
forget	like	matter	mean	mind	need
own	prefer	realise	seem	suppose	want

Some other verbs are like this depending on the meaning.

I see you're interested in politics. You're reading the biography of Mao. (see = notice)
He's seeing someone at the moment, so he's happy. (see = have a girl / boyfriend)
I have a VW at the moment, but I'm thinking of buying a BMW. (have = own / possess)
They're having a meeting about it now. (have = do)
It's really hot. Open a window. (verb + adjective)
Sorry, *I'm* just *being* silly. (temporary / unusual behaviour)

Other verbs like this are: feel, think, taste

Exercise 1

Choose the correct form.

1 A: What are the hours like where you work?
   B: OK. *I'm usually just working / I usually just work* nine to five, but this month *I'm doing / I do* a lot of overtime because we've got a really tight deadline to meet, so *I'm working / I work* from nine in the morning till nine at night or even ten most days.
2 A: Where do you work?
   B: Well, *I'm normally working / I normally work* in the centre of town, but this week *I'm working / I work* from home, because *they do up / they are doing up* our office.
3 A: What does your job involve exactly?
   B: Just general office work, *I'm answering / I answer* the phone and *making / make* appointments for my boss, that kind of thing, but *we're holding / we hold* a conference in a couple of months, so at the moment *I'm sorting out / I sort out* lots of things for that as well.

Exercise 2

Find the five mistakes and correct them.

1 Can you phone back? I have dinner.
2 Ignore him. He's just being silly.
3 Is she seeing anyone at the moment?
4 I'm annoyed with him. He's still owing me money.
5 I don't need any help thanks. I just look.
6 I go to the shops. Do you want anything?
7 I'm preferring coffee, if you don't mind.
8 I love cycling. I belong to a local cycling club.

Exercise 3

Complete these sentences by putting the words in brackets into the correct place.

1 I have lots of free time, but I'm studying really hard because I have exams. (generally, this month)
2 What are you doing? Are you studying? (these days, still)
3 I'm finding it quite difficult at home, because my husband does the cooking, but he's away for three weeks on business. (at the moment, normally)
4 I'm sorry, we're experiencing problems with the system. Can you call back in a half an hour? (currently)
5 They're doing building work outside our office. Honestly, it's driving me mad. (at the moment)
6 I go to my dance class on Tuesdays, but I'm working so I'm going to miss it. (usually, this week).

> **Glossary**
>
> **tight deadline to meet:** if you have a tight deadline to meet, you have to finish work in a very short time
> **do up:** if you do up a place, especially your house, you paint it and repair things to make it nice
> **experiencing problems:** experiencing problems is a formal way to say you are having problems

03 TIME OFF

Present perfect questions

To ask questions about people's experiences, use the present perfect simple. In the answers, we use a range of different structures.

Use the past simple to talk and ask about the details of the event.

A: Have you seen that new Spielberg film?
B: Yes, I *saw* it last week. It *was* OK, but it *wasn't* brilliant.

Use the present perfect to ask questions about recent activities.

Do not use the present perfect with past time expressions.

I have been there last month. ✗
I went ... ✓

Use questions to continue the conversation.

A: Have you ever been to Japan?
B: No. *Have you?*

A: I went to see Hamlet last night. Have you seen it?
B: Yeah. *What did you think of it?*

Use future forms to talk about plans or hopes.

A: Have you ever been to Australia?
B: No, but *I'd love to.*

A: Have you ever been to Paris?
B: No, but *we might go* in the summer.

Use the present simple to give your opinion.

A: Have you been there before?
B: Yeah, several times. *It's fantastic. I love it.*

Use expressions such as *supposed to* and *I was told* to report what you know.

A: Have you ever tried frogs' legs?
B: No, but *they're supposed to be quite nice.*

A: Have you been to the city museum?
B: No, but *I was told it was quite boring.*

We sometimes use the present perfect to emphasise a *yes* or *no* answer. The present perfect is also used in some other expressions to add information to a yes / no answer.

A: Have you finished?
B: Yes, *I have* now. Thanks.

A: Have you ever been to New Zealand?
B: No, *I've never really wanted to*. It's too far away.

Exercise 1

Correct the mistakes in B's answers.

1 A: Have you read *The Shadow of the Wind*?
   B: No, I haven't, but it's supposed to good. Is it?
2 A: Have you discussed the problem with Matt?
   B: Yeah, he's actually rung me about ten minutes ago to talk about it.
3 A: Have you been to that new market yet?
   B: Yes, I have, actually. I've been shopping there yesterday – and guess what? I bumped into Rick while I was there.
4 A: We went to see the musical *We Will Rock You* last night. Have you seen it?
   B: No, but I like to. I've heard it's really good.
5 A: We went to that Italian restaurant round the corner. Have you eaten there yet?
   B: No. What it's like?
6 A: Have you ever done a parachute jump?
   B: No never, but I always want to ever since I was a kid.
7 A: Have you ever been to that fish restaurant on the high street?
   B: Yeah! I went there loads of times. It's one of my favourite restaurants.
8 A: Have you ever been to Seoul?
   B: No, but I'll go there next week.

Exercise 2

Complete the dialogues by putting the words in brackets into the correct form.

1 A: I went to that bar in Hanway Street last night. ....? (you/be there)
   B: Yeah, of course. .... (I / be there / lots / times)
2 A: ....? She might want to come. (you / tell Agnes / we / go out)
   B: Yeah, ... She said she can't come. (speak / her this afternoon)
3 A: .... (eat / wild boar)?
   B: No, ...? (you)
   A: No, but .... (I / think / order it / my main course. / it / supposed / nice)
4 A: ....? (you / see / new Bond film)
   B: No, ..., so don't tell me too much about it. (I / actually / go / see it / Sunday)

> **Glossary**
>
> **bump into:** if you bump into a friend, you meet them by accident
> **round the corner:** if a place is round the corner, it is very close
> **do a parachute jump:** if you do a parachute jump, you jump out of an airplane with a parachute – a large piece of cloth that opens
> **loads of times:** an everyday way of saying lots of times
> **boar:** a boar is a large animal, a bit like a pig, that lives in the wild

THE FUTURE

There is no future tense in English and sometimes there is not much difference in meaning between two forms. Take any definition of future forms as just a guide, not as fixed rules.

Questions

To ask about plans, use the present continuous, *be going to* or *Have you got any plans?*

What *are you doing* now / later / tomorrow?

What *are you going* to do when you finish / when you go back / on Friday?

Have you got any plans for the weekend / for the holidays?

Definite plans

Do not use *I will* for plans you have already made.

A: What *are you doing* in the summer?

B: ~~I'll go~~ *I'm going* to Bulgaria. ~~I'll spend~~ *I'm going* to spend two weeks there.

Use *have / have got* with nouns such as *meeting / appointment / class*.

I have / I've got a dentist's appointment at 4 tomorrow.

She has / She's got a meeting at 4.30.

The present continuous and *be going to*

For arrangements with other people, use the present continuous.

We're having a party on Saturday night.

A few of us are meeting later, if you'd like to come.

We also use *be going to*. However, *be going to* has a wider use for plans further in the future.

I'm going to look for a job once my English is better.

I'm going to buy a house abroad when I retire.

Sometimes people use *probably* with this forms.

I'm probably just going to stay in.

Uncertain plans

These expressions show plans are incomplete:

I'm not sure.   I haven't decided yet.

I don't know yet.   It depends on the weather.

I haven't thought about it.   I've no idea.

These expressions are often used with: *I'm / We're thinking of*

Use this structure to talk about ideas you have had, but have not made any arrangements for yet. Native speakers sometimes use *I was thinking of* to show less certainty.

We're thinking of going to Morocco for New Year.

I was thinking of maybe going to Sri Lanka for a week or two this summer.

Will

Use *will* to make a decision at the moment of speaking.

I don't know what I'm doing yet. *I'll phone* you later.

Use *will* with an adverb to show uncertainty.

Maybe I'll go and see a film.

I'll probably go.

Will is also used in other ways, such as in conditional sentences. (See p. 146)

Might

Use *might* to show less certainty (50%).

I might just *stay in* and read. I'll see. It depends how I feel.

Exercise 1

Complete the conversation below with one word in each gap.

A: What are you doing today?

B: I think we're [1]......................... to go to the Roman ruins outside town and after that, I'm not sure. We [2]......................... just go to the beach. I [3]......................... probably be bored of sightseeing by then, but it [4]......................... on my husband – he might have other plans. What about you? What are you doing?

A: Well, we [5]......................... leaving tomorrow.

B: Already?

A: Yes, unfortunately. I've got to go back and study, I've [6]......................... some important exams in September.

B: Poor you.

A: Oh it's OK. Anyway, we're [7]......................... to the main square and the market down there. We saw some nice handicrafts, which we thought we'd take back as souvenirs and presents. Hopefully, we [8]......................... have time to go to the beach one last time, though. I don't want to spend all day shopping!

B: Well, in that case, we [9]......................... see you down there.

Glossary

handicrafts: nice, traditional art objects made by hand

souvenirs: you buy souvenirs when you go on holiday to remind you of the place when you get home

04 INTERESTS

Frequency

We can ask about frequency using these questions:
Do you play tennis *much*?
Do you go walking *a lot*?
How often do you do that?
Do you ever go swimming?
Do you often go there?

Use the present simple tense to ask about current habits.

We usually reply to these questions with one of the following expressions, and an example.

(Yes / Yeah)	*All the time.* Maybe three or four times a week.
(Yes / Yeah)	*A lot.* Maybe two or three times a month.
(Yes / Yeah)	*Quite often / Quite a lot.* I probably go once or twice a week.
(Yes / Yeah)	*Sometimes* – it depends how I feel.
(No)	*Not that often.* I don't have much spare time.
(No)	*Hardly ever.* The last time I went was about three years ago.
(No)	*Never.* I'm just not interested.

Do not use *Yes / No* when you answer *How often* questions.
Say: Once a month / three times a week
Say: Once every two months / Once every three weeks
Say small numbers first: once or twice / two or three times

We also often use comparatives and other expressions, such as:

Not as much as I'd like to.   Not as much as I used to.
Not as much as I should.   Not as often as before.

We can also answer *How often* questions with *whenever* to mean *every time.*
Whenever I can.   Whenever I get the chance.

To talk about present habits, use adverbs and the present simple tense.
I sometimes go cycling by the river. It's lovely there.
I never watch TV. I just don't have time.

> ### Glossary
>
> **exhibitions:** exhibitions are public shows of art or other interesting things that are put on for a temporary period so that people can go and look at them
> **therapist:** if you go to a therapist, you visit a professional who helps you with your physical, mental or emotional problems
> **unfit:** if you are unfit, you have not been doing enough exercise. You need to do more exercise – and get fit/get in shape

To talk about habits in the past, use the past simple or *used to.*
I hardly ever *used to go* swimming when I was younger. When I was a kid, we always *went* to Blackpool for our summer holidays. We usually *stayed* with my uncle.

Look where adverbs normally go. Notice the other time expressions that go with them:
We always go to that restaurant. Let's go somewhere different.
I nearly always go out on Saturday nights.
In my old job, *I sometimes had to work* late, but *I hardly ever worked* weekends.
When I lived in Leeds, *I usually just used to stay* in at the weekends.

Occasionally, you see adverbs in other positions, but normally they go in between the noun and the verb. *Hardly ever* always does. Putting the adverb in the wrong place does not usually cause misunderstandings.

Exercise 1
Correct the mistake with the frequency expression in each of these dialogues.
1 A: Do you ever go swimming?
   B: No, hardly never. I don't really like it.
2 A: How often do you go out?
   B: Not much often. I'm very busy with my studies.
3 A: Do you go and watch them play a lot?
   B: Yeah, basically once a two weeks.
4 A: Do you ever go to art exhibitions?
   B: Yeah, sometimes. Probably twice or once a year.
5 A: Can we meet on Tuesday evening?
   B: I'm sorry, I can't. Always I go to my therapist on Tuesdays.
6 A: So how often do you go walking?
   B: Whenever I will get the chance.
7 A: Do you go to the gym a lot?
   B: Not as much how I should.
8 A: Do you do much sport?
   B: Not as much as I used. I had a foot injury for a while which stopped me.

Exercise 2
Complete these sentences by putting the verbs in brackets into a correct form.
1 When I was a kid, my parents .... me stay out late. (never let)
2 My brother .... swimming every morning before I get up. (go)
3 I .... my parents as much as I used to, now that we've moved. (not see)
4 When I was at school, I always .... really hard, but now I'm at university I .... to. (study, not need)
5 I .... an hour in the gym every day, but I hardly ever .... now. That's why I'm so unfit. (spend, go)

Duration

To ask about the duration of an activity, use *How long?*
How long has she been learning English?
How long does it take you to get to work?

Present perfect continuous

Use the present perfect continuous to talk about activities that began in the past, but affect the present.
How long *have you been working* here?
I've been diving all day. (I'm tired now)

Some verbs aren't used in the present continuous.
How long have you *known* each other?

Some verbs can use either the simple or continuous. There's no difference in meaning.
I've been living here for six months.
How long *have you lived* in Italy?

Past simple

Use past tenses for activities which are finished.
A: I used to run in a team.
B: How long *did you do* that for?

Other tenses

Use the present tense to talk about the typical duration of regular activities.
How long *do you* usually *swim* for?

Use *be going to* to describe duration of future events.
How long *are you going to be* out?

for, during, since, till

For shows the length of time something lasted – whether the activity is finished or not.
I've been working as a teacher *for 6 years now*.
I do exercises *for 30 minutes* every morning.

Don't use *during* in this way. Use *for*.
I've been learning to drive ~~during~~ *for the last 6 months*.

Use *during* + noun to show an action which happened within that time or event.
He died *during the war*.
We were interrupted *during the meeting*.

We also use *during* + noun to mean throughout a time period.
I stayed at my mother's house *during the summer*.
I kept waking up *during the night*.

Since goes with present perfect tenses to show when the activity started.
She's been training for the Olympics *since she was 10*.
This government has been in power *since 2008*.

Don't use *since* with past tenses. Use *from*.
We were walking ~~since~~ *from* 7 in the morning.

Until or *till* shows the point at which a period finished.
We walked from 7 in the morning *till lunch*.
Until now I've never played tennis. This is a first.

Exercise 1

Write *how long* questions in response to each of the following.

1 I used to live in Munich, so I know it quite well.
.... ? (you / live)
2 He's very careful. It's the first accident he's ever had.
.... ? (he / drive)
3 It's my parents' wedding anniversary today.
.... ? (they / married)
4 I'm finding work very tough. I'm thinking of leaving.
.... ? (you / work / there)
5 She got divorced last year.
.... ? (she / married)
6 He's probably my oldest friend.
.... ? (you / know each other)
7 Are you still on the phone to your mum?
.... ? (Yeah. Why? / we / talk)
8 Her German is pretty good already.
.... ? (she / learn)
9 It was a nightmare getting to the airport.
.... ? (it / take you / get there)

Exercise 2

Complete each sentence by adding *for* or *since* and the most suitable time expression in the box.

over six hundred years	fifty years
2004	his heart attack
most of my adult life	a few weeks now
I last wrote to you	a couple of minutes

1 He's not here, I'm afraid. He's just gone out
.... Shall I ask him to call you back?
2 It's my grandparents' golden wedding anniversary today. They've been married ....!
3 He's stopped smoking and changed his diet a lot
.... He nearly died and that was obviously a real shock.
4 It's quite a historic building. There's been a church on this site ....
5 We moved to England when I was 12 and I've been here ever since, so I've lived here ....
6 I've been following the diet .... and I'm feeling much better. I've lost almost nine kilos already!
7 Dear Lorraine, I know it's been a while ...., but I think about you all the time.
8 There's been a ban on smoking in pubs and cafés in Ireland ....

05 WORKING LIFE

have to, don't have to, can

We use *have to* for things that we feel are essential for us to do. We also use *have to* to talk about rules. The past form is *had to.*

To collect the certificate, *you have to go* to Room 11 and talk to Ken.

Sorry I didn't come to your party. *I had to drive* a friend home.

If you *don't have to* do something, there is no obligation, but you can do it if you really want to. The past form is *didn't have to.*

Here's your homework. It's optional, OK, so *you don't have to do* it if you don't want to. It's up to you.

It was great! *We didn't have to pay* to get in. We just walked in!

Use *can* when the rules say it is possible to do something. *Can't* is used when the rules say it is not possible to do something.

I can start and finish when I like. My working hours are very flexible.

We can't work from home in my company.

The past forms are *could* and *couldn't.*

In my last job I had a lot of freedom. *I could do* whatever I wanted.

When we were at school, *you couldn't bring* mobile phones to class.

To ask about rules, use *Do you have to* + verb. Use this to ask if it is necessary to do things when you do not like doing them. Use *Can you* + verb to ask if it is OK for someone to do something they like doing.

Do you have to get up very early?

Can you work from home some days or *do you always have to travel* into the office?

Exercise 1

Correct the mistakes in six of the sentences below.

1 I'm really sorry, but you can't to leave your car here.
2 You're really lucky that you don't have to take work home with you.
3 She's really behind with her work so she have to work late this evening.
4 I don't usually have to spend more than thirty minutes on lunch. I just don't have time!
5 I'm so sorry I can't go out with you all last night, but I have to start work really early this morning. I was up at five!
6 I left my last job because I have to travel too much. I missed my family.
7 Can you take your lunch break whenever you want?
8 I can't come to the class next week. I have to take some important clients out for dinner.
9 Have you to wear any kind of uniform or can you wear what you like?

Talking about rules

As well as *have to* and *can't*, we use several other structures to talk about rules and regulations.

When the rule says it is OK to do something, people sometimes use *be allowed to* instead of *can*.

You are allowed to use these computers. It's OK.

We're allowed to get to work late if we then work later in the evening to make up the time.

A more formal word you may see written is *permitted*.

Smoking is only *permitted* outside. (= allowed)

If you *are not allowed to* do something, or *it is not allowed*, it is against the rules.

Sorry, but *you're not allowed to bring* dogs in here.

We use *be not really supposed to* and *should not really* to talk about rules we often break.

I should really get back to work, I suppose.

We're not really supposed to talk about the work we're involved in, but sometimes people do, of course.

As well as *Do you have to...?* and *Can you...?* people use *be allowed to* to ask about rules.

Are you allowed to use a dictionary in the exam?

Am I allowed to have visitors at any time?

Exercise 1

Complete the sentences with one word in each space. Sometimes there is more than one possible answer.

1 .... children allowed to watch this film?
2 I'm afraid students aren't .... to log on to these computers. You have to go downstairs.
3 I .... really do 35 hours a week, but I often do less.
4 Smoking is not .... in any work area.
5 Slow down! You're only supposed .... do sixty on this road. I hate it when you drive so fast.
6 I shouldn't .... help you. It's against the rules, but for you, I'll make an exception.
7 We .... not really supposed to let visitors in, but I'll make an exception for you.
8 He can be a difficult guy to work for, but at least we're .... to disagree with him!

Glossary

behind with your work: if you are behind with your work, you have not done as much work as you needed to. You need to catch up

up: if you were up at five this morning, you got up at that time

log on: if you log on to a computer, you enter the system, usually by entering your password

make an exception: if you make an exception, you treat a person in a more positive way than the rules normally allow you to

06 GOING SHOPPING

must

Using *must* to talk about obligation is far less common that using *must* to make guesses.
Petra's not in her office. *She must be* at lunch.
There's an enormous queue outside the cinema.
It must be showing a good film.

Because *must* carries the idea of strong personal opinion, it is mainly used to talk about things we feel we need to do ourselves. In this case, *must* means something like *I think it's very important to*. Here are some verbs commonly used with *must* in this context.
I must remember to phone and change the time of the meeting.
I must make sure I spell-check it before I print it out.
I must just let my parents *know* that I'm going to be home late tonight.
I mustn't forget to post this letter later on.

To talk about rules, we generally use *have to* or *be (not) supposed to*. To talk about obligation in the past, we usually use *had to*. Use *(will) have to* for the future.
I have to go for an interview next week.
We're supposed to start at nine, but it's OK if you're five or ten minutes late sometimes.
I'm sorry I didn't come. *I had to stay in* and babysit my little sister.
You'll have to get a visa to go to Nigeria.

To tell people we know quite well what to do – or what not to do – we often just use imperatives.
Don't send your bank details by email, whatever you do.
No, *don't put* that file there. It goes over there in the out-tray.

We sometimes use *You (really / simply) must* to strongly recommend things. We also often use *should* when recommending, as it sounds less direct.
It's an amazing place. *You really must visit* it if you get the chance.
It's a really good book. *You should try* and read it, if you have time.

To give people a better suggestion after they have told you an idea, use *You'd be better (off) –ing*.
You'd be better off storing all those files on a hard drive instead of keeping them on the desktop.
The course was a waste of time. To be honest, I think *you'd be better off* just *studying* at home.

Exercise 1

Complete the sentences with the verbs in the box. Then underline the expressions using *must / mustn't*.

ask	get	keep	forget	reply
remember	visit	let	tell	buy

1 I really must .... China sometime soon. It just looks amazing.
2 I must .... a haircut sometime soon. It's getting long!
3 That reminds me. I must .... someone in my class if I can borrow their notes from the lesson I missed yesterday.
4 Remind me later I must .... to Milo's email.
5 I must .... to give you back that CD you lent me.
6 Whatever I do, I mustn't .... to take the tickets with me!
7 I should go. I mustn't .... my friends waiting.
8 I must just .... my boss know I can't attend the meeting tomorrow.
9 I really mustn't .... anything else on the Internet for a while. I don't want to go into overdraft.
10 I must just .... you what happened to me while I was shopping yesterday. You won't believe it!

Exercise 2

Rewrite the sentences using the words in brackets so that they sound softer and more polite, as in the example.

1 You mustn't go there. It's too expensive! (wouldn't / if / you)
   I wouldn't go there if I were you. It's too expensive.
2 You mustn't pay the first price they ask. (don't)
   ....
3 You must take out travel insurance. (If / you / would)
   ....
4 You must pay in cash, I'm afraid. (have to)
   ....
5 You mustn't smoke in the building. (allowed)
   ....
6 You mustn't make any personal calls from the office. (supposed)
   ....
7 You must wear a suit to the meeting instead of those old jeans. (be better)
   ....
8 You must change some money before you go. The rates are much better here. (be better)
   ....

07 SCHOOL AND STUDYING

After, once and *when*

Use a present tense after *after, once, when* or *as soon as* and other time phrases when you are referring to a definite future event.

I'll tell him the news *when he gets* home.

We'll start cooking *as soon as the kids have got back* from school.

Where the future situation is only a possibility and not a certainty, use *if*.

Give this letter to your parents *if when you see* them.

If When I pass all my exams, my Dad's going to buy me a bike.

Instead of *if*, we sometimes use *as long as*.

I'll help you study for your exams *as long as you help* me improve my English.

Exercise 1

Choose the correct word.

1 I'll phone you *when / if* I can't come to the meeting.
2 I'll phone you *when / if* I get home.
3 I'm going to have a holiday *once / if* my final exams have finished. I deserve it!
4 I'm going to bed *as soon as / if* I get to the hotel.
5 If you're strict with them, you'll gain their respect – *as soon as / as long as* you're fair as well.
6 After I *will finish / finish* my master, I'm going to do a PhD.
7 I'm probably going to go to Canada to study English, before I *will start / start* university.
8 I'm going to take a nice, long holiday once the course *finished / has finished*.

First conditionals

Use first conditionals to talk about things that are likely to happen in the future. The *if*-clause talks about a possible future situation. Use present tenses in this clause.

The other part of the sentence talks about the future result. Use *will, be going to*, and *might* in this clause.

If I fail the exam, *I'll just re-take* it in the autumn.

If I'm feeling bad tomorrow, *I'm going to phone* in sick.

If I get 6.5 in my IELTS exam, *I might apply* for a master's in the UK.

Either part of the sentence can come first. When the *if*-clause comes first, add a comma after it.

You won't gain the students' respect if you're not strict.

If you're not strict, you won't gain the students' respect.

Instead of *if* + negative, we use *unless*.

The college won't accept you for the course *unless* you get 6.5 in your IELTS exam.

Exercise 1

Decide which six sentences are incorrect. Correct them.

1 If you want to get a good grade, you'll have to work a lot harder!
2 If he'll find a job, he might move out.
3 If you won't have your passport or some other kind of ID, they'll refuse to register you on the course.
4 They told us if he skips any more classes, they're going to throw him off the course.
5 Your students don't behave better if you don't set some clear rules.
6 What you will do if you don't get offered a place on a masters?
7 I won't can finish this essay by tomorrow unless you give me some peace and quiet!
8 You'll fail the exam if you revise properly.

Zero conditionals

Use zero conditionals to talk about things that are always (or generally) true. Both the *if* clause and the result clause use present tenses: the present simple or present continuous. When the *if*- clause comes first, add a comma after it.

If you arrive late, *you have to sign in* at the school secretary's office.

The football match *is* always cancelled *if it rains*.

Other conditional sentences with present tenses

It is common to tell people what to do with *if*- clauses in a present tense followed by imperatives, *should* or *can*.

If they can't help, come and have a chat with me, OK?

If you want to study in the States, *you should do* the TOEFL exam before you apply for your course.

If you tell me the problem, *I can* probably *help* you.

Exercise 1

Complete the sentences with the pairs of verbs.

be + working	fail + re-take
become + leave	feeling + miss
borrow + need	make sure + share
be + cheat	should stop + finding

1 You can always .... my notes from the lecture if you .... to.
2 If I'm not .... very well, I can always .... the occasional lecture.
3 If you .... the end-of-year exams, you have to .... the whole year all over again!
4 In my opinion, you deserve to .... thrown out of university if you .... in an exam.
5 You .... drinking coffee if you're .... it difficult to get to sleep.
6 My personal tutor can .... quite strict if he thinks you're not .... hard enough.
7 Revision can .... stressful if you .... it till the last minute.
8 .... you keep your valuables safe if you

08 EATING

.... a flat or house.

tend to

Tend to is used to talk about general truths. The negative form can be *don't tend to* or *tend not to*. *Tend not to* is more common.

We *tend to eat* quite late.
I *tend not to eat* after seven at night.
I *don't tend to eat* after seven at night.

There are several other ways of doing this as well. They basically mean the same thing.
I don't *generally / usually / normally* eat after seven.
Generally speaking, I don't eat after seven at night.
Most of the time, I don't eat after seven at night.
On the whole, I don't eat after seven at night.
As a rule, I don't eat after seven at night.

Exercise 1

Complete the sentences with the correct positive or negative forms.

1 I don't like cooking, so I .... eat out a lot.
2 I try to eat as healthily as I can and I .... eat fatty or fried things, if I can help it.
3 I had a bad experience with oysters a few years ago and I .... avoid them ever since then!
4 When I was a kid, I .... eat much foreign food, but I've become much more adventurous as I've got older.
5 There was a big news story about mad cow disease a few years ago and since then I .... eat much beef!
6 Even before I became a vegetarian, I .... eat lot less meat than the rest of my family.

Second conditionals

Use second conditionals to talk about things that are unlikely to happen. The *if-* clause talks about an unlikely / impossible situation. Use the past simple, past continuous or *could* in this clause. The other part of the sentence talks about the imaginary result. We use *would* or *might* in this clause. When the *if-* clause comes first, add a comma after it.
If I ate this kind of thing every day, *I'd get* really fat!
If I wasn't working part-time in the restaurant, *I wouldn't be able to pay* my university fees.
I'd go there more often *if it wasn't* so expensive!
It'd be better *if they served* bigger portions.
You're so unadventurous! *If you* actually *tried* it, *you might like it!*

Either part of the sentence can come first. When the *if*-clause comes first, add a comma after it.
I'd buy more organic food if it was / were cheaper.
If it was / were cheaper, I'd buy more organic food.

Using *If I / he / she / it was* like this is very common. In exams and writing, it is better to use *If I / he / she / it were.*

Exercise 1

Decide which six sentences are incorrect then correct them.

1 I will really miss eating fried chicken if I were a vegetarian!
2 You'd be in trouble if you had to use chopsticks all the time!
3 I wouldn't eat tripe even if you'd pay me!
4 You might lose weight if you didn't drink so much!
5 They would can make more money if they started stocking more foreign food.
6 If I would be better at cooking, I might invite people round for dinner more often.
7 I'd be happy to pay for dinner sometimes – if you wanted me to!
8 I would go crazy if I had to go on a diet!
9 I wouldn't ask you if I wouldn't really need your help.
10 If I am you, I'd just do what it tells you to do in the book.

Exercise 2

Complete 1–6 by putting the verbs in brackets into the correct form.

1 I'd love to come tonight, but I'm afraid I have to take an important client out to dinner. If it .... (be) anyone else, I .... (cancel) it, but I really can't. Sorry.
2 It's not really my kind of place, to be honest. Perhaps if I .... (be) a bit younger, I .... (enjoy) it, but it's just a bit too trendy for me now.
3 Thank you so much for inviting me to dinner, but I'm afraid there's no way I can make it. I .... (come) if I .... (not / be) so busy at the moment, but I honestly don't have the time.
4 I .... (be) happy to have the party at our place if our flat .... (be) a bit bigger.
5 I'd love to come out with you tonight, but I really can't. If I .... (not / be) so broke at the moment, I .... (try) to come along, but I really can't afford to.
6 Bill said sorry, but he's not going to be able to come tonight. He said that if he .... (not/work), he .... (love) to come, but there's no way he can get out of it.

Glossary

take someone out to dinner: if you take someone out to dinner, you take them to a restaurant and you pay for everything

there's no way I can make it: if there's no way you can make a meeting or a party or an appointment, it is impossible for you attend it

broke: if you are broke, you do not have any money

get out of: if you get out of (doing) something, you manage to avoid doing something you do not want to do

09 HOUSES

COMPARING THE PAST WITH NOW

Making comparisons using adjectives
Add –er to one-syllable adjectives and –ier to two-syllable adjectives ending in –y. Use than to make comparisons with another time.
It's much quicker to get across the city now they have a metro.
It's far easier to find work than it was five years ago.

Add more to longer adjectives.
It's a bit more interesting round there than it used to be.
It used to be a lot more isolated than it is now.

You can also make negative comparisons using less.
The city's less safe than it was before.

Use far, much or a lot to show there is a big difference. Use a bit or slightly to show there is a small difference.

Use (just) as + adjective to explain that two things are equal.
The supermarket brand is just as good as other famous brands.

Use not as + adjective (+ as) to explain that two things are not equal.
It's not as nice as it was when I was a kid.
It's not quite as expensive as it used to be.

Not nearly or nowhere near show a big difference.
Not quite shows a small difference.
It wasn't nearly as touristy in those days.
It was nowhere near as good as the last time we went.

Making comparisons using nouns
You can use more before countable or uncountable nouns.
There was more crime than there is now.
There are more cars than there used to be.

With negative comparisons, notice the different usage:

Uncountable nouns
There's less crime than there was in the past.
There isn't as much crime these days.

Countable nouns
There are far fewer cars in the city centre since they started charging car drivers to go in.
There aren't as many cars now.

Using less with countable nouns (e.g. less people) is very common, but some people say it is wrong. In exams and writing it may be better to use fewer.

Time phrases
Here are some expressions used to compare times:
than / as it used to be   than / as it is now
than / as there was before   that / as there are now
than / as it is nowadays   than / as when I was a kid

'Double' comparatives
We often use 'double' comparatives to show a change is continuing. Note the tenses and time phrases we use.

With nouns:
More and more people are moving out to the suburbs.
Fewer and fewer people are voting in elections.

With adjectives:
Over recent years, the city has just got bigger and bigger.
Buying a house is getting more and more expensive.

Exercise 1
There is one word missing in each sentence in 1–8. Add the word in the correct place.
1 It used to be a lot greener it is now.
2 It wasn't nice as the last time we went there.
3 There's not as people living here as when I was a kid.
4 It's far multicultural than it was ten years ago.
5 There are more restaurants than were before.
6 The area isn't as working class as used to be.
7 There isn't as pollution round here since the government tightened the laws.
8 There use to be as many shops here as there are now.

Exercise 2
Complete the sentences by making 'double' comparatives with the words in the box, as in the example.

less	expensive	few
late	more	sophisticated

1 Children are leaving home later and later, with the average home-leaving age now over 30.
2 Despite the government's attempts to reduce traffic, there are .... cars on the road.
3 .... people can afford to buy a home these days as prices continue to rise.
4 The cost of weddings is getting .... as people go for ever bigger parties.
5 Computer technology is becoming ....
6 As there is .... space available in the city, they're having to build ever taller skyscrapers.

Glossary
tighten: if you tighten a law or rule, you make it more difficult to do something
ever: if something is ever bigger, it means it is increasingly big

10 GOING OUT

There are several ways of referring to future plans, promises or predictions that we made in the past.

future	future in the past
I'm going to go out later	*I was going to go* out.
I'll do it later, OK.	*He said he'd do* it.
I'll probably see you there	*He said he'd probably see* us there.
I might come later.	*She said she might come.*

Plans / arrangements

She had 50kg of luggage because *she was going to spend* a year abroad. She had to pay €300 extra at the airport.

This form often shows something you planned, but then did not do.

A friend was going to come for dinner, *but* he rang to say he couldn't make it.
I was going to go swimming, *but* in the end I was too tired.

Use *was supposed to / was meant to* to talk about arrangements that did not take place. In this context, they are synonyms for *intended to* or *had planned to*.
I was supposed to help him, *but* I didn't have time.
I was meant to meet a friend of mine, *but* just forgot about it!

Reporting promises

He promised he wouldn't be late.
You told me you'd wait.
I said I'd do it – and I will.

Reporting predictions

The play *was better than I thought it would be.*
I was hoping the concert *would be better than it was.*
I honestly *didn't think they'd win.*
The forecast *said there was going to be* a storm.

Other verbs and structures to report the future in the past

The following verbs are often used with *to-* infinitive to talk about the future in the past:

want	plan	intend	promise
expect	hope	mean	

I didn't expect it *to last* so long.
I was hoping to see him there, *but* he didn't go.
I didn't mean to cause any trouble.
They promised to improve things.

Was / were (just) about to + infinitive is used to talk about something you were going to do just before something else happened.
We were waiting for ages and *we were (just) about to leave when* they finally gave us a table.

Exercise 1

Match 1–8 with a–h to make complete sentences.

1 I only expected there to be about 20 people,
2 I was going to buy her a present,
3 I was going to call you,
4 I was about to leave the house,
5 I was about to say yes,
6 I thought it'd be rubbish,
7 He promised he'd be there,
8 He said he'd pay me back,

a but I'm still waiting for the money.
b but he never turned up.
c but I actually really enjoyed it.
d but I wasn't sure what she'd want.
e but then he said something which put me off.
f but the place was packed.
g but I had my mobile stolen.
h when they called to say the meeting had been cancelled.

Exercise 2

Rewrite 1–6 using the words in bold and three or four other words, so the sentences have a similar meaning.

1 He promised to help me later.
   said
   He .... me later.
2 We hadn't planned to return now, but we ran out of money.
   stay
   We .... longer, but we ran out of money.
3 Just before I was going to phone him, he called me!
   about
   I .... when he called me!
4 I expected him to be rubbish, but he was quite good.
   thought
   His performance was much better .... be.
5 I was surprised how much it cost.
   expect
   I .... so much.
6 It's so sunny! The forecast was for rain.
   to
   They said ...., but it's turned out really nice.

Glossary

turn up: when someone turns up, they arrive – often unexpectedly late, or not at all
put me off: if someone puts you off something, they stop you liking it. Things can put you off your food or an idea
had my mobile stolen: if you have your mobile stolen, somebody steals it

11 THE NATURAL WORLD

When two things happen at the same time, we often use the -ing form for one of the verbs. The main clause usually comes first. The -ing clause comes second.

When she saw the spider, she ran out the bathroom *screaming*.

This huge snake was just lying on the roof of my car *sleeping*.

If the clause contains a verb and an object, we usually put a comma before it. If it only contains a verb, we tend not to.

Exercise 1

Complete the sentences below with the correct form of the verbs in the box.

chase	circle	crawl	eat
jump	look for	make	stare

1 I was woken up by the cats .... a terrified mouse around.
2 This deer was just standing there in the middle of the road .... at us.
3 It was horrible. This huge rat was sitting in the middle of the kitchen .... a piece of cheese.
4 It was amazing. As we were sailing along, we saw a group of dolphins .... out of the water.
5 I think there's something wrong with the dog. It was up most of the night .... a terrible noise.
6 About an hour after we finally gave up looking for it, the dog just walked into the house .... for its dinner!
7 When I was walking up in the mountains, I saw this huge bird .... overhead. It stayed for about ten minutes.
8 I saw a cockroach .... across the restaurant floor! It really killed my appetite.

> ## Glossary
>
> **up:** if you are up most of the night, you do not sleep, usually for unpleasant reasons
> **overhead:** if something is overhead, it is above your head, usually in the sky
> **killed my appetite:** if something kills your appetite, it stops you wanting to eat. It puts you off your food
> **nest:** a nest is the home birds build to keep their eggs in
> **investment:** if there is a lot of investment in an area or a country, lots of money is spent improving it and making it more successful
> **raid:** if police raid a building, they enter it by surprise, because they want to search it

Passives

Look at the ways we make passive sentences from active ones.

The police arrested him for smuggling exotic animals.
He was arrested for smuggling exotic animals.

Something delayed our plane for two hours.
Our plane was delayed for two hours.

We make passive sentences with *be* + past participle.

Intransitive verbs (verbs that do not have an object) are never used in the passive form. For example: *arrive, become, cry, die, disappear, fall, happen, lack, rise, wait.*

A passive is used instead of an active because:
– it is not clear who or what did the action
– we do not know who or what did the action
– we want to emphasise who the action was done to.

Although you can say who or what did the action with by after the verb, this is not always necessary.

Look at how we make passive sentences in different tenses:
English is spoken all over the world now.
The animals are bred in zoos and *are* then *released*.
My car is being repaired at the moment.
The temple was built in the ninth century.
My mail was being sent to the wrong address!
My flight has been delayed, so I'll be late getting in.
You'll be met at the airport *and taken* to your hotel.

Exercise 1

Complete the sentences with the correct form of the verbs in the box.

arrest	give	release	see
smuggle	keep	search	create

1 When the house ...., police found over two hundred cats living in terrible conditions.
2 The eggs were taken from the eagle's nest. Police believe they will now .... out of the country and sold abroad.
3 I just heard on the news that someone .... and charged with the murder.
4 He .... last Friday after a year in prison.
5 With the recent investment in the area, plenty of new jobs .... at the moment.
6 When the police raided the farm, they found that crocodiles .... in a small lake.
7 He's an amazing performer. His show really has to .... to be believed.
8 I don't know why he was surprised they sacked him. He .... several warnings about lateness.

12 PEOPLE I KNOW

Used to, would and the past simple

Used to, would and the past simple are all used to talk about repeated actions in the past. See also the grammar reference on pp. 136–137.

My parents *used to take* us to the cinema every Saturday.
My gran *would always bring* cakes whenever she visited.
My brothers *fought* a lot when they *were* younger.

Look at the different ways the negative of *used to* is formed.

We *didn't use to get* pocket money when we younger.
Mum *never used to let me wear* make-up when I was a kid.

It is very common to introduce memories with *used to* and to then explain details with *would* or the past simple.

A friend of mine always *used to get into* trouble at school. *He'd always make* jokes or refuse to do what the teacher told him. He *got punished* a lot, but it *wouldn't stop* him.

Do not use *would* to describe character or possessions in the past.

My sister ~~would be~~ / *was* / *used to be* very spoilt when she was little.
I ~~would have~~ / *had* / *used to have* a car when I was at university.

Do not use *would* or *used to* for single events.

I ~~would meet~~ *met* my mum's dad once.
We used to go to the beach all the time, but I only ~~used to go~~ *went* twice last year.

Exercise 1

Complete the conversation with one word in each space.

A: Arnedo's a lovely place, isn't it? How do you know it?
B: Well, my parents used to ¹.......................... a little house near there. We ².......................... go there every summer for a month.
A: Really? Whereabouts?
B: The house ³.......................... actually just outside the town.
A: Lovely. Did you ever go walking round there?
B: Not really. In fact, we ⁴.......................... use to do that much. We'd ⁵.......................... swimming in the river or sit around and read. Sometimes we ⁶.......................... for a bike ride, but to be honest, none of us ⁷.......................... to like walking.
A: What a shame. So ⁸.......................... your parents sell the house?
B: Yeah. As we got older, we used ⁹.......................... complain about going. We ¹⁰.......................... keep asking not to go. In the end, they got fed up and sold it, yes.

Regrets and wishes

We use the past perfect (h*ad* + past participle) after the word *wish* to talk about things in the past that we now regret.

I wish I'd been a bit stricter with my children.
(= I was very soft with them and they became spoilt)
I wish I hadn't eaten so much. (= I ate a lot and now I feel sick)
I wish I'd never asked. (= I asked a question and he gave a very long, boring answer)

Look at these other ways of expressing regret.

I really regret not ask*ing* for her phone number.
(= I wish I'd asked her for her phone number.)
It's a shame I didn't think of that.
(= I wish I'd thought of that.)

Exercise 1

Choose the correct form.

1 I often wish I *had / hadn't* travelled more when I had the chance, but it's impossible with the children.
2 I wish I *had / hadn't* gone. It was such a waste of time.
3 All the flights are really expensive. I wish I *had / hadn't* left it till the last minute to book them.
4 I wish I *had / hadn't* brought up my children in the country. It's healthier and they would've had more freedom.
5 I wish I *had / hadn't* ignored him. He was right.
6 Thanks. You've really put my mind at rest. I wish I *had / hadn't* spoken to you earlier.
7 I really shouted at her and I wish I *had / hadn't* now.
8 I never really pushed my children, but I sometimes wish I *had / hadn't*. They would've thanked me for it.

Exercise 2

Rewrite the sentences so they have a similar meaning.

1 I really regret starting smoking.
   I really wish ....
2 I really regret not asking her.
   I wish ....
3 It's a shame you didn't tell me.
   I wish ....
4 I regret being so hard on my children.
   I wish ....
5 It's a shame I lost touch with them.
   I really wish ....
6 It's a shame I didn't move when I had the chance.
   I wish ....

> ### Glossary
>
> **brought up:** if you bring up a child, you look after them at home until they become an adult
> **put my mind at rest:** if you put someone's mind at rest, you say something to make them stop worrying

13 TRAVEL

Third conditionals

In third conditionals, the *if-* clause of the sentence uses the past perfect to talk about imagined things in the past. In these examples, the real situations are in brackets:

If I *had known* ... (= I didn't know)
If *he'd been driving* more slowly... (= he was driving fast)
If *we'd been given* more information... (= we weren't given much information)

The second part of the sentence shows the possible consequence of the *if-* clause. Use:
– *would + have* + past participle (definite)
– *could / might + have* + past participle (possible)
If I'd known the weather was going to be so bad, I *would've stayed* at home.
He *wouldn't have crashed* if he'd been driving more slowly.
If we'd been given more information about the delay, we *might not have got* so angry.

Do not use *would* in the *if-* clause:
If we ~~would've left~~ *had left* earlier, we wouldn't have missed the plane.

If the result of the condition refers to a present situation, we use *would* + verb.
If he hadn't helped me, I *wouldn't be* here now.

Exercise 1
Correct the six mistakes in the sentences below.
1 If you'd asked me earlier, I could come yesterday, but I didn't have time to rearrange my meeting.
2 If we would set off at nine, we would've missed the rush hour.
3 It would've been worse if she wasn't wearing a seatbelt.
4 I don't know what I would've did if I hadn't come here.
5 If it hadn't been for that long journey, we might never have got to know each other.
6 If there'd been a traffic jam, I might've got there on time.
7 We wouldn't have got lost if we'd given better directions by the conference organisers.
8 I wouldn't be alive today if I hadn't had that operation.

Exercise 2
Complete the sentences with the verbs in brackets.
1 I .... you last night if I .... your number. (call, had)
2 I .... if I .... she was going to be here. (come, know)
3 If you .... your bag in such a stupid place, I .... over it. (leave, trip)
4 If he .... more attention instead of talking on his mobile, he .... (pay, crash)
5 If there hadn't been so much traffic, I .... that plane which crashed, and I .... alive today! (catch, be)

Should have

We use *should've / shouldn't have* + past participle to talk about things that went wrong in the past.

Should've explains good things that people failed to do or were unable to do.

Shouldn't have explains things people did which were bad. There is often a present reason that make us state these regrets.
My mobile's dead. I *should've recharged* it before I left.
I overslept. I *should've set* my alarm clock.
I *shouldn't have eaten* so much earlier. I feel dreadful.

You can also use *never* to make a negative.
I *should never have started* smoking!

We also use *should've* and *shouldn't have* with continuous or passive forms of the verb.
You *should've been working*, not surfing the Web.
(= you weren't working when he saw you)
They *shouldn't have been arrested* for demonstrating against the government.

Notice we prefer to use *so* instead of *very* after *shouldn't have*.
He *shouldn't have been driving so fast*.
I *shouldn't have eaten so much*.

Exercise 1
Choose the correct form.
1 It's crazy! They *should've / should never have* let so many people onto the ferry.
2 Look at the traffic! I knew we *should've / shouldn't have* taken the train.
3 I don't know whose fault it is, but we *should've / shouldn't have* been told earlier about the change.
4 It's my own fault. I *should've / shouldn't have* tried to overtake on a blind corner.
5 It's your own fault. You *should've / shouldn't have* been watching where you were going!
6 It's my fault. I *should've / shouldn't have* been so stupid.

Exercise 2
Rewrite the sentences using *should have / shouldn't have.*
1 We didn't set off early enough.
   We .... earlier.
2 I wish I hadn't left it till the last minute.
   I .... till the last minute.
3 It's a shame you didn't get here earlier. It was great.
   You .... It was great.
4 I wish we hadn't gone there. It was a rip-off.
   We .... somewhere else. It was a rip-off.
5 I could've helped if you'd told me.
   You .... me you needed help.
6 If you hadn't been in such a rush, you wouldn't have crashed.
   You .... in such a rush.

14 TECHNOLOGY

-ing forms

-ing forms are also known as gerunds. They can be used as the subject or object of a clause.
Using energy-efficient bulbs saves a lot of electricity.
If you ask me, *being short* is a disadvantage in our society.

Use -*ing* forms following prepositions.
I felt a bit sick *after* eat*ing* so much.
We were all involved *in* organis*ing* the event.
I just don't agree *with* eat*ing* meat.

These adjective + preposition combinations are followed by -*ing* forms:

pleased about / at	useless at	capable of
upset about	involved in	scared of
sorry about / for	bored of	wrong with

The adjective *be / get used to* is followed by -*ing*.

These verb + preposition combinations are often followed by -*ing* forms:

think of	ask about	apologise for
blame s.o. for	succeed in	cope with
complain about	push s.o. into	

Several phrasal verbs are also followed by an -*ing* form. For example:

carry on	look forward to	give up
take up	end up	

to- infinitives

We use a *to*- infinitive to explain the reason or purpose of doing something.
I need to go to the bank *to sort out a problem.*
I burned a CD of my own music *to give to my mum.*

They are also used after some adjectives without a preposition, and following *too* or *enough.*
It's important *to recycle* as much as possible.
I'm *too busy to think* about that now.
We're still *not doing enough to stop* global warming.

-ing forms or to- infinitive?

Both -*ing* forms and to- infinitives can follow verbs with no preposition. There are no fixed rules.
He always avoids *do*ing the washing up.
We've arranged *to meet* at nine outside the station.

Other verbs that can be followed by -*ing*:

be caught	can't stand	deny	fancy
feel like	involve	mind	miss
recommend	risk	spend	suggest

Other verbs that can be followed by to-infinitive:

agree	arrange	ask	decide
deserve	fail	hope	intend
learn	manage	persuade	plan
promise	refuse	threaten	want

Exercise 1
Complete each sentence with the correct preposition and a verb in an -*ing* form.

study	fly	let	set up	shout	give up

1 There's nothing wrong .... kids play computer games so long as you control it a bit.
2 I was involved .... the website at work.
3 He always has to travel by train because he's so scared ....
4 My parents pushed me .... Computer Engineering, but personally I would've preferred to study Chemistry.
5 I'm thinking .... basketball because I can't get into the team.
6 She's apologised .... at me now, so we've made up and we're friends again.

organise	talk	work	be	store	have to

7 The phone is capable .... 500 photos.
8 I'm fed up .... weekends! It's too much.
9 She always blames me .... late, but it's often her fault.
10 I can't cope .... the wedding all on my own.
11 He's useless .... to people. It's embarrassing.
12 My son even complains .... tidy his room.

Exercise 2
Choose the correct form.
1 My job involves *travelling / to travel* a lot.
2 Do you fancy *going / to go out* somewhere this evening?
3 Sorry. I've arranged *meeting / to meet* a friend.
4 I'd rather stay in. I don't feel like *going / to go* out.
5 They finally agreed *paying / to pay* the staff more after three days of negotiations.
6 He played well. He didn't deserve *losing / to lose.*
7 I asked her very politely *emailing / to email* me a response, but I still haven't heard back from her.
8 I avoid *talking / to talk* to him as much as I can.
9 Unless you want to risk *losing / to lose* your work, you should set your computer to save automatically.
10 They're threatening *firing / to fire* anyone who's caught surfing the Internet at work.

Glossary

get into the team: if you get into a team, you are selected to play for it
make up: if two people make up, they become friends again after having a big argument and then not talking to each other for a long time
capable: if a machine is capable of doing something, it has the ability or power to do it

15 INJURIES AND ILLNESS

Reported speech

We report what people said using a verb + (*that*) clause. Some verbs with this pattern are:

admitted	said	told s.o.	warned
agreed	claimed	explained	promised

When reporting things that have finished or which we believe to be untrue now, use past tenses. Move one tense back.

Present simple	→	Past simple
Present continuous	→	Past continuous
Present perfect	→	Past perfect
Past simple	→	Past perfect
be going to	→	was going to
will	→	would
can	→	could
must/have to	→	had to

"I'm going to Poland tomorrow."
I saw him last week and *he said he was going to Poland.*

"We travelled twelve hours to be there."
They told me they'd travelled twelve hours to be there!

"I can't come now. I'm studying"
He said he couldn't come because *he was studying.*

A: I hate football.
B: I thought *you said you liked it.*

The following stay the same in reported speech.
The doctor told me I should rest.
He claimed he used to be very rich.
He agreed that he might be wrong.

When what is being reported is still true, you can use present and future forms in the normal way because we are talking from the point of view of now.
She said she lives in Madrid now.
They said they can't come tomorrow because they're working.
He said he's already seen the film and *he doesn't want to see* it again.

Reporting verbs

Some reporting verbs can be followed by a *to-*infinitive or *-ing* form.

+ *to-* infinitive

agree	offer	refuse	advise s.o.	told s.o.
claim	promise	threaten	persuade s.o	warn s.o.

+ *-ing*

admit	deny	recommend
apologise for	insist on	suggest

Verbs often have more than one pattern.
Our doctor *recommended* trying a different medication.
The doctor *recommended that I use* cream from now on.
My doctor *recommended a* specialist based in Kraków.

Exercise 1

Complete the reported speech by adding the verbs in the box in the correct form. You may need to use a modal verb.

be	have	qualify	not want	take	suffer

1 A: He's suffering from depression.
   B: Really? He told me he .... from a hormonal condition.
2 A: She's having an operation to sort out the problem.
   B: I thought she said she .... one already.
3 A: He's looking really well, isn't he?
   B: I know, it's amazing! The doctors told him it .... him years to recover.
4 A: He's got his final exams next month.
   B: I thought he said he .... them already.
5 A: I feel guilty because we didn't help.
   B: You shouldn't. We did offer, but he said he .... fine.
6 A: Can you pass me the sugar?
   B: I thought the doctor said you .... sugar in your coffee anymore.

Exercise 2

Choose the correct verb.

1 I'm not surprised you're ill. I did *warn / threaten* you not eat the food at that place!
2 My dad has finally *insisted / agreed* to go and have a check-up at the doctor's.
3 My dentist *suggested / told* me to start brushing my tongue – as well as my teeth!
4 The doctor *said / recommended* that I cut down on salt and caffeine.
5 I've finally managed to *advise / persuade* my grandmother to get a hearing aid!
6 My girlfriend has *threatened / offered* to leave me unless I stop smoking.
7 You *promised / suggested* to pick up my prescription for me! How could you forget?
8 I asked if I could be moved to another hospital, but they *refused / denied* to even talk about it!

> ### Glossary
>
> **have a check-up:** if you have a check-up, the doctor looks at your body to find out if you are healthy
> **cut down on:** if you cut down on something, you use less of it
> **a hearing aid:** you need to wear a hearing aid if you are going deaf
> **prescription**: a prescription is the piece of paper a doctor gives you saying what medicine you need

16 NEWS AND EVENTS

Defining relative clauses

We use relative clauses to add information after a noun. We use different relative pronouns (*who, which, that,* etc.) in the clause depending on the noun we are adding information to, or depending on the following information.

To add information about a person, use *who* or *that*.
He's a famous scientist *who discovered* radiation.
She's the woman *that spoke* to me earlier.

To add information about a thing, use *that* or *which*.
She wrote a book *that was a* huge best-seller.
It's a government scheme *which helps* unemployed people.

To show that something belongs to a person or thing, use *whose*.
That's the couple *whose child went missing* last year.
He made a film *whose main character couldn't speak, see or hear!*

To add information about a place, use *where* or *that* + preposition.
That's the hospital *where I was born!*
That's the hospital *that I was born in.*
What's that bar *where you went* for your birthday?
What's that bar *that you went to* for your birthday?

When talking about places, you can replace *where* with *that / which* + preposition. You can also leave out *that / which,* but you then need to keep the preposition.
Is that the flat *where you lived* last year?
Is that the flat *which / that you lived in* last year?
Is that the flat *you lived in* last year?

To add information about a time, use *when* or *that*.
I remember *the day when Princess Diana died* very clearly.
At *the time that he was writing,* there was a war going on.
That's when I realised I'd made a mistake.

We tend not to use relative pronouns when they are the object of the clause that follows. In these cases, the noun that comes after the relative pronoun is the subject of the clause.
It's one of the best films *(that) I have ever seen.*
(subject = I, verb = have seen, that = object)
We stayed in a hotel *(which / that) a friend had recommended.*
(subject = a friend, verb = had recommended, which / that = object)

Exercise 1

Match the sentence starters 1–6 with the pairs of relative clauses a–f.

1 Did you apply for that job
2 Did you read about that guy
3 What's the name of that company
4 We met that woman
5 We went to that bar
6 He's the writer

a you recommended. It was really good!
  where all the stars go, but we didn't see anyone famous!
b which went bankrupt last week?
  Maria works for?
c whose novel was banned by government.
  who won the Nobel prize a couple of years ago.
d you were telling me about?
  that was advertised in the paper yesterday?
e who works with you. I've forgotten her name!
  you said you're interested in.
f they arrested for that big robbery?
  who was awarded the Nobel peace prize?

Exercise 2

Complete the film review with appropriate relative pronouns. Which one of the pronouns in 1–8 could be left out?

Lorenzo's Oil is a film [1]......................... tells the true story of a couple [2]......................... child develops medical problems at the age of 7. The first doctors [3]......................... see him have no idea what is causing the problem, but he is eventually diagnosed with a disease [4]......................... is called ALD and is incurable. They ask about hospitals [5]......................... they are doing research on this disease, but they are told it is so rare that no one will pay the money [6]......................... is needed to investigate it. The couple, who have no medical training, then start to study medical literature to find something [7]......................... will help their son. I love this film because at the time [8]......................... I saw it I was also quite ill, and it was very uplifting. Like the boy in the film, I eventually got better.

> ### Glossary
>
> **bankrupt:** if a company goes bankrupt, it loses all its money and closes
> **banned:** if a book is banned, you are not allowed to sell it or read it
> **robbery:** robbery is the crime of taking money – often from banks. Robberies often involve threats or violence

FILE 1

Unit 3 p. 23 Speaking
Student A
You are Maggie, a personal assistant (PA) from the UK. Read about your holidays and then discuss them with Student B and Student C. Answer the questions on p. 23.

I do take my full entitlement, but the problem is trying to get time off as a family all together. I have 20 days. My husband has a better job than me and he gets 30 days off, but my children have over ten weeks throughout the year. Most of the time, my husband has to take time off at a different time to me so we can look after them. The other thing is the prices of flights always go up in the school holidays, and so we can't afford to go away unless we go before the official holiday starts. The last time was three years ago. We went to Disney World in Florida, but the school complained about the kids missing classes.

FILE 2

Unit 6 p. 43 Conversation practice
Student A
You are the customer. Decide:
- how much you currently pay for your phone.
- how many text messages you get per month: 100? 200? 300?
- how many minutes you get per month: 100? 200? 300?
- Then decide what questions you want to ask about the new phone:
  - camera?
  - kind of battery?
  - MP3 player?

FILE 3

Unit 8 p. 56 Reading
Group B

Ya-Wen (Taiwanese)

I work for a big accounting firm and they transferred me to the States a couple of years ago. It's been quite a shock! For one thing, the portions here tend to be enormous. You see people with steaks the size of their plate – and they eat it all. It's really off-putting. Even worse is steak with blue cheese sauce. I can't stand the way it smells! Why you would put something which is basically mouldy cow fat in your mouth? And it's served with French fries all the time! I really miss having rice with my meals.

Of course there's good food here too. To begin with, there are some good Taiwanese restaurants here! There are also lots of amazing health food shops. I've also got some friends who are great cooks and they often have me round for dinner. Back home, we tend to meet in restaurants, so it's a lovely thing to do.

One last thing that I sometimes find frustrating is the way people usually order things individually for themselves. Sometimes you choose something which doesn't turn out to be that nice and the food goes to waste. It would be better if people shared more. That way, everyone would get something they like.

Alan (Scottish)

One of the first things I saw when I came to Valencia to teach English was people pouring oil on their bread. I thought it was really weird, but then I tried it and I quite like it now. It's not so different to spreading butter on bread.

In general, there's a lot more good food here and people tend to buy fresh food every day and cook, rather than buying lots of ready meals from the supermarket. Eating out is also good. I always enjoy ordering *tapas* – lots of little dishes that you share.

Having said that, it's not very good if you're a vegetarian. A friend of mine came over and they were always giving him 'vegetable' dishes with bits of ham or sausage in them. It's quite strange – they don't seem to think of ham as meat! The other thing is, it's difficult to get food which isn't Spanish – maybe because there's a lot of regional variation. I love curry, but there are hardly any Indian restaurants here and the curry is never spicy enough!

One last thing is that I'm still not used to having dinner so late. When we eat out, we sometimes don't get to the restaurant until around 11, and I'm usually starving by then!

FILE 4

Unit 6 p. 44 Reading
Answers to the Shop till you drop! questionnaire.
Add up your score.
Answers a = 1
Answers b = 3
Answers c = 5

18–29
You really can't stand shopping. Some people might even say you're mean because you never spend money, although you might say it's for political reasons such as protecting the environment. Fashion doesn't interest you and some might think you look scruffy or old-fashioned. You're only interested in getting the cheapest things available.

30–53
You don't mind shopping, but you're quite careful with your money and you often keep an eye out for bargains. You want to look good, but you also want clothes to last, so the latest fashions don't interest you so much. There's more to life than shopping.

54–71
You're quite fashion conscious and love shopping. It's one of your main leisure activities and it often cheers you up. You might have a particular obsession – shoes, shirts, DVDs. Although you try to control your spending, you sometimes get into debt. Sometimes you rush into buying something and then realise it's a bad idea.

72–90
Your only interest is shopping and fashion and you are seriously out of control! You can't go shopping without buying something – even if you don't need it. You follow all the latest fashions and have drawers and wardrobes full of clothes you hardly ever wear. Your buying habits are getting you into debt. You should get some help!

FILE 5

Unit 3 p. 23 Speaking
Student B
You are Luca, a civil servant from Italy. Read about your holidays and then discuss them with Student A and Student C. Answer the questions on p. 23.

As well as some breaks during the year, we always take the whole of August off. It's an Italian tradition. We usually go to the seaside. We meet the same people: eat, enjoy some good wine, go to the beach, play tennis – just totally relax. There has been some talk about stopping people taking such long holidays. I have heard some businessmen in Italy say they can't get anything done or that it's expensive. I think this is just an American idea of work. It's bad. Life is not all about work.

FILE 6

Unit 4 Pronunciation
Final consonant sounds which are not pronounced are in **bold**. Words that join together are shown with the symbol ‿.

A: So did you have a nice weekend?

B: Yeah, it was OK. Nothin**g** special really.

A: No? Wha**t** did you do?

B: Well, I wen**t** roun**d** to a friend's for dinner on Saturday, which was nice.

A: Yeah.

B: An**d** then on Sunday I playe**d** football.

A: Really? I didn'**t** know you playe**d** football. Where do you do that?

B: Oh, I play for a local team in a Sunday league.

A: Oh yeah. So are you any good?

B: I'm OK. I'm qui**te** good in defence, but I'm useless at shooting. I think the las**t** time I scored a goal was about three years ago.

A: So how long have you been playing?

B: Well, in this team, abou**t** five years, but I played at school before that. Do you play at all?

A: No, I'm rubbish at football. I do a bit of swimming, though.

B: Yeah? How often do you go?

A: Well, not as often as I use**d** to. Since I started this job I haven'**t** had much time. I actually went on Saturday, but I think tha**t** was the firs**t** time in abou**t** three weeks. I use**d** to go three or four times a week.

FILE 7

Unit 3 p. 23 Speaking
Student C
You are Ethan, a marketing manager from the United States. Read about your holidays and then discuss them with Student A and Student B. Answer the questions on p. 23.

I don't take all the holiday I could. Back in the States, I worked for the same company that I'm working for now and took ten days a year. As a result, it's quite strange for me to suddenly get more than twice that, just because I'm working in London at the moment. I do take more than ten days, though! I want to take advantage of my time in Europe. A couple of weeks ago, we went on a one-week tour of Italy and Austria. It was wonderful. We went to Rome, Florence, Pisa, Sienna, Venice, Milan, Salzburg, Innsbruck and Vienna.

FILE 8

Unit 6 p. 43 Conversation practice
Student B
You are the salesperson. Decide what functions the phone you are selling has:
- camera?
- MP3?
- email?

What makes it better than other phones:
- battery?
- price?

How many text messages per month you can offer: 100? 200? 300?

How many minutes per month you can offer: 100? 200? 300?

What price can you offer everything for?

FILE 9

Unit 8 p. 54 Vocabulary

1 olives

2 oysters

3 raisins

4 squid

5 shrimps, prawns

6 corn on the cob

7 peanuts

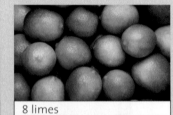
8 limes

9 kebabs

10 spinach

11 trifle

12 tripe

13 blue cheese

14 radishes

FILE 10

Unit 11 p. 76 Vocabulary

1 squirrel

2 lizard

3 bear

4 eagle

5 dolphin

6 cockroach

7 deer

8 whale

9 wolf

10 crow

11 crocodile

12 parrot

13 snake

14 scorpion

15 rat

UNIT 01

♻ 1.1
G = Guy, O = Olga

G: Hi. Come in. Sit down. Take a seat.

O: Thank you.

G: So...um...what's your name?

O: Olga.

G: Right, OK. And where are you from, Olga?

O: Russia.

G: Oh OK. Whereabouts?

O: Saratov. It's maybe 500 kilometres from Moscow. Do you know it?

G: No, sorry. I'm afraid I don't. My geography of that area's not great! So how long have you been learning English, Olga?

O: About 10 or 12 years on and off.

G: OK. So have you been to the UK to study before?

O: No, no. In fact this is my first time in an English-speaking country.

G: Really?! That's amazing, because your English is really good. I mean, you haven't got a very strong accent.

O: Thanks. I had really good teachers at school.

G: Yeah? Mine weren't that good, but then I wasn't a very good student either!

O: Yes. I was lucky.

G: So how long are you going to stay here?

O I'm not sure. I'd like to do a degree here – maybe in business management, but I'll see. It depends on my husband as well. He's looking for work here.

G: Oh OK, So how old are you, if you don't mind me asking?

O: I'd rather not say.

G: Oh right. OK, fair enough. Anyway, I think that's all I need to ask. I'm going to put you in the top class. Is that OK?

O: Fine. Thanks.

♻ 1.2

1 A: What do you do?
  B: I'm a computer programmer.
  A: Oh yeah? Do you enjoy it?
  B: Yeah, it's OK. It pays the bills!

2 A: Have you studied here before?
  B: No. Never.
  A: So where did you learn your English?
  B: I lived in Canada for a year and I just picked it up there.

3 A: What do you do when you're not studying?
  B: I like going shopping, going out with friends, that kind of thing, but I've also got a part-time job in a café.
  B: How long have you been doing that?
  A: Only about six months.

4 A: Have you got any brothers or sisters?
  B: Yeah, seven!
  A: Seven! Older or younger?
  B: I'm the youngest, so, as they like to remind me, I'm the baby of the family.

5 A: What did you do at the weekend?
  B: Nothing much. I went shopping on Saturday, but that's all.
  A: Oh right. Did you get anything nice?
  B: Yeah, I did actually. I got this really nice T-shirt in the market.

6 A: What are you studying?
  B: Media studies.
  A: Oh right. What does that involve? I've never heard of that subject.

B: Really? It's quite popular here. You study everything about TV, newspapers and advertising. Some of it's practical, and some of it is more theoretical, almost like philosophy. It's really interesting.

♻ 1.3
M = Martin, A = Anna

M: Sorry, but I've forgotten your name.

A: Anna.

M: Oh yeah, sorry. Hi.

A: So what did you do in the first half of the class?

M: I don't know. I missed it as well.

A: Oh dear. Why was that?

M: Well, I was late getting up and then I rushed out of the house to get the train, but when I got to the station, I realised I'd forgotten my book. So I went back home to get it and then I realised I didn't have my keys either! I rang the bell, but my flatmate was sleeping so he didn't answer. I was banging on the door and shouting, but nothing.

A: He must be a really heavy sleeper!

M: It's not that, really. He works nights, so he doesn't get home till five o'clock in the morning.

A: Oh right. So did you get in the house?

M: No, in the end, I stopped trying, but by then I'd missed my train to get here and I had to wait another twenty minutes before the next one came.

A: Oh right. Whereabouts are you living?

M: Moncada. It's only about twenty minutes by train from here, but the trains only run every thirty minutes. So anyway, what about you? What's your excuse?

A: Sorry?

M: What's your excuse for being late?

A: Oh right. Sorry. Well, I'm looking for a flat to rent and I was phoning round a few places this morning before class.

M: Right. So did you have any luck?

A: Not really. I'm going to see one later near the centre of town, but it's quite expensive.

M: Mmm.

A: Actually, Frank – the German guy in class – was telling me that you're looking for another person to share your flat.

M: Yeah, well, we've got a spare room and it'd be good to pay less rent.

A: So how much would it be?

M: I guess about forty euros a week.

A: Really? That's really cheap! So what's the room like?

M: It's all right. It's quite big. The only problem is, it's an internal room. I mean, it doesn't have any windows to the outside, so there's no natural light.

A: Oh right. And how many people live there?

M: Oh, just the two of us. Me and this Spanish guy, Pedro.

UNIT 02

♻ 2.1
Conversation 1
R = Ryan, C = Clara

R: Hey, Clara!

C: What is it, Ryan?

R: Have you seen Karim this week?

C: Yeah, I saw him yesterday. Why?

R: Is he OK? I haven't spoken to him for a while, but the last time I saw him he seemed a bit down.

C: Hmm. I know. I think it's his mum. Apparently, she's quite ill and he's just very worried about her.

R: Oh no. What's wrong with her? Is it very serious?

C: I think it must be. He was quite upset when I spoke to him, and he didn't want to say much.

R: Oh dear. That's awful. I feel a bit guilty now that I haven't rung him, because I had a feeling something was wrong.

C: Why?

R: Well, I met him outside the university with Chris. Chris and I were chatting, but Karim didn't say much. In fact, he hardly said anything at all.

C: Really?

R: And Karim is normally really chatty.

C: I know. Well, he probably isn't in the mood to talk to anyone at the moment.

R: Oh dear. Well, if you see him, tell him I'm thinking of him. Say 'hello' to him from me.

C: Sure.

Conversation 2

B = Belinda, A = Alisha

B: Hello Alisha! How's it going?

A: Great actually, Belinda. I've just finished all my exams!

B: That must be a relief. How did they go?

A: Quite well, I think. I was really pleased with how I did.

B: That's great.

A: Are you all right? You look a bit fed up.

B: Yeah, sorry. It's not you. I'm just having a few problems with my accommodation.

A: Oh dear. What's the problem?

B: Oh, I've just found out I can't continue to stay where I am at the moment.

A: What a pain! How come?

B: I don't really want to explain. Basically, I need to find something else and, to be honest, I just don't need the stress.

A: I can imagine. Can I do anything to help?

B: No, it's OK. I'm sure it'll sort itself out, but thanks.

A: Well, at least let me buy you a drink.

B: OK. That'd be nice.

A: What would you like?

B: A cappuccino would be good.

A: Anything else? A bit of cake? Go on. It'll cheer you up.

B: Well, I have to say that chocolate cake looks very nice.

A: I think I'll join you – to celebrate finishing my exams.

🎧 2.3

S = Sarah, L = Louise

S: Hello Louise!

L: Oh Sarah. All right.

S: How's it going?

L: OK. I'm a bit stressed to be honest. I'm working quite hard at the moment. We're finishing at nine most days!

S: Really? What a pain. You must be exhausted.

L: Yeah, I am. So what are you doing here? Are you window shopping?

S: What? No, no. Not really. I'm just meeting a friend here. I'm a bit early.

L: Oh right. Hey listen, Sarah. I've rung you a few times recently, but you always seem to have your phone switched off or you don't answer it.

S: Oh right, yeah, Sorry about that.

L: So why aren't you answering it? Don't you want to talk to me?

S: No, no, it's not that!

L: I mean, you usually answer it on the first ring!

S: I know, I know.

L: So what? Is it work?

S: Sort of.

L: What do you mean, 'sort of'?

S: Well, if you must know, I'm seeing someone from work.

L: Oh right! But why are you being so mysterious about it? It's unlike you. You normally tell me everything.

S: Well, it's just ... well, it's my boss!

L: You're going out with your boss? So how long has this been happening?

S: About three weeks.

L: That's not long.

S: No. That's why I don't want anyone to know for the moment. I've just changed jobs too.

L: Oh really? I didn't know that. What are you doing now? Did you get promoted?

S: No, the new job isn't really a promotion. I'm not getting any more money. I'm just doing something different. It's more marketing than sales.

L: And you studied marketing, didn't you?

S: Yeah, that's right. I prefer marketing, so it's a good change. I'm really enjoying it.

L: Well, with your boss, it sounds like you're having a great time!

S: But I didn't get the new job because of my boss. I was promoted by Head Office.

L: Oh right.

S: But you see, this is why I don't want people to know about the relationship! They'll think I've got the job because I'm going out with the boss. It's really annoying.

L: OK, OK, I'm sorry. It was a stupid thing to say. Listen, what are you doing on Friday? Do you fancy meeting? It'd be nice to hear more of your news.

S: I'm afraid I can't. I play badminton on Fridays. And this Friday we're going for a meal afterwards.

L: Oh right. That's a shame. Maybe next week sometime.

S: Yeah ... yeah.

L: So ... when am I going to meet your boss?

S: Er...Um... er ... now. There – coming towards us.

L: Wait! That's your boss!

UNIT 03

🎧 3.1

C = Claire, R = receptionist

C: Hello there. I wonder if you can help me. I'm thinking of going sightseeing somewhere today. Can you recommend anywhere good to go?

R: Well, it depends on what you like. There are lots of places to choose from. What kinds of things are you interested in?

C: I don't know. Erm ... something cultural.

R: Oh right. OK. Well, quite close to here is St. Mary's Church. It's Kraków's most famous church – and very beautifully decorated. You can walk there in five or ten minutes.

C: OK. I'm not really a big fan of churches, to be honest.

R: That's OK. I understand. Of course, the most visited place near here is Auschwitz. There's a day tour leaving soon.

C: Actually, we're planning on going there later in the week.

R: Well, in that case, you could try Kazimierz, the old Jewish Quarter, where Steven Spielberg filmed some of *Schindler's List*. It's actually quite a lively area now. There are lots of good bars and restaurants round there.

C: Oh, so that might be nice for this evening, then.

R: Yes, maybe. Let me know if you want more information about places to eat or drink there. Erm... Then, if you'd prefer something a bit different, how about a guided tour of Nowa Huta - the old communist district? They'll show you what life was like in the old days there.

C: Oh, that sounds interesting. How much is that?

R: About €40. I can call and book a place for you, if you want.

C: What times does that leave?

R: Every two hours from outside the hotel – and the tours last around 90 minutes. They leave at 10 o'clock, 12 o'clock, 2 o'clock and 4 o'clock.

C: OK, that's great. Can you book me onto the 2 o'clock tour? Then I can do some shopping in the main square in town beforehand.

R: Sure.

3.2

C = Cristina, A = Andrew

C: Oh don't believe it!

A: What's up?

C: I'm just checking the weather forecast for next week!

A: Oh right. Is it going to be bad?

C: Well, not here, it's not. Apparently, it's going to be boiling here: 27 degrees on Monday!

A: Really? That's great!

C: Great for you, but I'm not going to be here. I've got a week off work. I'm going to Italy and apparently it's going to pour down most of the week!

A: Oh dear. I forgot you were going away. Whereabouts are you going?

C: Sicily. I mean, it's in the south! It's supposed to be really sunny at this time of year. I was hoping to go to the beach and get a suntan, you know.

A: Oh no. Well, it'll probably clear up later in the week. It's not going to be wet for long.

C: I hope not, because I don't think there'll be much to do there.

A: Why? Where are you staying?

C: Some little village on the coast. We're also thinking of going to Palermo for a couple of days. It depends on the weather.

A: Well, maybe you could go to Palermo first. There'll probably be museums you could visit if it's wet.

C: I suppose so. I prefer the beach, though.

A: Oh, OK. Well, maybe the forecast will be wrong and it'll turn out really sunny.

C: Mmm. So what are you doing over the Easter holiday? Have you got any plans?

A: Well, I've got to work on Saturday, and I'm having lunch with my parents on Sunday, but apart from that ... I don't know. I don't usually do much on bank holidays, but if it's going to be hot, I might go for a picnic in the park. I might even go to the beach. I guess it depends what time I get up on Monday! But honestly – 27 degrees! That's mad for this time of year! It's actually a little bit worrying, really.

C: Or annoying!

UNIT 04

4.1

Conversation 1

A: So what did you do last night? You didn't come to Gary's party.

B: No. I was too tired. I just stayed in and went to bed early.

A: Oh right. Are you OK?

B: Yeah, I'm fine. I just had a really busy week and I didn't feel like going out.

Conversation 2

C: Did you have a nice weekend?

D: Yeah, it was OK. I didn't do that much. I went shopping on Saturday and that was all, really.

C: Oh right. Did you get anything nice?

D: No, I didn't see anything I liked.

Conversation 3

E: So what did you do after we left you?

F: We went to the cinema.

E: Oh right? What did you see?

F: *The Lives of Others*. It's a German film.

E: Oh yeah? I've been thinking about going to see that. Is it any good?

F: Yeah. It's brilliant.

Conversation 4

J = Jason, M = Mohammed

J: So did you have a nice weekend?

M: Yeah, it was OK. Nothing special really.

J: No? What did you do?

M: Well, I went round to a friend's for dinner on Saturday, which was nice.

J: Yeah.

M: And then on Sunday I played football.

J: Really? I didn't know you played football. Where do you do that?

M: Oh, I play for a local team in a Sunday league.

J: Oh yeah. So are you any good?

M: I'm OK. I'm quite good in defence, but I'm useless at shooting. I think the last time I scored a goal was about three years ago.

J: So how long have you been playing?

M: Well, in this team, about five years, but I played at school before that. Do you play at all?

J: No, I'm rubbish at football. I do a bit of swimming, though.

M: Yeah? How often do you go?

J: Well, not as often as I used to. Since I started this job I haven't had much time. I actually went on Saturday, but I think that was the first time in about three weeks. I used to go three or four times a week.

4.2

I = Ian, R = Rika

I: Am I imagining things, Rika, or did that guy just ask you for your autograph?

R: You saw that? Oh, I'm embarrassed now, Ian!

I: Why? How come he knew you?

R: You won't believe me when I tell you!

I: Go on! What?

R: Well, in my other life, away from selling books, I'm kind of famous! I do judo and last week I was on TV and that guy recognised me from there. That's why he wanted my autograph.

I: Seriously? That's amazing!

R: Oh, it's no big deal. I didn't even win the tournament. I lost in the semi-finals, but at least the girl who beat me went on to win the whole thing, so it wasn't too bad!

I: So you got to the semi-finals! I can't believe it! You don't look big enough to fight – if you don't mind me saying.

R: Well, that's why I love judo. It's nothing to do with how big you are. It's all about balance. You learn how to take advantage of your opponent's strength and size to throw them off balance.

I: Oh right. I see. So how long have you been doing that, then?

R: Ever since I was a kid. I used to get into fights when I was at school because I was so small. The big kids used to bully me, so my dad suggested I started doing a martial art and that was it, really.

I: You've kept very quiet about it all the time I've known you!

R: Yeah, well, I don't like to talk about it. People might think I'm being big-headed. I don't really feel like it's connected to what I do at work.

I: So, how often do you have to train?

R: Oh, well, I usually practise all the techniques for at least an hour a day – once I get home in the evening – and then two or three times a week I go to a special judo school to spar, you know, to practise fighting.

I: I'm speechless, Rika, I really am!

R: Yeah, well. There you go!

I: And this tournament the other week… what was it exactly? Was it a big thing?

R: Um… Yeah… It was the women's national final!

I: No!

R: Yeah, honestly! I'm actually quite annoyed. I think I had a chance of winning it, but I hurt my back quite badly last year fighting in a competition. I didn't warm up properly before the fight, so my body wasn't really ready for it, and when I fell I injured myself a bit. I didn't fight for a couple of months after that and it took me a while to get used to competing again.

I: I can imagine!

R: Yeah, but I've been doing quite a lot of yoga for the last few months, and that has really helped a lot.

4.4

1 How long was your flight delayed?
2 How long do you want to stay?
3 How long were you waiting?
4 How long did it take you to get home?
5 How long are you going to go for?
6 How long will it take to repair?
7 How long have you been seeing Dan?
8 How long does it take you to get here?

REVIEW 01

R 1.3

1 I suppose a lot of people would've been fed up to travel that far and find the weather is quite grey and chilly, but to be honest I can't really deal with the heat. I like to spend my time walking along the beach and looking at the wildlife and so it was just what I needed after all the stress at work.

2 I'm still not really sure how to greet people here in England even after years living here. Often they don't do anything – just smile – sometimes they kiss you once on the cheek and occasionally twice. Quite often I change my mind in mid-kiss and I end up either

banging my nose on their nose or kissing the air, which makes me feel a bit stupid.

3 I play for a local volleyball team. I find I really need to play to relax at the weekend because I have a very stressful job. I hardly ever miss a game, so it's really annoying that I've got injured and I can't play for six weeks. And they're playing in our local cup competition on Saturday and I was really looking forward to it. It's a real shame.

4 It was a bit frustrating when I started the job. I could get by outside the office, but it was more difficult being in a meeting where everyone was talking and I couldn't express myself. I pick things up quite quickly, though, and I did extra classes in the evenings. After a year I've become quite fluent so I'm really happy.

UNIT 05

5.1

I = Ivan, A = Amanda

I: So what do you do, Amanda?

A: I work for a mobile phone company.

I: Oh yeah. Doing what?

A: I work in the design department. I'm involved in designing what you see on the screen of the phone. You know, all the graphics and icons.

I: Oh right. Sounds interesting. How did you get into that?

A: Well, I studied graphic design. After I graduated, I worked for a company that designed websites. Then one day I saw Vodafone were recruiting people so I applied and I got a job. They gave me some training and I just got into it that way.

I: So how long have you been working there?

A: It must be seven years now. Wait! No, eight! I was 25 when I joined. Time goes so fast!

I: You must enjoy it.

A: Yeah, I do generally. It's quite varied because they're constantly changing the phones and designs, and of course it's quite a creative job, which is nice. But, you know, it's like any job. It has its boring moments and the hours can be quite long.

I: Really? How long?

A: Well, it depends if we have a deadline to meet, but sometimes I do something like fifty or sixty hours a week.

I: Really? That must be stressful.

A: Yeah, it can be, but you get used to it. In fact, I sometimes need that stress to work well, you know. I sometimes work better under pressure.

I: Really? I can't work like that.

A: So what do you do?

I: Oh, nothing! At the moment, I'm just studying.

A: Really? How old did you say you are?

I: Thirty.

A: Really? You look younger.

I Thanks.

A: So were you working before?

I: Kind of. I worked in a law firm two years ago, but it was really insecure. They said I would get a permanent contract, but then it never happened and it was really badly paid. I got almost nothing.

A: That's terrible!

I: Yeah, but you know, it happens quite a lot. Anyway, now I'm preparing for government exams, so I can get a civil service job. It's much more secure. It's almost a job for life.

5.2

1 A: I'm the sales manager for Europe. I'm in charge of thirty reps.
  B: That must be quite stressful.
  A: It can be, but I like the responsibility and my own manager is quite supportive if there are any big problems.
2 C: I travel a lot round Europe and the Middle East.
  D: That must be really interesting.
  C: Not really. A lot of the time all you see is the hotel. You get fed up with it quite quickly.
3 E: I care for people who are dying.
  F: That must be quite upsetting.
  E: It can be, yes. Er,... but when you work as a nurse you have to get used to working in emotional situations.
4 G: Basically, I just sit in front of a TV screen all day.
  H: Yeah? That must be quite boring.
  G: It can be, but I read quite a lot, which is good.
5 I: I often can't explain myself clearly in English.
  J: That must be really frustrating.
  I: Yeah, it is. I often get quite annoyed with myself.
6 K: I really see the kids develop and improve.
  L: That must be really rewarding.
  K: Yeah, it is. I wouldn't do any other job.

5.3

Conversation 1
D = Dom, L = Laura

D: Did you hear about Patrick?
L: No. What?
D: Apparently, he's been reprimanded.
L: You're joking! What for?
D: He was going on the Internet all the time to buy concert tickets and book holidays. And he was always sending personal emails.
L: No! But everyone does that, don't they?
D: Yeah, well, you're not supposed to use the company computers like that. Not in his company, anyway.
L: That's a bit unfair, isn't it?
D: I know. Actually, I think the problem was that he visited some site and got a computer virus and then it infected the whole system. Apparently, the company have had to spend over £20,000 to sort out the problem.
L: Oh right. I can see why they might be a bit angry, then!

Conversation 2
F = Francesca, J = Jade

F: Are you thinking of buying that?
J: Yeah, what do you think?
F: Very smart. I don't usually see you wearing stuff like that.
J: No, I know, but I've got this new job working in a law firm.
F: Oh really? That's great news! What are you going to be doing there?
J: Just admin work really, but they have a strict dress code – you're not even allowed to wear smart trousers. You have to wear skirts!
F: You're joking! Is that legal?
J: I guess. They can do what they want, can't they?
F: You think?
J: Well, anyway, I need the job, and I've been looking for ages so I'm not going to complain!

Conversation 3
A = Adam, B = Bill

A: Bill, sorry to interrupt, but can I have a quick word?
B: Yes, of course. What's up?

A: Listen, I need to take the day off on Friday. My son's performing in a school concert.
B: Friday? I'm afraid that's impossible.
A: Are you sure?
B: Sorry, Adam. It wouldn't be a problem normally, but we've got a bit of a crisis. Vicky's off sick and we really need to complete this order by Saturday.
A: Can't someone else help? My son will be so disappointed if I don't watch him play. And I do have some holiday left for this year.
B: I'm sure. But if we're late with this order, we might lose the whole contract.
A: I see.
B: You should really arrange time off with me a month in advance, you know.
A: I know, I know. It's just I've asked you at short notice before and it hasn't been a problem.
B: Well as I say, normally it isn't.
A: Well, I guess that's all. I don't know what I'll tell my son.
B: I'm sorry. You'll be really helping me and the company.

UNIT 06

6.1

A: Do you like it? OK?
B: Yeah, it's nice. How much is it?
A: Five hundred.
B: Five hundred! That's really expensive.
A: It's very good quality. Feel it.
B: Yeah, I know.
A: Real silk and it's hand-woven. You see here, it's a bit uneven, whereas this one, it's machine-woven, so it's all the same.
B: Uh huh.
A: This one, the colour, it'll last longer.
B: Sure. It's nice. But five hundred?
A: How much do you want to pay?
B: Well, I was thinking one hundred dollars.
A: One hundred! Come on!
B: OK, one fifty.
A: You're insulting me. I won't make any money like that. Listen, I'll give it to you for four hundred.
B: Two – I've seen similar ones for that price.
A: Similar, but not as good. Go then! Go and buy it. You're wasting my time ... OK. I tell you what, I'll give you it for three fifty.
B: Three hundred. I don't have much money left.
A: No. Three hundred and fifty. Final offer. Take it or leave it. Three fifty. I'm giving it away. I have children. Look, feel it. It's beautiful.
B: It is nice ... OK, three fifty.
A: Three fifty. You are a difficult man. It's a very good price, eh. My wife, she'll kill me! You want anything else? Very nice plates, hand-painted ...

6.2

A: Can I help you?
B: Yeah, I'm thinking of changing phone companies.
A: Who are you with at the moment?
B: Blue. but I'm looking to see if there are any better deals around.
A: I'm sure we can find you something. What phone have you got now?
B: This one, but they've offered to upgrade it to the S620.
A: OK, that's a nice phone. And what are your monthly payments?

B: £20 a month.

A: OK, well, I think we could offer you something better. For example, this one – the N5703.

B: All right. What's the difference? They look pretty similar.

A: Well, with this one, the N5703, you get greater functionality, like email, and on the whole it's much better quality. For example, this has a lithium battery, whereas the other phone uses a nickel cadmium one, which isn't as good. The lithium one lasts a lot longer.

B: Oh, OK.

A: And then the camera is almost twice as powerful. So this one is 3 mega-pixel and it has a digital zoom, whereas the one on the S620 is just 1.7.

B: Right. And how many pictures can the N5703 store?

A: Well, on the phone itself, not that many, but it comes with a memory card which stores up to 700 photos and 250 songs, whereas the S620 doesn't have a memory card – I guess that's because there's no MP3 – so you can only store about 15 photos.

B: OK, so this one has an MP3 player as well.

A: Yes, of course.

B: I'm sure the sound quality isn't as good as my normal MP3 player, though.

A: Maybe not, but it is good quality. I use my phone all the time now to listen to music. It's maybe slightly worse than your MP3, but it's a lot more convenient. I mean, you've got everything in one package. You don't really want to carry round a separate phone, MP3 and camera all the time, do you?

B: No, I suppose not. What about calls and text messages? How many can you offer me?

A: Well, for £20 a month we could give you 150 free minutes and 100 texts.

B: 150! That's quite a lot less than Blue are offering me.

A: Well, I'm not sure we can give much more for that phone. What do you get with them?

B: 200 free minutes and 150 texts.

A: OK. Well, we could probably match that and still give you the better phone.

6.3

L = Leo, N = Noel

L: Hey Noel, can you remind me later? I must try and book some tickets for a gig next week.

N: Yeah, of course – assuming I remember myself, that is! Who are you thinking of seeing?

L: Oh, it's a German group called *The Brain Police*. I don't know if you know them.

N: Yeah, of course I do! They're great. I've been into them for ages. I've already got tickets for the gig next week, as it happens.

L: Oh really? How much did you pay for them?

N: Twenty each, but I'm pretty sure they've sold out now.

L: What? But they've only been on sale for a day.

N: Yeah, but you know what it's like, Leo. Things sell out so quickly. I had to queue for an hour to get mine.

L: Oh no! I was going to take my girlfriend as a birthday present! She would've loved it. She's a huge fan. I don't suppose you want to sell yours, do you?

N: No chance! Nice try, though. Why don't you look online? You must be able to get tickets somewhere. Try looking at one of the auction sites – like eBay or something.

L: Yeah, but things cost a fortune on there.

N: Well, not necessarily, and anyway what other options have you got?

L: No, I guess you're right.

N: And if you really can't find anything on the Internet, then I suppose you could go down to the venue next week. Hang around outside for a while and try and buy tickets from someone. There are sometimes people outside selling spare tickets they've bought.

L: What? You mean buy them from a ticket tout? Isn't that a bit risky? I mean, I don't want to buy a ticket and then not get in because it's a fake or something.

N: Well it's up to you. I'll tell you what, though, if you like *The Brain Police*, you must go and see *Spook Train*. They're brilliant and they're playing next week. I'm sure you'd be able to get tickets for them. Maybe you'd be better just trying that instead.

UNIT 07

7.1

D = Daniel, P = Paulina

D: So how's the course going? Are you enjoying it?

P: I am, yeah, but it's hard work. I have to go in to college almost every day for a lecture or a seminar or just to use the library, so I've been pretty busy lately.

D: Wow! It sounds quite demanding.

P: Yeah, it is, but it's also really interesting. The course is pretty flexible, so there's a wide range of different modules we can take, which is great. I've just started doing a module in Marketing Psychology, which is fascinating.

D: It sounds it. So what does that involve, then? I mean, what kind of things do you have to study?

P: Well, we have to look at different kinds of shoppers, the relationship between advertising and shopping, that kind of thing. It's brilliant.

D: Oh, that's great. I'm glad it's going well. And what are the other students like? Do you get on with them OK?

P: Yeah, they're mostly really nice and friendly.

D: Mostly?

P: Well, there are one or two guys that never really talk to anyone or help, but generally everyone's very supportive. I mean, we're all in the same situation, so ...

D: Sure. And what about the tutors? What are they like?

P: They're great. They're all so helpful and dedicated. I feel really lucky to have such knowledgeable people teaching me.

D: It sounds great. So how long does the course last? When do you finish?

P: Not for another few months yet. The final exams are next April. I've got plenty of work to do before then!

D: I bet! And what are you going to do once the course has finished? Have you decided yet?

P: Well, actually the first thing I'm going to do is take a long holiday. I think I deserve it.

D: Right. Where are you thinking of going?

P: Well, I'm going to fly to India and then travel through Asia to Australia. When I'm there, I might look for a job.

D: Doing what?

P: Oh, I don't know. Bar work or something. Whatever I can get. And then after I get back from Australia, I'll just start looking for a proper job.

7.2

Conversation 1

A: How's the class?

B: Awful! They just don't pay attention. If I try to explain something, they sit whispering to each other. It's so rude! And then there's one boy who always walks in 20 minutes late. He doesn't apologise. He just puts his mobile on the table, takes off his iPod and his Armani sunglasses – and then he sits there looking bored, because he thinks he knows it all. He's got no pen, no paper, nothing. It's really annoying!

A: I think you need to set some rules. If they talk, send them to the headmaster or give them a detention.

B: Maybe. I don't want to be too strict.

A: But you have to be! If you're strict from the start, you'll gain their respect. Obviously, you need to be fair as well.

Conversation 2

C: Are you OK? You look a bit fed up.

D: I've just got the results of my English test.

C: Oh dear. What did you get?

D: A 6. And I needed a 6.5 to do a Master's.

C: Oh no! I'm sorry. But you worked so hard. I was sure you'd get at least a 7.

D: I know. I was so stupid. I misread one of the questions. That probably lowered my score.

C: Oh dear. So what are you going to do now?

D: It depends. I'm going to ring the course leader and see if they'll accept me with a 6. If they don't accept me on the course, I'll either re-take the test or I might look for another master's.

Conversation 3

E: Right, there are a number of things I need to tell you about assessment. Firstly, 50% of your final marks are based on your essays during the course. Because of that, we're very strict on deadlines. If you miss a deadline that your tutor has set, you will be given a zero. No arguments! Secondly, er … yes.

F: Yes, sorry to interrupt, but what if you have a family crisis or something?

E: Well, obviously we'll make an exception for certain cases affecting your immediate family. Also, we won't accept any excuses to do with illness unless you produce a doctor's certificate within two days of the deadline. Does that answer your question? Good. I should say, while we're on the subject, that if you have any problems which are affecting your coursework, you should contact the student counselling service. Their number is …

Conversation 4

G: So how's Angela doing at her new school?

H: Oh, much better, thanks. I'm so glad we decided to move her to St James's. The teachers seem a lot better prepared. And they push the kids. I think Angela was just a bit bored at her last school.

G: Well, she's a bright kid.

H: And that other school was quite rough. I was always hearing about fights in the playground and kids skipping classes.

G: Well, St James's has a very good reputation.

H: Yes. Discipline is very good there. And I think they look so much smarter in a uniform.

G: Mmm.

🎧 **7.3**

1 If I try to explain something, half of them just sit there whispering to each other.

2 If they talk, just send them to the headmaster or give them a detention.

3 If they don't accept me on the course, I'll either re-take the test or I might look for another Masters.

4 If you miss a deadline that your tutor has set, you will be given a zero.

5 If you have any problems which are affecting you're coursework, you should contact the student counselling service.

UNIT 08

🎧 **8.1**

A = Aurora, C = Claes

A: They don't have an English menu, I'm afraid, Claes – just a Spanish one.

C: That's OK. You'll just have to talk me through it.

A: No problem. Well, for starters they've got *Papa Rellena*. That's balls of mashed potato, stuffed with beef, raisins and olives, and then deep-fried.

C: OK. That sounds very filling for a starter!

A: It can be, yeah. Then there's *Anticuchos*. That's a bit like a Peruvian kebab. It's sliced cow heart, very tender and juicy, grilled on a stick.

C: Right. To be honest, Aurora, I don't really like the idea of eating heart. I don't know why. I just don't.

A: That's OK. No problem. There are plenty of other dishes to choose from.

C: Sorry. Anyway, what's next? What's *Ceviche*?

A: *Ceviche*! That's Peru's national dish. Have you never tried it?

C: No, never.

A: Oh, you really should. It's delicious. It's basically raw fish marinated in lime juice or lemon juice and served with the local kind of potato and corn. You get lots of different kinds of *Ceviche*, using different fish and seafood.

C: OK. Well, I'll go for that, the ceviche. What are you going to have?

A: The *Tallarín Con Mariscos*. It's a kind of spaghetti served with shrimps and prawns and squid.

C: Sounds great. And what about the main courses?

A: Well, the *Bistec Apanado*. That's steak, sliced very thinly and then fried and served with rice.

C: OK.

A: And then there are two rice dishes – *Arroz Con Mariscos*, which is rice with fresh seafood. It's a bit like a Spanish paella, but spicier. Then there's *Arroz Con Pato*, which is rice with duck. The *Lomo Saltado* is a kind of steak dish.

C: Another one? I don't really eat steak very much, to be honest. I tend to find it quite bland.

A: Bland? Not this one. It's cooked with tomatoes and onions and spices and things. It's really good. Honestly!

C: I'll take your word for it, but I don't really feel like steak tonight anyway.

A: OK. Well, finally, there's *Seco De Cabrito*. It's a kind of stew with goat meat in, young goat meat – and they serve it with beans on the side.

C: That sounds very tasty. And quite unusual too. I'll have that.

🎧 **8.2**

Conversation 1

A: Where shall we go, then?

B: How about that bar on the corner?

A: Mmm. The music's a bit loud in there. It's not very good if you want to chat. I'm not sure they do much food either.

B: Oh right. Do you have somewhere else in mind then?

A: Well, if you don't mind walking, I know this really nice café. It has a terrace that looks out over the river.

B: Well, that'd be nice.

A: Yeah, and they do some really nice snacks.

B: Great. So how far is it?

A: Well, it is a twenty-minute walk.

B: That's OK – the walk will give us an appetite!

Conversation 2

C: Have you been to that restaurant in the main street?

D: Yeah, a couple of times.

C: Is it any good?

D: Yeah. The menu's a bit limited. I mean, there aren't really any options if you're vegetarian, but it's good home-style cooking.

C: Right. It's just that I went past and it was almost deserted.

D: I know. I'm surprised they stay in business, to be honest. They should advertise in the paper or something, because the food's nice, and they're very friendly.

C: Well, they might attract a few more people if they redecorated, even if they just re-painted it.

D: That's true. I suppose the restaurant doesn't look very inviting.

Conversation 3

E: How's your fish?

F: It's OK, but it would be better if it didn't have so much sauce on it!

E: There is a lot of it.

F: Yeah, and it's really overpowering. I mean, the sauce is quite spicy so it really overpowers the taste of everything else.

E: Oh dear. Do you want to try some of mine?

F: Go on then. Here, try some of this as well. It's not that bad. Mmm ... that's gorgeous! That steak is so tender! You don't want to swap, do you?

E: Erm, no thanks. I think I'll stick with my one. You can have another bite, though.

Conversation 4

G: When did we ask for the bill?

H: I don't know. At least half an hour ago!

G: I know they're busy, but this is ridiculous. I think we should just go ...

H: What? Without paying? Are you mad?

G: Well, they don't seem to want our money, do they?

H: Don't be ridiculous. I mean, what would happen if they called the police?

G: They wouldn't do that. Anyway, the restaurant doesn't deserve the money. I mean, the food wasn't that great.

H: The asparagus was OK.

G: Yeah, but the portions weren't very generous and the rest of the food was pretty bland. Those vegetables were really overcooked.

H: Yes, but you can't just leave without paying, can you?

G: Hu. No, I suppose not!

8.3

I think it's a really serious problem nowadays. People are just obsessed with being thin. I know lots of teenage girls who say they are on a diet when they don't really need to lose weight. I blame the media. I recently heard of a reality TV show here in Germany where they were trying to find the next top model. Apparently, one girl was voted off the show because she was too fat. I think she only weighed something like 50 kilos and she was 1 metre 70 tall. That's terrible! No wonder girls get eating disorders! It's difficult to know how to stop this, but maybe they should just ban adverts featuring really thin models – make them completely illegal. If they had bigger, more normal looking people as models, perhaps girls wouldn't worry about their weight so much.

REVIEW 02

R2.2

Speaker 1

I love it – you have to love it, really, to cope with working such long hours. Sure, some of the work is quite repetitive, but it's also very creative as everyone in the kitchen is involved in creating the menus. It does annoy me how badly paid it is though, especially when the waiters get tips. OK, service is important, but surely people are eating out for the food – and most waiters haven't studied as much as I have.

Speaker 2

I'm lucky, because I've always loved eating, but I'm one of those people who never puts on weight even if I don't always have a balanced diet. I'd never do this job if I had to starve myself like some girls do. I only really do it for the money anyway – I'm not that interested in fashion. Outside my job, I don't wear very trendy clothes and never wear high-heels. I'm happy doing it till I'm 30, but then I'll find something else.

Speaker 3

Domestic science used to have a bad reputation, but these days the course is much more than learning how to roast a chicken – we cook dishes from all over the world. We also cover hygiene and the science behind having a healthy diet. Some of the kids think I'm quite strict, but you have to be. If you can't control the class here with hot ovens and hot fat, people can get hurt.

Speaker 4

I never used to eat out that much, because I couldn't really afford it. However, since I've been working here, we quite often take out clients or potential customers for lunch to discuss business. In fact, I need to watch my weight because I tend to eat more when I go out. This particular place is my favourite. The service is great, and I love Moroccan food and it's maybe a bit different to the restaurants my clients normally go to, which is nice.

Speaker 5

It took a while to get used to working nights, but I quite like it now, because for every ten days I work, I get a week off. It is quite boring though, packing boxes all night, and I sometimes get backache from bending over and lifting a lot. People often say it must be great to work where they make chocolate. I did used to eat some when I first started here, but you quickly get fed up with it – and of course it is fattening! I hardly ever eat it now.

UNIT 09

9.1

G = Gavin, L = Lynn

G: Did I tell you I went round to see Nick and Carol the other day?

L: No, you didn't. How are they? I haven't seen them for ages.

G: Oh, they're fine. They said to say 'Hello' to you. You know they've moved recently, don't you?

L: Oh really? No, I didn't, actually. The last time I heard from them they were still in that place near the centre.

G: Oh, OK. Well, yeah, they moved, um I think it was last month. To be honest, they seem much happier now.

L: Oh, that's good. So what's their new place like? Is it nice?

G: Yeah, it is. It's OK. It's quite a lot bigger than their old place. The front room is huge – it's about twice the size of this room – and the whole place is pretty spacious.

L: That must be nice for them, now the kids are growing up.

G: I know. They said the old place was getting a bit cramped for them all. They wanted separate rooms for the kids. They didn't want them sharing forever! That's the main reason they moved out.

L: So what kind of place is it? I mean, is it a house or a flat?

G: Oh, it's a flat. It's on the third floor of an old block. It's a little bit run-down and it does need a bit of work done on it, but they've actually bought it, so they can do what they want to it.

L: Lucky them! All those weekends spent painting and decorating to look forward to!

G: I know! I don't envy them! It has got real potential, though. It's got a great kitchen – it's a similar size to yours, maybe a bit bigger – and it's got these lovely old wooden floors throughout – and huge windows, so they get a lot of sunlight coming in, which is great. Then there's a little balcony where you can sit and eat in the summer, and a shared garden out the back where the kids can play and everything.

L: Oh, it sounds lovely. I must go round and see them sometime soon.

G: Yeah, I'm sure they'd like that. The only problem is, though, it's not as central as their old place was. It's quite a lot further out, so it takes quite a long time to get there.

L: Oh, OK.

9.3

Conversation 1

A: I live near the port.

B: What's it like round there? I've heard it's quite dangerous.

A: I know it has that reputation, and there are still bad things about it but it's better than it was before. There used to be a lot of problems with drugs, but the police have done a lot to clean up the area. There's nowhere near as much crime as there was five years ago. And the government's invested quite a lot of money to improve the local facilities.

B: Oh right. I didn't know.

A: Yeah. I mean, there are still some rough streets that I would probably avoid at night, but everywhere has some crime, doesn't it? I know someone who lives in quite a posh area of the city and he got robbed, so, you're never completely safe anywhere.

B: I guess that's true.

A: And where we live is convenient for the centre of town and it's not far from the beach, and on top of all that it's still quite cheap, so it's good. I like it. It doesn't matter to me that some places are still a bit run-down.

Conversation 2

C: I live in an area on the outskirts of town.

D: Oh yeah? What's it like?

C: It's OK. It's just a normal residential area – it's very green, there are plenty of places for the kids to run around and play. I mean, we live on a very small side street, so there's hardly any traffic. The kids just play in the street a lot of the time.

D: Sounds nice.

C: Yeah, on the whole we love it, even though it's not as quiet as it used to be.

D: How come?

C: Well, we're close to the airport. When we moved here the airport was quite small and there were far fewer flights than there are now. Then one of the budget airlines started using the airport and over the past few years it's become bigger and bigger. So it's often quite noisy . You kind of get used to the noise after a while, but it's still quite annoying – especially late at night.

D: I can imagine.

C: Still, I can't complain too much. I certainly wouldn't want to move.

UNIT 10

10.1

D = Dan, J = Jason

D: Do you fancy going out later?

J: Yeah, maybe. What's on?

D: Well, do you like horror films?

J: Yeah, if I'm in the right mood. Why?

D: Well there's this Brazilian film which is on in town that I'd quite like to see. It's got English subtitles, so it should be OK.

J: Oh yeah? What's it about?

D: Apparently, it's about zombies taking over Brasilia.

J: Oh right. That sounds fun. When's it on?

D: There's a showing at just after 9 and then a late one at 12.

J: OK. Well, I'm not sure I want to go to the late one. I need to be up quite early tomorrow.

D: That's OK. The ten past nine showing is good for me.

J: Where's it on?

D: The Capitol.

J: Oh, er, OK. Great.

10.2

D = Dan, J = Jason

D: Do you know where the cinema is?

J: I think so. Isn't The Capitol that one near the river?

D: Er ... no.

J: Oh right. Well, in that case, no, I'm not sure.

D: It's in the centre – on Crown Street.

J: No, I don't know it.

D: You know Oxford Road, yeah? That's the main street which goes past the railway station.

J: Yeah, yeah.

D: Well, if you have your back to the station, you turn right down Oxford Road. You walk about 200 metres and you go past a post office.

J: OK.

D: And the next street after that is Crown Street. The cinema's along there, about halfway down.

J: Oh yeah. I think I know the place now. There's a big sweet shop right opposite, isn't there?

D: That's the one.

J: OK. So what time do you want to meet?

D: Well, the programme starts at 9.10, so shall I just meet you on the steps outside at 9?

J: Can we make it 8.30? We want to be sure we get a ticket.

D: I doubt it'll be that busy, but I suppose we could get there a bit earlier. We can always get a coffee before the film starts.

J: Exactly. Maybe whoever gets there first should start queuing, OK?

D: OK, but I don't think we need to worry. I don't think that many people will want to see a Brazilian zombie movie!

J: You never know!

10.5

Conversation 1

A: So how was it?

B: Brilliant – it was much better than I thought it would be.

A: Really. I'd heard it wasn't that good.

B: Well, me too, but I really enjoyed it.

A: So what was so good about it?

B: The story, the acting, everything. It's just really funny and it's quite exciting too. I don't know. Maybe it was because I wasn't expecting very much.

A: I know what you mean. You see so many films these days where there's so much advance publicity – especially from Hollywood. It's all in the papers and everyone's saying "you must see it". And then you go and you just think it's a bit overrated. It's nice to have the opposite experience.

Conversation 2

C: Did you have a good night out? How was the gig?

D: Oh, we didn't go in the end.

C: Really? What a shame.

D: No. Hans had promised me he'd pick me up at 7, but of course he was late! He had to finish some work at the office and by the time we got there, there was a massive queue for tickets. So we decided we weren't going to get in, and we went to a club instead.

C: Oh right. So what club did you go to?

D: Radio City.

C: Well, that's supposed to be really good – it's quite trendy, isn't it?

D: That's what they say, but I hated it!

C: Really? What was so bad about it?

D: The people, the music, everything – it's awful. It's one of the worst clubs I've been to.

C: Really?

D: OK, maybe I'm exaggerating a bit. I mean, it was OK to begin with, but then it got absolutely packed, so you couldn't really dance properly. And it was boiling hot, so you were sweating like crazy. And then they changed the music later to this heavy techno stuff, which I hate. And the drinks were a rip-off...

C Oh dear. Maybe you just went on the wrong night.

Conversation 3

E: I'm a bit tired. I was out late last night.

F: Really? I thought you said you were going to stay in.

E: Yes. I was going to stay in, but I was talking to Clara on the phone last night. She mentioned she'd got a spare ticket for this play in town and I said I'd go with her.

F: Not *A Man for All Seasons*?

E: Yeah that's the one.

F: Oh I've been wanting to see that for ages! It's had some excellent reviews in the papers. How was it?

E: Brilliant! It's one of the best things I've seen in a long time.

F: That's what I'd heard.

E: Yeah. It's so moving. Honestly, I was in tears at the end. And the whole staging – the lighting, the costumes, everything – it's just really well done.

F: I'll have to go.

E: Yeah, you should.

UNIT 11

11.1

Conversation 1

A: You'll never guess what happened last night.

B: Go on. What?

A: Well, I was writing some reports on my computer at home when I suddenly noticed a group of crows looking quite excited. They were all making this dreadful noise, so I went outside to see what was happening.

B: And?

A: Well, the crows were chasing a little parrot up and down the street.

B: A parrot? What was it doing there?

A: I have no idea. I guess it must've escaped from somewhere. Anyway, it was obviously very scared and cold. I felt really sorry for it, so I chased the crows away. I then spent two hours trying to get the parrot off my neighbour's roof.

B: Yeah? So what happened in the end? Did you catch it?

A: Yeah, eventually it came down and I managed to catch it and put it into a box. We've got it at home now!

B: Wow! That's mad. Actually, it reminds me of something I saw a few weeks ago. I was coming home from work on my bicycle when...

Conversation 2

C: How was your journey? Was it OK?

D: Yeah, it was fine, but I did see something really strange on the way.

C: Yeah? What was that?

D: Well, at about midnight last night, I was driving along next to a field and the road was quite narrow. In front of me, I suddenly saw this huge snake lying across the road.

C: Ugh! Really?

D: Yeah! I mean, it was obviously dead, but next to it, I could see what I thought was a cat, eating part of the snake. As I got nearer, though, I realised that it was actually the largest, most disgusting rat I have ever seen in my life, staring up at my car. It was so horrible! Actually, I was so shocked, I almost ran it over. I just managed to avoid it and it disappeared into the long grass!

C: Oh, nasty! It actually reminds me of something my brother once told me, about when him and some friends of his were camping in...

Conversation 3

E: I really thought I was going to die. Honestly, I hope I never see another crocodile in my life!

F: I can imagine. That's awful! It actually reminds me of something that happened to me last year in Indonesia.

E: Oh yeah? What was that?

F: Well, I was there on holiday, and I'd decided to spend a few days trekking through the jungle. On the second day, we were walking along a path through the rainforest when suddenly these huge lizards came running out of the bushes from all sides. They were enormous – much bigger than me! Everyone ran away, leaving me with three of these monster lizards running towards me. I tried to scream, but just couldn't! I really thought they were going to eat me.

E: God! That sounds terrifying! So what happened?

F: Well, luckily, the guides managed to stop the lizards with these big sticks they had, and so I managed to escape.

11.2

1 A: You'll never guess what happened last night.
 B: Go on. What?
 A: Well, I was walking home from the bus stop when I suddenly saw a horse, standing there in the street!

2 C: I saw something really strange while we were away.
 D: Oh yeah? What was that?
 C: We saw this whale stuck on the beach.
 D: Seriously? Still alive?
 C: Yeah! It was actually quite upsetting! We phoned the police to see if they could organise help.

3 E: I was just about to put my shoes on when I found a scorpion hiding in one of the shoes!
 F: Really? God! What was that doing there?

E: I don't know. I guess it was just looking for somewhere to sleep.

4 G: We spent hours trying to persuade the cat to come down from the tree, but it refused to come.

H: Oh no. That's awful! So what happened in the end?

G: Well, eventually, we gave up. But an hour later it walked into the kitchen, looking for its dinner!

11.3

S = Suzie, A = Al

S: Oh wow! They're so cute!

A: I know. They're great. They're only three weeks old.

S: What breed are they?

A: Siberian Huskies.

S: Really? So what are you going to do with them?

A: Well, I wish I could keep them, but it's too much. They grow so big.

S: Mmm.

A: So, I guess we'll just sell them or give them away. You don't want one, do you?

S: Er ... no! I'm actually more of a cat person.

A: Really? I can't stand cats myself.

S: Why?

A: I just find them annoying. They're only interested in people so they can get food. You know what I mean? Most of the time, they're out of the house. They only come back when they want to be fed.

S: Oh, come on! They're not that bad. They like to be stroked – and it's good anyway, that independence. I mean – don't get me wrong – I do like dogs, but they're very demanding. They always expect you to play with them or take them for walks. And they're always jumping on top of you and licking you. I could do without it.

A: Oh, I like that about them! Dogs are more rewarding – you develop a relationship with a dog.

S: Well, I prefer my relationships to be human!

A: OK, but you know what I mean.

S: I suppose so.

A: So have you got a cat, then?

S: No. We had one when I was younger. In fact, my parents still have him, but it's not fair to have a cat in my flat. Cats need some freedom. And then the litter tray's really smelly!

A: I can imagine. So you don't have any pets?

S: Well, actually, I've got a snake.

A: A snake! You're joking. I'm terrified of snakes.

S: There's no need to be – the one I've got isn't poisonous.

A: OK, but how big is it?

S: About a metre. It's a bit shorter than that table.

A: Well, that's big enough. Where do you keep it?

S: It's in a tank in my bedroom. It doesn't need much looking after. I just give it a mouse every month or two.

A: A mouse? You don't have to catch them, do you?

S: No! I buy them frozen from the pet shop and then I defrost them in the microwave.

A: Oh, what? That's so disgusting!

S: What's so disgusting about it? It's no different to the tinned food you give your dog. It's only meat.

A: I know, but ... I don't know. So, do you ever take it out?

S: Yeah, of course! I've taken it to university a few times to show people. People like to have their photo taken with it around their neck.

A: Not me!

S: It's fun!

A: Forget it.

S: Actually, the last time I took it out at home, it disappeared behind the cooker and wouldn't come out.

A: You're joking! How did you get it out?

S: I had to leave a mouse on the floor to persuade it to come out.

A: Oh man! That's horrible.

11.5

I don't really like dogs, but I really hate some dog owners. They can be so annoying – the way they talk about their pets like they were actually human beings! They say things like, "Oh my little baby. You're so beautiful! Yes, you are. Yes, you are." Oh, it's so stupid. What really annoys me, though, is the way they let their dogs run out of control. They even let their dogs jump on top of you. Then, if the dog bites you, they actually blame you. They say you scared the dog!

UNIT 12

12.1

L = Lewis, J = Jessica

L: Where did you disappear to?

J: Sorry, I went out to phone my brother, Noel. It's his birthday today.

L: Oh OK. It's just that you were a long time.

J: I know. I was only going to be five minutes – just wish him 'happy birthday' – but once he starts talking, he doesn't stop!

L: Oh, that's like my mum. She could talk for hours. I sometimes think we could be on the phone and I could go and have a coffee and then come back and she'd still be talking! She wouldn't have noticed I'd gone!

J: Right. I'm not sure he's quite that bad.

L: No? Well, maybe I am exaggerating a bit, but she is very chatty. So do you and your brother get on well?

J: Yeah, really well, but unfortunately I don't see him that much now because he's living in the States.

L: Really! What's he doing there? Is he working?

J: No, he won a scholarship to study Physics.

L: Wow! He must be very clever.

J: Yeah, he's really bright. He was always top of his class – but he's not really intense with it. He's very funny, very outgoing.

L: That's good. So have you got any other brothers or sisters?

J: Yeah, I've got a younger brother – Greg.

L: And what's he like? Do you get on well with him too?

J: OK, I suppose.

L: You don't sound too sure.

J: No. I mean, we used to be quite close. We were both quite sporty – we would go to the beach a lot, we'd play tennis together and that kind of thing – but he's not interested now.

L: Really?

J: No, he's become a bit of a dropout. It's not that he isn't bright – he's just very lazy. He failed most of his exams last year – and then he's really got into politics. He's always going on demonstrations and complaining about me using the car too much and about me wanting to work for big business.

L: Maybe it's just a phase he's going through. How old is he?

J: 17.

L: Well, he might grow out of it.

J: I hope so. He can be quite boring sometimes.

L: Mmm.

J: Anyway, what about you? Have you got any brothers or sisters?

L: Yeah. Actually, there are six of us!

12.2

We used to be quite close. We were both quite sporty – we would go to the beach a lot, we'd play tennis together and that kind of thing – but he's not interested now.

12.3

1 Doug

I met him while doing a summer job in England. We were both working in this café – he was in the kitchens and I was a waiter. Our boss was a bit of an idiot. He was really strict – he was always shouting at us and was just horrible. Anyway, we used to go out after work and we'd sit and complain about our boss. We'd talk about the things we wished we'd said to him. Nicolas was always very funny about it.

2 Sandra

We were going out for a while. I met him when we were studying in Rome on an Erasmus programme. It was a great few months. We tried to keep the relationship going after he went back to Belgium, but it's difficult maintaining a long-distance relationship. We couldn't afford to visit each other very often and in the end, we split up. We've remained friends – which I suppose is important – but I sometimes wish we'd stayed together. Yeah, I wish we hadn't split up.

3 Shane

I met him while I was backpacking. We were staying in a hostel and we had to share a room. We got talking and found we had a lot in common. We ended up spending a couple of weeks sightseeing until I went back to Australia. We kept in touch via email after that and two years ago I moved to Britain. Since then, I've been over to Belgium to see him a couple of times.

4 Brigitta

We met at university. We didn't have much to do with each other at first. We're a bit different – I'm quite quiet and, as you know, he's very outgoing. It's not that we didn't get on at all. We'd see each other in class and in the library and we'd chat a bit. Over time, though, our chats got longer, and then just before we left university, he asked me out on a date. We've been seeing each other for about two years now. It's a shame it took so long for us to get together, really!

5 Franck

I met him through a friend, Jef, who he was sharing a flat with. We all used to go out quite a lot so I'd talk to Nicolas and got to know him very well. At some point, I had an argument with Jef. It was about something stupid, but we basically stopped talking to each other. We're both very stubborn and I didn't want to be first to apologise, but of course, neither did he! I regret that, really. Anyway, to cut a long story short, I haven't seen Jef for years, but I'm still friends with Nicolas.

REVIEW 03

R3.2

1 Oh, the special effects were incredible and it had a great soundtrack as well. The whole cast was great, but I think Asia Argento was particularly good in it. It's funny, really, because he's certainly not my favourite director, but it really was much more interesting than I thought it would be.

2 The costumes were marvellous and the scenery was fairly spectacular, I suppose, but the acting was just dreadful. Honestly, it was truly terrible! It had had great reviews as well. They said

it was supposed to be a romantic comedy, but no one in the audience laughed at any point. In the end, I left about half an hour from the end.

3 We keep him outside. Whenever we have let him into the house, he's made a terrible mess everywhere. He does make a noise out there and the neighbours have sometimes complained, but what can you do? We tend to just give him leftovers or tinned food, but we do have to take him for a walk every day. He's quite demanding like that.

4 It was just an incredible time. We'd all get up early and start driving. It used to get really hot around twelve, so we'd usually stop for a while and have something to eat. During the time we were there, we saw all sorts – snakes, lions, zebras, everything. Amazing! And most of us have stayed in touch as well. The shared experience helped to bring us all closer together.

UNIT 13

13.1

Conversation 1

M = Maria, B = Belinda, A = Andre

M: Thanks for picking us up. It's really kind of you.

B: That's OK. It's no problem. So how was your journey?

M: Oh, quite stressful, actually. It's a relief to finally be here.

B: Oh no! What happened? You weren't delayed or anything, were you?

M: No, no. It wasn't that, thank God, but everything else that could go wrong, did! To begin with, we almost missed the flight – because Andre didn't want to spend too long hanging around at the airport.

A: I've already said I'm sorry!

M: He said we'd be OK if we got there an hour and a half before take-off, but there was a huge queue at the check-in desk – and then another one going through security, so in the end we only just caught the flight.

B: Oh, it's horrible when that happens, isn't it?

M: Yeah – and then the flight was dreadful as well. As we were coming over France, we hit a big storm and it was really bumpy. Honestly, at one point, I thought we were going to crash.

B: Oh, that sounds terrifying.

M: It was! I don't want to go through that again, I can tell you!

B: I'm sure. What do you want to do now? Do you want to go to the office, or do you want to check in at the hotel first?

Conversation 2

L = Lara, K = Karen

L: Hi. There you are! I was starting to worry.

K: Yeah, sorry I'm so late. I had a bit of a nightmare getting here.

L: Oh really? How come?

K: Well, to begin with, it was still dark when we set off.

L: Really? What time did you leave?

K: Six. And then it immediately started to pour down, so the roads were really slippery.

L: Oh, I hate driving in the rain – especially in the dark.

K: So do I. That's probably why I took a wrong turning. I got completely lost and ended up going round in circles for ages. I couldn't work out where I was or where I was going! Then, when I finally got back onto the right road, I almost had an accident.

L: Seriously? What happened?

K: Oh, it wasn't anything bad. It was just this stupid guy in a big expensive car who drove straight across me. I had to brake to avoid hitting him. I wasn't hurt or anything, but I did have to stop and park the car for a few minutes to calm down.

L: Oh, you poor thing. That's awful – but that's male drivers for you!

13.3

Conversation 1

A: What was the weather like in Peru? Was it hot?

B: No, it wasn't, actually. We arrived at night, and it was freezing. Then, during the day it was still chilly and cloudy.

A: Oh dear.

B: I wish I'd taken some warmer clothes – I only had T-shirts and one thin jacket.

A: Oh no!

B: It was stupid – I should've thought more carefully about what to pack. I knew we'd be in the mountains and could've checked the forecast.

A: I guess, but South America – you assume it'll be hot.

B: Exactly! It's silly, really! Anyway, we still had an amazing time!

Conversation 2

D: Hello.

C: Hello, mum. It's me. Alan.

D: Oh hello. I was worried. Did you arrive safely?

C: Yeah, sorry, we got here late – that's why I didn't phone.

D: Oh right. So, is everything OK? Are you both well?

C: Yeah, fine, except for the cockroaches in the hotel.

D: Cockroaches!

C: Yeah. We stayed in this little place last night and the room was filthy.

D: That's horrible!

C: We were silly. We should've looked around more, but because we got here so late, we just chose the first cheap place we came across.

D: Oh Alan!

C: Don't worry – we'll check the place out better next time.

D: I hope so.

Conversation 3

E: How was Greece? Nice and hot?

F: Yes, it was. It was boiling!

E: Lucky you! I bet that was nice.

F: It was, but I did get sunburnt on the first day.

E: Oh no!

F: It was really hot and I was sunbathing and just fell asleep. The next day, my skin went purple! It was horrible.

E: Oh, you poor thing!

F: Oh it was my own fault. I shouldn't have stayed in the sun for so long, especially with my skin! I should've at least put on some sun cream!

Conversation 4

G: Hello, Sir. You're flying to Prague.

H: That's right.

G: Is that your only bag to check in?

H: Yes.

G: I'm afraid there's an excess baggage charge of €200 to pay.

H: What? But there's three of us! The baggage allowance is 15 kilos each.

G: I'm sorry sir, but the rules are very clear: the maximum for any one bag is 15 kilos. You can transfer some weight to your hand baggage, if you like.

H: How can we fit 15 kilos in there – it's tiny!

G: Well, in that case you need to pay the excess.

H: That's ridiculous.

G: I'm sorry, but it really isn't my fault. The ticket conditions are very clear. I'm afraid you have to go back to the desk over there and pay the excess.

H: But the queue's huge!

I: I told you we should've brought another suitcase.

H: I just thought it would be easier with one.

I: €200! That's such a rip off!

UNIT 14

14.2

J = Jirka, E = Ella

J: Hello. Jirka Kaspar. IT.

E: Oh hello, Jirka. This is Ella. From Marketing.

J: Hi. What can I do for you?

E: Well, I've actually got a fairly major problem. My computer crashed yesterday and when I turned it on again today I seem to have lost all my really important files.

J: OK. Well, firstly – don't panic! I'm sure everything will be in there somewhere. What makes you think you've lost them?

E: Well, the folders I keep all my files in have just disappeared from the screen.

J: OK. Have you made back-up copies at all? Haven't you copied them onto an external hard drive or onto online storage or anything?

E: I was worried you might ask me that! It's stupid of me, but I haven't, no. I just kept all my files on the computer.

J: Ah! OK. Well, in future, you might want to think about backing the files up more! Anyway, you say it crashed yesterday.

E: Yes, but it'd been strange all week. The screen kept freezing and I kept having to re-start it all the time.

J: Right. And was it slow?

E: Yes, very.

J: That might be because the memory was full.

E: Ah, OK. And then I turned it on today and everything had gone. I'll be in such trouble if I can't find things again!

J: Have you done a search for them?

E: Kind of, yeah. I've tried searching for specific files, but nothing comes up.

J: And have you tried re-booting at all?

E: Um . . . what does that mean?

J: Turning it off and then turning it on again.

E: Oh, OK. I need these things in plain English, you see! But yes, I have – and it didn't make any difference.

J: Right. Well, in that case, Ella, I think the best thing to do is just leave it as it is. Don't touch it or do anything else to it and I'll come down to you as soon as I have a minute and have a proper look at it. I can't promise anything, but I'll see what I can do.

E: Oh, that's great, Jirka. Thank you so much for that. I really appreciate it.

J: That's OK. It's why I'm here.

14.3

1 A: Are those solar panels on your house?

B: Yeah. The whole place runs off them.

A: Very green.

B: Lots of people have them in Germany. Look – you can see them on those houses there as well.

A: Oh yeah! You don't see them much in Britain.

B: That's because you don't have any sun!

A: Very funny. Germany's not exactly the sunniest place in the world either! I mean, how much electricity do they produce? Isn't it very expensive?

B: I can't remember exactly how much they were to install – a few thousand euros – but they reckon you can get back the money you invested within ten years.

A: Really? But my electricity bill isn't that much.

B: No, no. It's not like that. You actually end up saving on electricity because you sell it back to the company for three or four times more than the normal price.

A: So it's subsidised by the government?

B: Kind of. And the price is guaranteed for twenty years.

A: Wow! But you still need the cash to install the panels.

B: Sure.

2 C: I got completely lost in the one-way system. I was going round in circles for ages. Then I must've taken the wrong turning and I ended up on the motorway going out of town!

D: Haven't you got a GPS?

C: No. I did consider getting one at one point, but I decided it wasn't worth it. I just don't drive that much.

D: They're not that expensive. They've come down in price a lot, you know. And they're very straightforward, very easy to use.

C: Right, but even so, I think I can do without one.

D: But think of the time you'd save.

C: Well, today maybe. But don't you worry about all those satellites tracking you all the time?

D: Now you're just being paranoid.

3 E: What's this?

F: That? It's for making boiled eggs.

E: You're joking! What's wrong with just putting them in some water?

F: I don't know. You forget to check the time when you put it on, and then you don't know how long it's been cooking, if it's hard or soft …

E: Well …

F: But with this, you just set the timer and then it switches itself off when the egg's ready. You just stick the egg in there, press the button and you're done! And you don't have to bother with water or pans or washing-up or anything.

E: Oh, come on! It's not that much trouble. You only normally have to rinse the pan quickly in some water.

F: And dry it and put it back in the cupboard.

E: Man, you're so lazy!

F No, it's like a toaster. And using this is more energy-efficient than boiling eggs in water. And the egg never cracks. If you want to have the perfect boiled egg …

E: I don't know. It just seems a waste of money to me. They should invent something really useful like a self-cleaning floor, so you don't have to mop or vacuum.

Unit 15

🎧 15.1

Conversation 1

A: Hello. Mr Gomez?

B: Yes?

A: I'm sorry. Have you been waiting long?

B: About two hours.

A: I'm sorry, we're quite busy today. You've done something to your ankle?

B: Yes.

A: Mmm, it's quite swollen. Does this hurt?

B: Yeah, it's very painful.

A: Can you put any weight on it at all?

B: No, no. It hurts too much.

A: Mmm. And how did you do it?

B: I was just coming out of the hotel and I slipped on the stair and my ankle … It just …

A: You just fell over on it. Nasty. Well, I think we should have it X-rayed. It might just be badly sprained, but it could be broken. You'll have to wait again, I'm afraid, but I'll give you something for the pain in the meantime.

B: Right. How long will I have to wait for the X-ray?

A: Hopefully, it won't be more than half an hour. Are you on any medication?

B: Er, I take something for my asthma.

A: That's fine. Any allergies?

B: No.

A: You've never had any adverse reactions to any drugs – paracetamol or anything?

B: No, never.

A: OK fine. Well, I'll get the nurse to give you some painkillers and then have you sent down for the X-ray.

Conversation 2

C: Hello.

D: Hello.

E: Hello.

C: Take a seat. What seems to be the problem?

D: It's my boyfriend. He's been up all night throwing up, he's hardly slept, he had a high temperature – 39 – he was sweating.

C: And how long have you been like this?

D: Sorry, he doesn't speak much English. He first said he felt a bit sick yesterday afternoon and then he threw up about 7 and he hasn't really stopped since.

C: Oh dear. Any diarrhoea?

D: No, none actually.

C: And has he been able to drink anything?

D: No, that's the problem. When he drinks water, he's sick again.

C: Right, well let's have a look. Can you just take off your jumper and sit up here? Open your mouth and stick your tongue out. Lovely. And now take a deep breath. Again – breathe in … and out. Just lie down. I'm just going to press. Does this hurt at all? And here?

E: Mmm. It's OK.

C: Maybe a bit uncomfortable – but no pain.

E: Yes … no pain.

C: OK, you can put your jumper back on. I think it's viral gastroenteritis, so there's no need for antibiotics. I'll give him an injection to stop the vomiting and then he just needs to rest and take lots of fluids. Can you explain for me?

🎧 15.2

A = Anna, D = Dan

A: How was your holiday? You went mountain biking in Austria, didn't you?

D: That's right. It was great, except for James's accident.

A: God! Why? What happened?

D: Well, we'd been cycling in the mountains round Kaunertal, and we were going back to the hotel down this steep road. James went round this tight bend too fast and he went off the road into some bushes and fell off. It was horrible.

A: It sounds it! Was he badly hurt?

D: Well, we thought so. He kept saying he was OK, but you could see that his knee was really swollen. He also had quite a few cuts and bruises and was bleeding quite a bit. The problem was, though, we were still miles from the next village.

A: So what happened? How did you get him to a hospital?

D: Well, luckily, we were actually on a road and a car came past a minute or two later. It stopped and the woman driving offered to take James to the nearest hospital. He kept saying he'd be OK, but she insisted on taking him and in the end we persuaded him to go – just to be safe. We got him into the car – and she took my mobile number and she promised to call me once there was more news.

A: Wow! That was nice.

D: I know. It was really kind of her. Anyway, we then cycled back to our hotel and waited to hear from them.

A: And did they call?

D: Yeah, they did! After a couple of hours, they rang and told me they'd given James an X-ray and there was nothing broken. They said he needed to stay there a bit longer, though, as he was waiting to have a few stitches in the cuts.

A: Oh, poor guy!

D: Yeah, I know. In the end, he spent the rest of the holiday hanging around the hotel. He was desperate to go out with us, but the doctors told him not to cycle for a week and rest the knee. It spoilt his holiday really.

A: I bet!

D: And on top of all that, I spoke to him yesterday and he said he's going to have to buy a new bike now because of the accident. He's found out the bike frame's broken.

A: Ouch! That actually reminds me of something that happened to some friends of mine when they went camping in Croatia.

Unit 16

16.1

1 A: Did you see that thing in the paper about Shaynee Wilson?
B: No. What was that?
A: Well, you remember she got married last September, right?
B: Yeah, I think so. It's hard to keep up.
A: Well, she's just got divorced! Apparently, she found out that her husband was having an affair with another Hollywood actress.
B: God, that didn't last long, did it? So did he get much of her money?

2 C: Did you see that thing on TV about the mobile phone factory closing down?
D: No. What was that?
C: Oh, one of the biggest factories in the country is closing down, which means about five thousand people will be made redundant.
D: That's bad news, isn't it?
C: Yeah. It must mean the economy is starting to slow down.
D: What's the employment situation like in that area? Do you think people will be able to find new jobs?

3 E: Did you see that thing on TV about the murder last night?
F: Yeah. It was shocking, wasn't it? Stabbed fifteen times and left to die in the street.
E: I know. The victim was only 16 as well. And apparently they think his attackers might've been even younger.
F: Oh, it's depressing, isn't it? Do you know if they've arrested anyone for it yet?

4 G: Did you see in the paper that Sven Larstrom passed away? His funeral is next Saturday.
H: No, I didn't. Who is he? I don't think I've heard of him.
G: Sven Larstrom. He was a really great Swedish director. He made some of my favourite films. Haven't you ever seen *Oranges in August*?
H: No, never.

G: Or *Anna and Maja and Jens*?
H: No. Sorry. So how did he die?

5 I: Hey. Did you see that we've finally signed Geraldinho?
J: No, I missed that. Who is he again?
I: Oh, he's a Brazilian midfielder. He's supposed to be great.
J: Yeah? How much did you have to pay for him?
I: Thirty three million euros! It's a new club record.
J: Yeah? That's a lot for a player I've never heard of! Has he played for the national team yet?

16.2

1 I know. It was dreadful, wasn't it?
2 Yeah. It was incredible, wasn't it?
3 I know. It was funny, wasn't it?
4 Yeah. It was a lot of money, wasn't it?
5 Yeah. It was a disaster, wasn't it?
6 I know. It's crazy, isn't it?
7 I know. It's ridiculous, isn't it?
8 Oh, it's depressing, isn't it?
9 I know. It's looking bad, isn't it?
10 Yeah. It's becoming a major problem, isn't it?

16.3

Conversation 1
A: Who's the statue of?
B: That's Garibaldi.
A: Garibaldi?
B: You've never heard of him?
A: No, I don't think so. Who was he?
B: He was a military leader in the nineteenth century who helped unify Italy. He's like a national hero. He fought in South America as well. He was part of some liberation struggles in Brazil and Uruguay. I think his first wife was even Brazilian. I'm surprised you haven't heard of him.
A: Well, I'm not really interested in history.

Conversation 2
C: You've been away, haven't you?
D: Yeah, I went to Germany as part of a Comenius project.
C: Comenius project?
D: Yeah, it's a European Union scheme which provides grants to teachers so that they can go on courses or set up partnerships with other schools abroad.
C: Sounds interesting. I've never heard of it. Why Comenius then? What does that mean?
D: He was a Czech writer who wrote about education. Apparently, he's seen as the father of modern education.
C: Oh yeah? I've never heard of him.
D: To be honest, neither had I before I went on this course. He sounds incredible, though. He wrote in the seventeenth century, but even then he was arguing for education for both boys and girls, and he was against just learning by heart. You know, he wanted to teach kids by doing things and encourage them to think for themselves. He was really ahead of his time.

Conversation 3
E: So what are you going to do while you're in Brussels?
F: Work mainly, but I'm hoping to go to the Eddy Merckx metro station while I'm there.
E: Really? Why do you want to go there?
F: It's where they have Eddy Merckx's bike, which he used to set the hour record.